THE JOURNALS

OF

MAJOR JAMES RENNELL

FIRST SURVEYOR-GENERAL OF INDIA

THE JOURNALS

OF

MAJOR JAMES RENNELL

FIRST SURVEYOR-GENERAL OF INDIA

**WRITTEN FOR THE INFORMATION OF
THE GOVERNORS OF BENGAL DURING HIS SURVEYS OF
THE GANGES AND BRAGHMAPUTRA RIVERS
1764 TO 1767**

EDITOR

T. H. D. LA TOUCH

GYAN

Published by

Gyan Publishing House
5, Ansari Road
Daryaganj, New Delhi-110002
Phone: 011-47034999, 9811692060
E-mail: books@gyanbooks.com

Distribution Network
gyanbooks.com
India, USA, Canada, UK, Australia

ISBN: 978-93-7133-460-0 (PB)

First Published, 1910

2nd Impression 2025

Printed at: Gyan Press, Delhi.

THE JOURNALS OF MAJOR JAMES RENNELL, FIRST SURVEYOR-GENERAL OF INDIA
Editor: T. H. D. LA TOUCH

THE JOURNALS

OF

MAJOR JAMES RENNELL

FIRST SURVEYOR-GENERAL OF INDIA.

WRITTEN FOR THE INFORMATION OF THE GOVERNORS OF BENGAL
DURING HIS SURVEYS OF
THE GANGES AND BRAHMAPUTRA RIVERS
1764 TO 1767.

EDITED BY
T. H. D. LA TOUCHE,
Geological Survey of India.

CALCUTTA:
PRINTED AT THE BAPTIST MISSION PRESS, AND PUBLISHED BY
THE ASIATIC SOCIETY, 57, PARK STREET.
1910.

Major James Rennell, F.R.S.,

'The first great English Geographer'.

Reproduced from a Medallion in the possession of the Asiatic Society of Bengal.

James Rennell

Engraved & printed at the Offices of the Survey of India, Calcutta 191[illegible]

PREFACE.

The Journal of Major James Rennell now published is contained in a small quarto volume bound in parchment, and is written throughout by his own hand. Inside the cover is the book-plate, dated 1840, of his daughter Lady Rodd, who in 1809 was married to Admiral Sir J. Tremayne Rodd. The book was presented by her grandson, the Rt. Hon. Sir James Rennell Rodd, G.C.V.O., British Ambassador at Rome, to the Victoria Memorial Collection accumulated under the auspices of Lord Curzon in 1906, and came into my hands through Sir T. H. Holland, Director of the Geological Survey, who asked me to discover whether it contained any matter of geological interest. This I found not to be the case, except as regards the striking and important changes that have taken place, and are still in progress, in the courses of the rivers of Bengal since the Journal was written. But it is so different in many respects from the other contemporary records of that most interesting period of the British occupation of India that have been preserved, concerning itself not with the political and social events of the time, but with the physical aspects of the country, its climate, crops, and communications, that it seemed to me to possess a quite unique interest; and I am greatly indebted to the Council of the Asiatic Society of Bengal for their permission, freely accorded, to edit the Journal as one of the Memoirs of that Society.

In many respects the picture of Bengal, as given in the Journal, differs very slightly from its aspect of the present day, in spite of the advance of Western civilisation, of our railways and our steam-boats. The first journey that I myself made in India was from Dacca to Maimensingh by way of the 'Luckya' river in a 'budgarow,' which might have been the very one, so far as appearance and construction went, in which Rennell made the passage. Since then I have travelled many a mile in the same unwieldy craft, which still remain the chief means of transport on the waterways of the delta. Still, on either side of the rivers, 'padda' fields stretch to the horizon; and the mat-built villages, with their groves of bamboos and betel trees, remain as they were. Notwithstanding the uniform flatness of the ground, the scenery is often charming; as Rennell more than once remarks in some such phrase as this :—"There is a very pleasant Prospect, the River being transparent and serpentine, and flowing through a Countrey made up of pleasant Meadows interspersed with Groves and Villages." The only innovations worth mentioning are perhaps the growing of jute, which now almost overshadows that of rice, and the nearly complete extermination of the 'Tygers,' which were so frequent a cause of apprehension to Rennell and his men.

I felt much hesitation in deciding how to deal with the mass of miscellaneous notes which follow the Journal; whether to arrange them under separate heads or to omit some that did not appear to possess much interest. But the topics dealt with are so varied that what seemed to myself to be superfluous might be the very subjects to which others might wish to devote particular attention. For this reason, and because I think that the notes, as they stand, give us some insight into Rennell's attitude of mind, testifying to his ardour in collecting every item of information that might assist him in the preparation of his 'Memoir' and other works, I have thought it better to make no alteration in the text.

In conclusion, I must express my gratitude to Mr. F. D. Ascoli, I.C.S., who as Assistant Settlement Officer in Faridpur has acquired an intimate knowledge of the vagaries of the great rivers in that neighbourhood since Rennell's time, and has kindly corrected many of the notes I had compiled from information which, though not many years old, is now quite out of date; to the Revd. W. K. Firminger, Editor of "Bengal, Past and Present," who has given me many valuable suggestions; and to Mr. J. T. Rankin, I.C.S., who has kindly identified several of the villages in the Dacca District mentioned by Rennell.

T. H. D. L.

CALCUTTA,
June 1910.

CONTENTS.

ILLUSTRATIONS.

INTRODUCTION.

A very complete biography of James Rennell, the writer of this Journal, has been published by Sir Clements R. Markham, and it will therefore be sufficient to give only a brief sketch of his career in this place. He was born on the 3rd of December, 1742, near the village of Chudleigh in Devonshire, his father being John Rennell, a captain in the Artillery. In 1756 he entered the Navy as a midshipman on board the *Brilliant* frigate, under Captain Hyde Parker, and was present at the landing of the Duke of Marlborough's troops in Cancale Bay, near St. Malo, in June 1758, at the taking of Cherbourg in August, and at the disastrous action at St. Cast on the coast of Brittany, in September of the same year. During this action Rennell was employed in making a survey of St. Cast Bay, and prepared a plan dedicated to Lord Howe, a copy of which is still preserved.

At the end of 1759 Rennell volunteered for service in the East Indies under Captain Hyde Parker in the *Norfolk*, 74, but that ship having sailed before he could join her he went out to Madras in the *America* frigate, and after a six months' voyage joined Captain Parker on the *Grafton*, 68, in September. During the next two years he saw a good deal of service and spent his leisure time in making surveys of the harbours visited by the fleet.

In 1763 he entered the sea service of the East India Company, and went on a voyage to the Philippine Islands as surveyor. On his return to Madras he obtained his discharge from the Navy and received command of a ship, but on the 21st October, 1763, she was lost in a hurricane. Fortunately for himself Rennell was on shore at the time, and soon after was appointed to the *Neptune*, a small vessel owned by a merchant of Madras, in which he surveyed the Pamben Channel and Palk Strait.

Early in the year 1764 Rennell went to Bengal, where he met with friends through whose influence, chiefly that of Mr. Topham, who had been a midshipman with him on board the *Brilliant*, he received a commission as Probationer Engineer in the Fort and was ordered by Mr. Vansittart, then Governor of Bengal, to make a survey of the delta of the Ganges.[2] Sir C. Markham quotes a letter of Rennell himself, but without giving the date of it, in which he says that his friend Captain Tinker, in command of the king's squadron, "procured me a commission as Surveyor-General of the East India Company's dominions in Bengal," and alludes to the share that Mr. Topham took in promoting his interests[3]; but from the Journal now published it appears that he was not appointed Surveyor-General till the 1st January, 1767,[4] just before the departure of Lord Clive at the end of his second administration of Bengal.

1 Major James Rennell and the Rise of Modern English Geography, Century Science Series, Cassell & Co., London, 1895.

2 Journal, p. 9.

3 *Op. cit.*, p. 41.

4 Journal, p. 86.

There are two references to this appointment in the old Records of the Government of Bengal, which are interesting not only because they give further particulars regarding an event which may be described as epoch-making in the history of the British occupation of India; since from Rennell and his four assistants sprang that vast edifice the 'Survey of India', which now employs nearly 150 Europeans besides a veritable army of native Surveyors and servants, and has carried its labours far into the surrounding regions as well as throughout the whole of India; but also because they show clearly the estimation in which the services of James Rennell were even then held; and the expressions conveyed in them must have been the more gratifying, since the minutes of the Council at that period seem to have more often been directed towards the admonishment of their servants for lapses of conduct, than to rewarding them for zeal and industry.

The first of these extracts runs as follows [1]: —

Proceedings in Council, January 8th, 1767.

"Mr. James Rennell having, in the surveys which have lately been carried on under his direction, given sufficient proofs of his abilities and assiduity in that branch, which may prove of great consequence to the Company's possessions under this Presidency, —It is agreed that he be appointed Surveyor-General, with the rank of Captain, and a salary of Rs. 300 per month in consideration of his merit and the labour of that employ."

The second extract gives, in a letter to the Court of Directors, the reasons of the Council for granting Rennell so high a salary, for though it may seem meagre enough according to modern ideas, it was exactly the same that Warren Hastings drew as a Member of Council in 1764.[2]

Letter to Court of Directors, March 30th, 1767.[3]

"So much depends upon accurate surveys both in military operations and in coming at a true knowledge of the value of your possessions, that we have employed everybody on this service who could be spared and were capable of it. But as the work must ever be imperfect while it is in separate and unconnected plans, we have appointed Captain Rennell, a young man of distinguished merit in this branch, Surveyor-General, and directed him to form one general chart from those already made, and such as are now on hand as they can be collected in. This though attended with great labour does not prevent his prosecuting his own surveys, the fatigue of which with the desperate wounds he has lately

[1] Rev. J. Long—Selections from the unpublished Records of Government for the years 1748 to 1767 inclusive, Calcutta, 1869, No. 940, p. 492.

[2] *Ibid.*, Introduction, p. xxvii. It must also be remembered that the Company's servants in those days, above a certain rank, were allowed to participate in the profits derived from the trade in salt, betel, and tobacco; and it is probably for this reason that Sir C. Markham states (James Rennell, p. 45) that Rennell's allowances on his first appointment in Bengal were from £900 to £1,000 a year. The numerous references to these commodities in the Journal perhaps indicate the personal interest that the writer must have taken in their production.

[3] *Ibid.*, No. 929, p. 487.

received in one of them have already left him but a shattered constitution. This consideration and his being deprived of every means of advantage while he is thus continually moving up and down a country unexplored by Europeans, to the utmost risk of his life, we hope will justify us for increasing his salary to Rs. 300 per month, which indeed may be considered as only a just reward for past services and sufferings. We beg leave to recommend it as a measure well worth your attention, the keeping your Corps of Engineers constantly supplied with young gentlemen properly instructed in that particular branch."

Rennell was first employed on the survey of the Ganges delta with the special object in view of finding a shorter passage suitable for large vessels from the Ganges to Calcutta, than that through the Sunderbans and the Meghna. The Journal gives a detailed account of this voyage and of three subsequent expeditions, during which he surveyed a great part of Northern and Eastern Bengal, penetrating beyond Goalpara on the Brahmaputra which was then on the frontier of the Assamese kingdom. It was while he was engaged on this duty on the frontier of Kuch Behar that he met with the accident referred to in the letter quoted above. He was surrounded by a party of Sunyasi Fakirs, a fanatic tribe then in rebellion, and was desperately wounded, barely escaping with his life. A full account of this skirmish is given in the Journal (p. 74), and further details in Sir C. Markham's biography.[1]

The Journal ends in March 1767, when Rennell was engaged in completing the survey of the rivers of the Ganges delta, but was forced to desist by a severe attack of fever, to which he was continually subject. An account of his further service in India will be found in Sir C. Markham's Biography. In 1771 he was sent in command of an expedition against his old enemies the Sunyasi Fakirs, with complete success; and a year later he married Miss Jane Thackeray, whose brother, William Makepeace Thackeray, grandfather of the novelist, was secretary to Mr. Cartier, the Governor at that time, an old Dacca friend of Rennell's.

Rennell retired from the service in 1776, shortly after being promoted to the rank of Major in the Bengal Engineers, with a pension granted to him by Warren Hastings.[2] He was elected a Fellow of the Royal Society in 1781 and took up his residence in London, where his house became a meeting-place for travellers from all

---

[1] *Op. cit.*, p. 47.

[2] Through the courtesy of Mr. B A. Gupté, the officer in charge of the Victoria Memorial collection in Calcutta, I am enabled to transcribe Rennell's application for a pension, the original of which is preserved in that collection :—

To the Honble Warren Hastings Esqr President and Governor, &c.. Council of Fort William.

Honorable Sir and Sirs,

My Circumstances and Situation in Life reduce me to the necessity of making the following Application to You, in hopes that by the favor of your Patronage, my Case may be represented to my honorable Employers; from whose Justice and Humanity alone I may expect the accomplishment of my just Desires: namely, the being enabled to retire from this Country; where, by means of a painful and labourious Service of 13 Years, and by various Accidents of Wounds and Sickness, my Health is so bad, that I am advised by my Physicians to lose no Time in quitting a Place, in which I have experienced no tolerable degree of Health for these eight Years past: and in which, if hard Necessity compels me to stay, I can only expect to linger out a few Years longer.

Yet, however necessary it may be to change my Situation, the slenderness of my Means will not permit me to live in England, encumbered as I am with a large Family, and disabled from pursuing any active Employment

parts of the world. The remainder of his life was devoted to the study of comparative geography and to literary pursuits. His first great work, the "Bengal Atlas, containing Maps of the Theatre of War and Commerce on that side of Hindoostan," was published in 1779, and a second edition in 1781.[1] This was followed by the first approximately correct Map of India, with a Memoir[2] containing a full account of the plan on which the map was executed and of his authorities. He conceived a great scheme for a comprehensive work on the geography of Eastern Asia, and published two volumes dealing with the geography of Herodotus. He also devoted much attention to the geography of Africa, and in 1790 constructed a new map of the northern half of that country for the African Association, accompanied by a Memoir. In 1791 he received the Copley Medal of the Royal Society. The study of winds and ocean currents also occupied much of his time, and in 1810 he began to reduce his collection of observations to one general system. He was the first to explain the causes of the occasional northerly set to the southward of the Scilly Islands, which has since become known as 'Rennell's Current.' On this subject he read two papers before the Royal Society in June 1795 and in April 1815. He was made an Associate of the Institute of France in 1800, and in 1825 received the Gold Medal of the Royal Society of Literature. He died on the 29th March, 1830, at the advanced age of 88, and was buried in the nave of Westminster Abbey.

A few words may be added on the methods employed by Major Rennell in carrying out his surveys. The construction of scientific instruments had made very little progress when he was at work in India: indeed it was not until 1761, the year after Rennell went out, that the chronometer was first used for the determination of longitudes; and his surveys were made with a compass and chain, supplemented by a Hadley's Quadrant for the determination of latitudes. So badly equipped was the Government of those days in the matter of instruments that even in 1787 it was necessary to borrow a sextant, a watch, and a quadrant from different officers in Calcutta who happened to possess them, in order to fit out a Government Survey expedition for determining the positions of the principal places in Bengal.[3] Among the notes at the end of the Journal (p. 125) will be found measurements of the chain used by Rennell, from which it will be seen how inaccurate was even so simple an instrument. In spite of such disadvantages, however, his surveys were wonderfully accurate; so much so that my friend Captain F. C. Hirst, of the Survey of India, while investigating the changes in the course of the river Kosi, found that many of the towns and villages marked in Rennell's Bengal Atlas coincided exactly with their

---

by reason of my Maims, & the ruined State of my Constitution; unless my honourable Employers would generously assist me.

I will not, Gentlemen, take up your Time with a Detail of my Misfortunes and Sufferings, as the Particulars are already well known to you: nor, as the hon^ble^ Court of Directors have been pleased to approve of my Services, shall I plead the Merit of having done my Duty.

I am with the greatest Respect, Gentlemen, Your most Obed Servant,

Fort William, 25th Septr. 1774. J. RENNELL, *Surveyor-General.*

[1] A reprint of this valuable work is now in course of preparation under the orders of the Surveyor General in India.

[2] Memoir of a Map of Hindoostan, or the Mogul Empire, &c., London, 1783.

[3] Sir C Markham, Memoir of the Indian Surveys, 2nd Edn., London, 1878, p. 56.

positions on the modern maps. It was perhaps the accuracy that Rennell had attained to, by his skill and constant care in checking his observations, that led him to look with little favour at first on the triangulation surveys that were started in India at the beginning of the nineteenth century by Colonel Lambton. But long before his death he had become convinced of the superiority of Lambton's method.

Very few observations of purely historical or social interest will be found in the Journal. The fighting that was more or less continuously going on along the western frontier of Bengal during that period is not even mentioned, nor is the mutiny of officers on the occasion of the loss of double *batta*, which took place in May 1766. Rennell was at this time at Dacca recovering from the wounds he had received in February in the skirmish with the Sunyasi Fakirs, and he confesses in a letter quoted by Sir C. Markham[2] that it was only this circumstance that prevented his throwing in his lot with the discontented officers, for he felt very strongly on the subject. He concerns himself strictly with the day's work, observing each change of weather, of which the Journal gives an almost complete record for the whole period, and such incidents as immediately affected his surveys. It was no doubt this faculty for concentrating his attention on the matter in hand that, in an age unparalleled in Indian history for the unbridled luxury of the European population, enabled him to establish that character for assiduity and integrity which caused the Council, unaccustomed as it was to find such qualities displayed by its servants, to refer to him in such apprecia-tive terms as they have placed on record.

[1] *Ibid.*, p. 69. [2] James Rennell, &c., p. 52.

February 1767.

The 1st of Jany. 1767, I was appointed Surveyor Genl. & the Govr. (Mr. Verelst) appointed the several Surveyors that were to be employed under me (Viz.)

Capt. Lewis Dyglop — Lieut. — Carter
Capt. John Adams — Ensign Wm. Richards —

The three first had each a particular part of the Country allotted him to survey, & myself (with Mr. Richards as an Assistant) had another part. Mine was, to wit, first, the Roads from Calcutta to Nadgigunge; next the Cosa or Cossi River from its Conflux with the Ganges to the Northern Frontier of Bengall —

The 6th. Feby. sent Baggage off to Dumdum, the same Evening I joined it, in order to begin the Survey next Day from Gowreepore Bridge; Capt. Cameron having surveyed as far as that Island —

Plans No. 1 The 7th. began the Survey and at Night came to Barrasett which is [struck out] from Dumdum — This Country is a part of the Kistnagur Province —

After leaving Barrasett we seldom found the Roads good, they being excessive narrow, rough, & crooked,
M. F.
7. 3. 15 &

Facsimile of a page of the Journal

February 1766. 51.

then assured that the Enemy were hemmed in be-tween the forks of that River and the Durla. About 4 we entered the Village of Deen hatta where a Party of the Enemy had posted them-selves or rather as I am inclined to think had sat down to rest themselves. The sudden Approach of our People however roused them & they made a desperate Effort to defend them-selves, at the same time that they might have ran off, & probably escaped. In this Skirmish I had the misfortune to be surrounded by the Enemy, & received several Cuts from their broad Swords, one of which threatned my Death — Morrison pursued his Course towards the Durla the following two days the second of which at ten in the Morning he came to the Banks of that River & found difficulty in getting Boats to cross over, the River of

Facsimile of a page of the Journal

1764, 5.

JOURNAL

Of Proceedings on the Survey of the River Ganges from the head of Jelenghee River to its conflux with the Baramputrey or Megna; of the Megna and other Rivers from Luckeypour to Dacca; and of part of the Southern Creeks in tracing the nearest Passage from the Ganges to Calcutta in the dry Season.

JAMES RENNELL *Surveyor.*

JOURNAL of the first Expedition for the discovery of the nearest Passage from ye Ganges to Calcutta in the dry Season.

Copy of Orders from the Hon'ble Henry VanSittart[1] Esq. Governor of Fort William.

Fort William, 6th. May, 64

Sir,

The first Service on which you are to be employed is the Survey of ye great River (Ganges) to the Eastward of Jelenghee; & upon this Survey your Particular Object must be to find out the shortest & safest Channel leading from the great River to Channel Creek or Rangafulla.[2]

For this purpose you will coast along the South side of the great River & 2
examine every Creek or Nulla which runs out of it to the Southw^d.^, tracing them as far as you find them Navigable for Boats of Three hundred Maunds Burthen & informing yourself by Enquiry from the Countrey People whether they are like Navigable all the Year; of which Circumstance you may yourself form a tolerable Judgment by the Appearance and steepness of the Banks.

You will keep a very particular Journal of your Proceedings, noting the Appearance and Produce of the Countries thro' which you pass; the name of every Village, & whatever else may seem remarkable, of which Journal you will give me a Copy along with the Drafts you are to make of the Rivers and Creeks.

I am Sir

Yr. most Obed Sert.

HENRY VANSITTART.

Monday May 7th. set out from Calcutta in order to proceed by way of Jelenghee 3
in a small Budgarow,[3] together with 5 small Willocks[4] to carry the People &c.

---

[1] Governor of Bengal, 1760 to 1764.

[2] Rangafulla. A creek connecting the Hugli with the Sandarbans. It leaves the Hugli at Mud Point, about 60 miles below Calcutta, and is at the present day the route taken by river steamers proceeding from Calcutta to Eastern Bengal and Assam.

[3] Budgarow. Sometimes also called Buggalow. "A travelling boat, constructed somewhat like a pleasure barge. Some have cabins 14 feet wide, and proportionably long: and draw from 4 to 5 feet water" (Rennell, Memoir of Hindoostan, *note* p. 360). The 'Bajra' is still one of the most common forms of boat employed on the rivers of the delta, both for cargo and passenger traffic, and no traveller on the great water-ways can fail to be struck by the picturesqueness of these craft, with their mediæval-looking high poops and bellying square sails, as they work up stream under the influence of a favouring breeze.

[4] Willock. A smaller boat having a long narrow bow overhanging the water. The name is spelled in various ways, such as Woolock, Oolock, Hooluck, Ulauk, etc. The term now appears to be obsolete, but it is probably one of

Number of People as follows:

1 Assistant Surveyor	11 Sepoys
3 other Europeans	1 Interpreter
11 Lascars	In all 39 with myself.
11 Motias[1]	

We left the new Fort[2] at 3 PM, but the Tide prevented our Proceeding up the River this Night, so came to at Calcutta. Fine Weather all this day.

The 8th at one in ye morning I was awakened by an alarm of ye Budgarow's sinking, & indeed she was on the point of it, being 2/3 full of water. By this accident I had most of my Stationary spoiled, & likewise a great part of my Cloathes. Stayed at Calcutta this Day, & repaired the Leak. In ye Evening proceeded up the River, & put ashore at Serampour[3] for the Night. A smart NW Squall this Afternoon.

4 The 9th. fair Weather. In ye morning at 8 went to take a View of Ghyretty.[4] Dined at Chendanagore,[5] & went to view the Ruins of the Fort and Town. Passed by Chinsura[6] at 4 in ye Afternoon and at Night put into Baunchbaria[7] Creek. This Creek is now 5 Cubits[8] deep at H. water, neap Tides. The River seems to be well described in Capt. Polier's[9] Map. The Night clear. Fresh Breezes from ye Southw^d^.

The 10th. variable Weather. Passed by Betwallera Nullah, which appears to be nearly the same breadth as that of Baunchbaria. At 4 P.M. a smart Squall from the Southward whilst we were in the Betwallera Reach. The Budgarow sprung another Leak. Lay at Berespour this Night.

---

the forms known under the generic name of 'Dinghy.' It differed from the ordinary cargo-boat in having the planks laid edge to edge, and fastened by iron clamps (Hobson Jobson, p. 971).

1 Motia. *Hind.* Motiya, a porter or cooly.

2 The new Fort. This was the present Fort William, the building of which was begun by Lord Clive in 1757, to replace the old Fort, destroyed by Siraj-ud-Daula, the Nawab of Bengal, eight years previously. The new Fort was not completed, however, till 1773, during the Governorship of Warren Hastings.

3 At this time Serampur was a Danish settlement. It lies on the Hugli, about 13 miles above Calcutta.

4 Ghyretty, or Ghiretti, about 6 miles above Serampur. Here was situated the magnificent residence of the French Governors of Chandernagore, supposed to have been built by Dupleix. Only the merest vestiges of the building now remain. (Bengal, Past and Present, Vol. i, No. 1, p. 68, Pl. 4). Bishop Heber gives a description of the building in his Journal (Vol. i. p. 85). A portion of the European garrison was stationed here in Rennell's time, at the cantonment of Champdani (Vansittart's Narrative, Vol. iii, p. 277).

5 Chendanagore. This is a more correct spelling than the present Chandarnagar or Chandernagore. The name is properly Chandan-nagar = city of Sandalwood (Hunter, Imp. Gaz., Vol. iii, p. 356). It was bombarded by Admiral Watson in 1757, on the breaking out of war between England and France, and captured by Lord Clive. The fortifications and houses were afterwards demolished by Clive's orders, in retaliation for the conduct of Count Lally in Madras.

6 Chinsura. A Dutch settlement on the Hugli, a short distance above Hugli town. It was ceded to the British in 1825.

7 Bansberia. Noteworthy as the site of the first Native Church founded in Bengal, and for its Hindu temples (*see* Bengal, Past and Present, Vol. ii, No. 1, pp. 74, 105).

8 A cubit = 18 inches, *see* p. 25.

9 A Captain Polier is mentioned several times by Orme in his "History of Military Transactions in Indostan," but he appears to have been mortally wounded at the siege of Fort St. George in December 1758 (Vol. ii, p. 393). In his 'Memoir of Hindoostan' Rennell acknowledges in several places the assistance given him by "my friend Col. Polier" in obtaining material for the construction of his map. He was Chief Engineer at Fort William in 1762, but afterwards entered the service of the Nawabs of Oude, and of the Emperor of Delhi, and retired in 1788 (Buckland, Dict. Ind. Biography, p. 339).

The 11th. mostly fair Weather, having only one slight squall from ye Southward. This Forenoon passed by Amboa,[1] which lies on ye South side of the River in ye long reach between Cutchoa and Culna.[2] I observe that this Place is remarked in some of ye old maps of Bengall & therefore imagine that it must once have been a flourishing Village; however at present it contains only a few poor Huts Lay at Beldanga this Night.

The 12th. fair Weather all day, the Evening heavy & threatning. At 8 in 5
the Morning entered the Jelenghee River[4] The Cossimbazaar River[5] at its conflux with the Jelenghee appears to be very narrow: I judge it cannot at this Season be above 50 yards over. The People inform me that it is now navigable for middle-sized Boats.

In the Evening at Hautnagore measured a Base & found the breadth of the River (Jelenghee) to be 150 yards now & 270 in the Rainy Season; its depth 13 foot in the deepest Place. It appears by the Banks that it will rise 13 foot more with the Rains.

The 13th. very fine Weather all day. Wind from the South. The River grows very shallow, & so crooked that though we have gone 22 miles thro' ye River this Day, we have scarce advanced 10 in a right Line. Lay at Teegaree or Negarin this Night. At Sunset found ye variation of the Needle to be 3°-3′ East^ly by an Amplitude.[6]

The 14th. the Forenoon fair; in ye afternoon a hard Squall from the Westward with much Rain, Thunder, & Lightning. By reason of ye bad Weather, we have proceeded only 16 miles this Day. At Notydungah, where we lie this Night, the River is only 2 Cubits deep.

The 15th. very squally Weather, & much Rain. This, together with ye 6
shallowness & intricacy of the Channells of the River, retards our Passage much. In some Places the Channell is not five yards over. At Paunchdaddah measured the breadth & depth of the River, & likewise took ye altitude of the Banks. The breadth is now 200 yards; the depth nowhere more than 5 Cubits. By the Banks the River will rise by the Rains 26 feet more. By this, & the former Experiment made at Hautnagore (the 12th.), it appears that the River swells much more in the neighbourhood of the great River (Ganges) than in Places remote from it, & that the difference is so much as 12 or 13 foot in ye distance of 41 miles.

1 Amboa. Marked as a considerable village on Van den Broucke's map of 1660 under the name Ambowa. It is not shown in the modern 'Atlas of India.'

2 Kalna, a town of considerable importance on the right bank of the Bhagirathi. A large fort existed here in Muhammadan times.

3 Haldanga. A ferry a short distance below Nadiya.

4 The Jalangi, one of the three 'Nadiya Rivers,' the other two being the Bhagirathi and the Matabhanga. It flows from Jalangi village on the Padma (Padda) or lower Ganges along an exceedingly tortuous course to the south-west to Nadia, where it joins the Bhagirathi. The united rivers form the Hugli. In the hot weather it is little more than a string of marshes connected by shoals and is fordable at many points. (Imp. Gaz., Vol. xiv, p. 16).

5 The Bhagirathi.

6 This variation of the compass is quite abnormal (*see* p. 121). At most of the places where it was determined by Rennell it varied within 0 and 2° *West*. It is now about 1° 30′ *East*, on the average.

This Evening lay at Gowgatty, having this day proceeded only 10 miles. Here are 19 large Salt Boats[1] sunk in ye middle of the River. Some rain this Night.

The 16th. a fair Morning, the Afternoon & Evening wet & squally. This Morning we had much trouble in passing the Buxeypour Shoals on which there is now only 1½ Cubit water, so that the River here must be quite dry in ye dry Season, as we are informed that it has rose just 1½ Cubit since ye Rains began.

7 At noon passed Vheckery-Gunge,[2] where there are 9 or 10 Salt Boats sunk, & at Night put ashoar at Jagipour, having gone only 10 miles this Day. The River here is 4 Cubits deep. Much Rain this Night.

The 17th. fair Weather. This Day proceeded 11½ miles, but the River is so crooked, that we have gone only 6 on a strait line. The Country here is open, & extremely pleasant. This Night lay at a small Nullah near Sasteeapour. A fine Night.

The 18th. mostly fine Weather, the wind from ye South. In the Morning sent my Sircar[3] overland to Jelenghee Village in order to procure necessaries &c. against my arrival. This Day proceeded only 11 miles, as the River here runs very rapid, altho' it is broader & deeper than before. Lay near Doolampour, about 6 miles below Jelenghee, this Night. Fair Weather.

The 19th. fair Weather all day, the Wind in fresh Breezes from the Southward. About 3 miles below the head of the Jelenghee we found the Water so shallow that the Budgarow was scarce *waterborne* for a quarter of a mile.

We came into the great Ganges before noon, & arrived at Jelenghee[4] at one in ye Afternoon.

8 Before I left Calcutta the Governor informed me that a convenient Budgarow, together with as many Willocks as I should want, would be in waiting for me at Jelenghee; as the Budgarow I came up in, was the smallest that could be procured at Calcutta, in order that I might use all possible Expedition in proceeding up ye Jelenghee at a season when ye River was very low; but on my arrival at Jelenghee I found neither Budgarow nor Willocks. The People there indeed informed me that Capt. Widderborne (who lately went to Camp with the Voluntiers)[5] had pressed

---

[1] Conveying salt from the sea-board to Patna and other towns on the Ganges, *see* pp. 18, 19.

[2] Bickarygunge in Rennell's Atlas.

[3] Sircar—applied in Bengal to a domestic servant who keeps accounts of household expenditure, and makes miscellaneous purchases for the family. (Hobson Jobson, p. 841.)

[4] Jalangi: the village is not now on the main stream of the Ganges, but is separated from it by a large island.

[5] Capt. Wedderburn is mentioned in a letter from Dr. Fullarton, the sole survivor of the Patna massacre of 6th October, 1763, to the Board. He says: "The 25th after giving money to a jematdar that had the guard to the westward of the Dutch Factory, by the riverside, I set out in a small pulwar, and got safe to the boats, under command of Capt. Wedderburn, that were lying opposite to the city, on the other side of the river, and at 11 o'clock that night arrived at the Army, under the command of Major Adams, lying at Jonsy' (Vansittart's Narrative, Vol. iii, p. 378; Diaries of three Surgeons of Patna, 1763, Calcutta Hist. Soc., 1909, p. 70). Several references to him are to be found in the accounts of the loss of Calcutta in 1756 published in Wilson's Old Fort William (Vol. ii, pp. 57, 62, 81, 88, 143). The Volunteers consisted of the body of men raised from among the Company's writers who were thrown out of employment by the events of 1756 in Calcutta (*Ibid.*, p. 80). They are mentioned by Orme as having embodied themselves at Fulta, to the number of 70, on the arrival of Admiral Watson's squadron for the recapture of the city (History, Vol. ii, p. 121), and one of them, a Mr. John Johnstone, is recorded by the same historian as having "managed a field-piece" at the battle of Plassey, and having checked by its fire the advance of Mir Jafir's troops

all the Boats that he could find, & amongst them a large Budgarow; but whether that Budgarow was for me, I could never yet could get rightly informed. Certain it was, the Budgarow I came in was very unfit for me to do my Business in during ye approaching wet Season, both on account of its smallness, & leakyness.

Finding however that I had no time to lose, as ye River was daily rising, I set about getting some better Willocks for the Surveying People, but had little success, for during the three days I staid there, I could procure only 2; those were of 200 9
maunds each; besides these I kept 3 of the Calcutta Willocks, & sent the other two to Calcutta.

The 20th. we had fair Weather all day; the 21st. the forenoon the same, but in ye Afternoon a fresh Gale from ye SE, with frequent heavy Squalls, but no Rain. This Day wrote to the Governor, informing him of my Proceedings to this time, & enclosing a Copy of the Sections of the Jelenghee river.

The 22nd. all the Forenoon very fresh Gales from ye SE, which prevented our proceeding on ye Survey (as I intended) till ye Afternoon, when we began surveying from the head of the Jelenghee River, eastwards, having surveyed the head of that River, & ye Bank of ye Ganges a mile above it, yesterday.

This Afternoon we had a Specimen of the Weather that we might expect in ye great River at this Season; for in ye Evening in crossing ye River near Quemairree, a violent Squall from the SE drove all the boats ashoar on ye Jelenghee Sand, where they continued beating all Night; 2 men were blown overboard during ye Squall but 10
fortunately swam ashoar.[1]

The 23rd. a fine Morning. Employed in surveying the Southern Bank of the River, for the Particulars of which see the Map No. 1. This Day examined the Nullah of Mayescunda[2] which lies about 5 miles SE of Jelenghee & is the first Nullah (or Creek) that we have discovered. We found it only 2 Cubits deep at ye inlet, & almost dry a quarter of a mile up. There is much Padda[3] & Cotton sown in this Neighbourhood. From this Place to near 8 miles to the Eastward the course of the River is nearly East, and full of dangerous Sands, the River also is excessive rapid.

(*Ibid.*, p. 176). In 1763 they were sent up to Murshidabad during the course of the operations against Mir Kasim Ali in charge of a fleet of store boats, and perhaps it was while on this duty that they 'pressed' Rennell's boats (Blechynden, Calcutta Past and Present, pp. 202—205)

[1] In his "Memoir of Hindoostan" Rennell gives a description of these squalls. He says: "The rivers are in a tranquil state, from the time of the change in the monsoon in October, to the middle of March; when the *north-westers* begin in the eastern parts of Bengal (though later as we advance westwards), and may be expected once in three or four days, until the commencement of the rainy season. These *north-westers*, which have their denomination from the quarter they usually originate in, are the most formidable enemies that are met with, in this inland navigation, they being sudden and violent squalls of wind and rain; and though of no long duration, are often attended with fatal effects, if not carefully guarded against; whole fleets of trading boats having been sunk by them almost instantaneously. They are more frequent in the eastern than in the western part of Bengal, and happen oftener towards the close of the day than at any other time. As they are indicated some hours before they arrive, by the rising and very singular appearance of the clouds, the traveller has commonly time enough to seek a place of shelter. It is in the great rivers alone that they are so truly formidable; and that about the latter end of May, and beginning of June, when the rivers are much increased in width" (p. 359).

[2] Maheshkunda. This creek is the head of the Matabhanga, also known for the first 40 miles of its course as the Kumar (Comer or Comare of Rennell).

[3] Padda—Paddy: rice in the husk, or growing rice.

At Paunchiferra 8 miles ESE from Jelenghee a Creek falls into the Ganges; this Creek as I am informed runs out of the same River near Surda. This Evening the Weather threatning, we sheltered the Boats in a Creek of Beresgunge Sand.

The 24th. fair Weather all day. Employed surveying as yesterday. Passed the Villages of Horisongkor [2] & Callygunge. Here the River is divided into 2 Channels by a Sand Bank of 5 miles long: its Course is now NE and breadth in some places near 2½ miles in ye wet Season. The Country here is very pleasant, being chiefly Meadows, well stocked with Cattle The Banks are now near 30 foot high,
11 & are continually falling in, so that Boats should be careful to avoid coming too near them.[3] The Wind this day has been from the Southward, in light Breezes.

The 25th. the Forenoon excessive hot, the Afternoon stormy, and much Rain. This Evening came to Chocculo [4] a Village situated on ye Point of the North Reach. From hence the River takes an ESE Course for 5 or 6 miles, & is all the way divided into 2 Channels by a large Sand Bank. The North Channell is the deepest & best.

The 26th. fair Weather. Surveying the ESE Reach.

The 27th. fair Weather. Finished ye ESE Reach, & entered another whose Course is South for near 5½ miles,[5] the breadth not more than a mile & half in ye wet Season, & now in some Places not more than a quarter of a mile. The Countrey People deserting the Villages on our Approach, occasions some Delay in getting the Names of the Places. This Evening betwixt the Villages of Malacola & Selah [6] (the space of 2½ miles) I counted no less than 400 fishing Boats. Variation of the Magnetic Needle by the Evening Amplitude 0°-36′ Easterly.

The 28th. the Forenoon fair, the Evening wet & stormy. The Wind has been at South these 3 days past. Finished the Survey of the South Reach & came to Damadure, a Village situated at the bottom of it. From hence the River turns
12 quick round to the NE & continues that Course 9 miles. Rain all this Night.

1 This creek is not shown on Rennell's Map. Surda is on the left bank of the Ganges, about 12 miles above Jalangi, near the mouth of the Baral river.

2 Harisankra, shown in the Atlas of India about two miles south of the present bank of the Ganges, on the south side of the Sonakhundi lake, which is evidently an old bed of the Ganges.

3 To this cause, the falling in of high banks along the rivers of the delta, has been attributed by some the phenomenon known as the 'Barisal guns' (Proc. As. Soc. Beng., 1888, p. 99).

4 Chocula on the map. Close to the present village of Raita.

5 This is the reach crossed by the E.B.S. Railway ferry between Damukdia and Sara, where it is now proposed to bridge the river. The N-S reach is much longer now, extending to at least 11 miles. The changes in the course of the river in this neighbourhood are of interest, in view of the importance of obtaining a suitable site for the railway bridge. If the river in Rennell's time ran through what is now the 'Sonakhundi Lake,' as seems probable from his speaking of passing the village of Horisongkor (Harisankra) two days before, it must have come very near cutting a channel through the base of the Damukdia peninsula. This, however, it failed to do, and it has since moved northwards, probably as a result of the easing-off of the bend higher up, opposite the mouths of the Jalangi and Matabhauga rivers. The base of the Damukdia peninsula is therefore probably safe for many years: but as shown in the Atlas of India, published in 1863, the position of the head of the peninsula at Raita was then much the same as it was in Rennell's time, whereas more recent surveys show that within the last 40 years considerable erosion of the point has taken place. This seems to indicate that there are (or were) hard beds in the alluvium at Raita point which checked the erosion, but that these are gradually being removed. If this erosion is allowed to proceed much further, it would seem that there is little hope of saving the remainder of the peninsula.

6 Selah is probably a corruption of Sara. The village of Damadure is in the position now occupied by Damukdia.

The 29th. drizling Rain in y[e] Forenoon; the Afternoon several heavy Squalls from different Quarters of the Compass & much Rain, so that we could perform but little Business this Day. Much Rain this Night.

The 30th. tolerable Weather. Five Miles up the NE reach begins a large Island which extends to the Eastw[d]. & SE five Miles, making the River in some Places 3½ miles broad. The Southmost Channell is not navigable all the Year[1]; the Villages of Serampour & Gurgoree are situated at the extremities of it. The Country here pretty well cultivated, & mostly sown with Padda. This Day wrote to the Governor, informing him of my Proceedings &c.

The 31st. very fresh Gales of Wind all day from y[e] Southward. From the SE Point of the large Island the River proceeds with a South Course near 8 miles. The Western Bank is mostly covered with Jungle, but the Eastern one well cultivated & has 10 or 11 Villages on it. Custee Village[2] lies at y[e] end of this Reach.

June the 1st. & 2nd. fair Weather, the Wind fresh from the SSE. These 2 days
employed surveying the Western Bank of the South Reach, & in y[e] Evening of the 13
2nd. came to Custee, a large Village situated on the Western Bank opposite the turn
of the Reach.

The 3rd. a fair Morning. Came to the Head of Custee Creek[3] which runs out of the great River three quarters of a mile below the Village. We are informed that this Creek is navigable all y[e] year & that it communicates with that of Rangafulla[4]: if so, it seems likely to put a successful end to y[e] Expedition. The Creek is from 130 to 200 yards broad, & a ¼ of a mile up from 40 to 10 Cubits deep.

In y[e] Afternoon put over to y[e] East Side, in order to survey it from hence back to y[e] head of the Reach; in order should the Creek prove navigable it may be more readily found by Boats coming down the River.

[1] From recent maps it appears that the main stream of the Ganges now flows to the south of this island.

[2] Kushtia, an important seat of river trade, especially jute, on the southern bank of the river. It was the terminus of the Eastern Bengal State Railway until 1870, when the line was extended to Goalundo.

[3] Custee Creek, now known as the Garai river. The development of this river is a striking example of the changes that have taken place in the course of the rivers of the delta within the last century. In 1764 Rennell found it so shallow within two miles of the head that only the smallest boats could pass during the dry season, whereas at the present time and for many years past it has been the main route for steamers plying between Calcutta and the upper Ganges. In 1828 it was only 600 feet broad at Kushtia but in 1863 it had increased to 1908 feet. The change appears to have been a direct consequence of the alteration in the course of the Brahmaputra in the early years of the nineteenth century. This river, ponding back the waters of the Ganges, compelled it to deposit its silt in the reaches above the new confluence at Goalundo, and to seek another route to the sea for its waters, and for a time it seemed as if the Garai must become the main channel of the Ganges. So nearly did this happen, that in 1838 the Ganges itself was fordable at several places above the junction with the Brahmaputra. The causes that have prevented the complete desertion of the old channel were explained in 1863 by Fergusson. It happens that the Brahmaputra begins to fall at an earlier period than the Ganges, and that the silt deposited by the latter river when it is ponded back is thus swept out again every year. Otherwise Fergusson anticipated that the lower Ganges would become entirely silted up (Fergusson, Delta of the Ganges, Quart. Journ. Geol. Soc., Vol. xix, pp. 335-337). A position of equilibrium seems now to have been reached and the Garai is gradually silting up again. Lower down the Garai becomes the Madhumati, and discharges into the Bay of Bengal by the Haringhata estuary. The increase in the volume of water carried by the river was the cause of a succession of severe floods in the Jessor district in the early part of the last century.

[4] *See* note, p. 9.

At 4 a very hard Squall from the NNW which obliged us to bear away for Custee Creek, the long Reach affording no Shelter for Boats. Much Wind and Rain all Night.

14 The 4th. & 5th. fair Weather, the Winds variable. These 2 days employed in surveying the East Bank of the long South Reach, & in ye Evening went into Custee Creek.

The 6th. 7th. & 8th. employed in reducing the Original Surveys to smaller Scales, and copying the Journal, to send to the Governor. During this time we had much Rain. Employed some Carpenters to stop ye Budgarow's Leaks, & repair the Rudder.

The 9th. traced ye Creek a mile & quarter below the head, where we find very shallow Water. Upon a strict Examination I found only 4 & 5 Cubits Water opposite the Village of Cupadin, & I am credibly informed that the River has rose 4 Cubits since the beginning of the Rains. Besides this Circumstance, several Boatmen inform me that they have passed here in Dingeys[1] during the dry Season, & that oftentimes there is not Water enough for a loaded Boat of 90 Maund. Boats of 300 Maunds loaded draw from 2 to 2¾ Cubits.

15 The 10th. in ye Morning dispatched a Hircar[2] with ye Maps & Journal; in the latter I acquainted the Govnr with every Circumstance relating to Custee Creek. Fair Weather all this Day. In ye Afternoon began surveying to the Eastward of Custee Creek. The Course of the River is now NEBE for 8 or 9 miles.

The 11th. in ye Morning fresh Gales from the Eastwd. with hard Rain; the middle of the Day fair; the Evening Calm & Rainy. Employed on the Survey as before. From Custee Eastward, a large Dam is thrown up to keep ye River from overflowing the Countrey in the height of the wet Season. This Dam extends more than 5 miles; it is about 12 foot high & 14 yards thick. The River here is only ¼ of a mile broad in some Places.

The 12th. in the Forenoon frequent Squalls of Wind and Rain; the remainder of the Day fair.

This Day came to the head of Pubna Creek,[3] wch. runs out of the great River from ye North side, & lies from Custee NE½E 8 miles This Creek falls into the
16 Ganges again at Rottingunge, of which hereafter.

Pubna Village[4] lies on ye East side of the Creek & very near ye great River. At this place Boats are repaired & built.

From hence the River proceeds with a SEBS Course for near 9 miles; a Dam is thrown up on ye East side & continues for several miles. By the breaking off of it in several Places, it appears that the River has gained very considerably on ye East Bank since ye Dam was made, but how long since it was made, I cannot learn.

1 Dingey—*Beng.* dingi, a small boat or skiff. The term is now used for any of the small passenger boats plying on the Hugli, and in the Navy and Merchant service as the name of the smallest ship's boat.

2 Hircar *Hind.* Harkārā, a messenger or courier; also a spy. (Hobson Jobson, p. 430).

3 The Ichhamati, a large creek connecting the Ganges with the Harasagar, one of the branches of the Bramahputra.

4 Pabna, the headquarters of Pabna district. In the Atlas of India, Sheet 120, it is shown as lying about 4 miles north of the main stream, but the river has now reverted to its old channel.

From the 12th. to ye 17th. employed in surveying the abovementioned Reach; there is little remarkable in ye Country on both sides of it, there are several Villages & much cultivated Land, particularly on ye West side, where there is much Paddy sown.

The Weather during this time was very turbulent, having every day hard Squalls from ye SE^{t}. & much Rain.

From the end of the SEBS Reach the River turns quick round to the NNE & continues that Course 5 Miles; another Dam is thrown up on ye East side of this Reach also. 17

The 17th. came to Oddygya,[1] a Village on ye East side of this Reach. Here the River divides into two Channells, of which the Northmost only is navigable during the dry Season. The Island which separates those Channels is about 3½ miles long, & is pleasant & well cultivated.

The 18th. fresh Gales of Wind all Day & continual Rain, which obliged us to lie by.

The 19th. fair Weather. Employed surveying the Southern Channel of the River.

The 20th. fresh Gales all day from ye Southward, but dry Weather. In ye Morning finished the survey of the Southern Channell, & came into the main River near Habbaspour. From hence the River proceeds with a South Course. There is much Padda sown in the neighbourhood of Habbaspour.

The 21st. a fair Morning, but ye Afternoon Squally & Rainy. At the end of the Reach from Habbaspour we perceived the inlet of a large Creek,[2] & in ye Afternoon examined the head of it. It is in general 250 yards over, & nowhere less than 6 18
Cubits deep. Maudapour, a large Village, is situated a mile down ye Creek, on ye Western Bank. The Course of the Creek is to the SE^{t}. & we are informed that it is navigable all the Year, to Sunderbound.[3]

The 22nd. went into the great River in order to survey it a few more miles Eastwards, & lay down a large Island that lies in ye turn of the Reach opposite the

---

1 Ajoodeea on more recent maps. The correct spelling is Ajodhya. The name is not an uncommon one; the most important is Ajodhya on the banks of the Gogra in Faizabad district, from which the province of Oudh takes its name.

2 The head of the Chandna R. Fergusson explains (*op. cit.*, p. 335) how it happened that when the Brahmaputra changed its course, this creek, which was before that time the main route for boats travelling from the Sunderbans to the Upper Ganges, did not become the chief outlet for the Ganges. Its banks had become too much consolidated by the silt deposited on them to be readily eroded, and the surplus waters found an easier passage through the Garai channel.

3 Sunderbound. The Sundarbans, the vast tract of forest and swamp extending along the sea face of the Ganges delta. The etymology of the name is doubtful Rainey (Proc. As. Soc. Beng. 1868 p. 265) thinks that the true name is Sundarban, or beautiful forest, as preferable to Sundriban, forest of *sundri* (*Heritiera littoralis*). Blochmann, in the discussion on Rainey's paper, proposed the derivation Chandabhanda, from a semi-barbarous tribe formerly living in this part of Bengal. He discussed the etymology of the word in a paper on the Geography and History of Bengal, (Journ. As. Soc. Beng., Vol. xlii. pt. 1. p. 226). and says that the form 'Soonderbund', adopted by Europeans, is derived from Chandraband 'the embankment of the moon.' The application of the term to the whole sea-coast of Southern Bengal is modern. On the old Portuguese and Dutch maps no name is applied to the whole tract. It will be noticed that Rennell always refers to it as 'Sunderbound' without the article.

Creek: without this being done, the Map of the River would break off too abruptly to give a clear Idea of its Course from the inlet of the Creek, eastwards.

This Afternoon a smart Squall from the WNW with some Rain. Rain most of the Night.

The 22nd, 23rd. & part of ye 24th. employed in surveying the great River 3 miles to the eastward of the Creek, & likewise the East Side from thence back to ye Village of Sujanagore. From the head of the Creek the Course of the River is nearly East for some Miles.[2] The 23rd. in ye Afternoon another hard Squall from the NW^t. & the Morning of the 24th. we had fresh Gales, the remaining part of the
19 Day fine Weather. This Morning entered the Creek & continued the Survey of it a mile farther down; it is here very crooked. I allow at this time 5 Cubits for the rising of the Water, the Creek is now no less than 13 Cubits deep.

From the 24th. June to the 3rd. July, the Weather in general remarkably fine, having only a few slight Showers, & the Wind in moderate Breezes from the South East. During this time we traced the Creek upwards of 30 Miles; its Course in general SE, tho' these 2 days past we have found it very crooked, having gone the last 9 miles through 7 Reaches, & in that time have proceeded only 2½ miles in a direct Line. The Face of the Countrey through which we passed has had various Appearances, sometimes thick Jungles continuing for some Miles, & at others fine open Countrey, tho' in general very little cultivated. In the neighbourhood of Sunapara,[3] about 9 miles down the Creek, are several Groves of Betel or Areca Trees[4]; & at Serampour 7½ miles farther is a small white Pagoda, situated in a Peninsula formed by five small Reaches. This Creek abounds with Alligators & Turtle of both
20 of which we have seen great Numbers. The former are exceedingly shy, & dive under the Water upon hearing the least Noise.

This Creek is named by the Countrey People the Chunnunah,[5] & as we are informed, falls into the Comare Creek[6] four miles farther down. It is of a very regular breadth, of about 200 yards; its depth is very irregular, being from 50 to 6 Cubits.

The 26th. & 29th. of June met two Fleets of Salt Boats bound for Patna; the one came from Calcutta by way of Sunderbound & Culna[7]; the other from Jaynagore[8] by way of the Burrashee[9] Creek. One of the Boats was 3500 Maund,[10] & drew 4½ Cubits Water.

1 Sujainagar, a village on the left bank at the head of the Habaspur reach.

2 The E.B.S. Ry. terminus at Goalundo is situated at the eastern end of this reach.

3 Sonapur.

4 The trade in betel nuts was one of the principal monopolies of the E. I. Co. The commodity is frequently referred to in Lord Clive's letters and the resolutions of the Council, under the name of 'beetle.'

5 Chundnah of Rennell's map.

6 The Kumar R. For an account of the changes in the courses of these creeks see Hunter, "Statistical Acc. Bengal," vol. v, p. 204.

7 This is Khulna in the Jessore district, on the Madhumati R., not the Culna mentioned above on the Bhagirathi.

8 Jainagar. This village is not marked on modern maps. It was then a place of some importance, and lay a few miles N.E. of the village of Muhammadpur, on the Madhumati.

9 Burrashee Creek. The Barasia R., a branch of the Madhumati.

10 About 120 tons.

The 28th. at Podumdey[1] found the Magnetic Variation to be 0°-54′ Eastwardly.

The 29th. received a Letter from the Governor by 2 Hircars.

From the 3rd. to the 8th. July mostly rainy Weather, the Wind squally from the East & Southeast. Being prevented from going out, I began to copy the Map, of the Creek &c. to send to the Governor, & the 7th. at Night compleated them, & ye next Morning sent them away by the Hircars that brought the Letter.

* 141 tons.
† 6 ft. 10 in.

The 5th. a Salt Boat of 4000* Maund passed by for 21
Patna; she drew only 4¾† Cubits Water.

The 8th. went on with the Survey This day we had frequent Showers. I allow 6 Cubits for the Rise of the Water. This Afternoon saw a high Pagoda to the SEt. distant 2 or 3 miles. It lies near the Village of Motrapour.[2]

The 9th. in ye Morning a Squall from the Southwd. the forenoon fresh Gales from the same Quarter, with Showers; the Afternoon continual Rain. This day allowed 7 Cubits for the Waters rising. The Creek runs very crooked, the Countrey open & pleasant.

The 10th. Squally and Rainy. Passed the Pagoda of Motrapour which lies on ye East side of the Creek. Two Miles below this Pagoda, a large Creek turns away to the Eastward & is at this time navigable for large Boats, but in ye dry Season is quite dry in some Places. It proceeds by way of Jaynagore and Hobbygunge.[3]

Here the Creek that we are tracing loses its name of the Chunnunah, & receives that of the Comer,[4] or Comare, & now proceeds with a WSW Course 5 miles, being much narrower than before, but considerably deeper.

The 11th. a Squally Morning, the remainder of the Day fine Weather. 22
Passed the Village of Bandorse, or Gopalpour, which lies a large Mile below the head of the Eastern Comer, or Creek to Hobbygunge. Here are many Betel Trees.

The 12th. the forenoon fair, a Squall at Noon, the Afternoon very fine. This Evening came to a Place where this Creek divides into 2 Branches; the largest is named the Burrashee & winds round to the South & SE. It is reported to be navigable all the year, & that it runs near Jaynagore and Culna. The smallest takes its Course NWBW, & is deep, though but 70 yards broad in general. This Creek is named the Comare. As it appears by its Course to allow the shortest Passage to Calcutta, I judged it proper to survey it first, & should it not prove navigable, to proceed by way of the Burrashee.

1 Podumdey. A small village N. of Baliakhandi, on the west side of the creek.

2 Mathurapur, at the junction of this creek with the Kumar. The temple is said to have been built about 70 years before this by one Sangram Shah of the Baidya family, but was left unfinished because one of the masons fell from the steeple and died. (List of Ancient Mon. Beng., p. 224.)

3 Habiganj, Hobibgunge of Rennell's map. It lies to the S.E. on a dying course of the Arial Khan (Arika R. of Rennell p 92). It is to be noted that Rennell does not mention Faridpur, now the headquarters of the district, and a town of over 10,000 inhabitants. It is marked on his map as an insignificant village (Farridpour).

4 Comer. The Kumar R. This had evidently been at one time the course of the main stream of the Ganges.

The 13th. all day Cloudy and cool. Proceeded with the Survey of the Comer Creek & find from 14 to 21 Cubits Water wch. allowing 7 Cubits for the Rise, will be no less than 7 Cubits in ye dry Season.

23 Two miles & half above ye head of the Burrashee the Eastmost Branch of Custee Creek[1] falls into the Comer; the Water of it appears quite black at this Season: it is named by the Country People Lettydoman Creek. The Village of Lettydoman lies on ye East side of it, just where it joins the Comer. From hence the Course of the Comer is WBS for some Miles.

The 14th. a cool Morning; the middle of the day excessive hot. Three Miles West from Lettydoman the Creek turns to ye Northward, & continues that Course for 3 Miles more, & then goes to the SW for near the same Distance. We find the depths of Water from 34 to 8 Cubits (in ye dry Season), the Banks being mostly covered with Jungle we have very troublesome Work to survey them.

The 15th. the Forenoon again excessive hot, having mostly Calm Weather; the Afternoon and Evening cool & pleasant. Still following ye Course of the Comer Creek. We find abundance of Turtle here, some of them very large. The Countrey
24 People inform us that they never saw any Europeans pass this way before.

The 16th. the Morning & Evening fine Weather, the middle of the Day excessive hot. This Day in pursuing the Course of the Comer we came into another Creek which is much larger than that, & which comes from the Northwest. The Countrey People inform us that it is the Westmost Branch of Custee Creek, but cannot inform us how far up it is navigable, or whether betwixt this & Custee any Creeks run out of it to the Southwest. This Creek has likewise the name of Comer or Comare; & now the two Creeks of that name joining, they proceed with a rapid Current to the South & South East forming a large Creek or River known by the name of the Burrasaat.

Some Boatmen that we have met here inform us that the Burrasaat runs towards Backergunge, a large Village situated on ye Eastern Skirts of the Wood or
25 Sunderbound, that a few Coss down a Creek runs out from ye East Side & communicates with the Burrashee; & that three or four Days down, another Creek runs out from the West Side & goes either to Rangafulla or the Southern Lakes[3] by Calcutta. If this Information be true, we have yet Hopes of finding the desired Passage; & indeed by the Course of the Creek we have some Reason to believe it.

[1] The Garai river. Hunter says "during the rains so much water flows through the Kaliganga channel into the Kumar that at Ramnagar, near Magura, the latter has to get rid of the surplus, and discharges part of its water back again into the Garai channel." This may account for the black colour of the water noted by Rennell, the portion of the creek where he made this observation forming a kind of back-water (Imp. Gaz., Vol. v, p. 11).

[2] Probably the Nabaganga. According to Hunter, it is drying up year by year and is not navigable in the hot season. (Imp. Gaz., Vol. x, p. 125).

[3] The Salt-water Lakes, about 5 miles E. of Calcutta, part of which is now used for the disposal of the sewage of the city. They are connected with Khulna at the head of the Sunderbans, by canals, the traffic over which now averages 1,000,000 tons per annum, valued at nearly four millions sterling (Imp. Gaz., Vol. ix, p. 287). This route is referred to in Rennell's 'Memoir of Hindoostan' (p. 363) as the Baliagot Passage, now the Baliaghata canal. In the same place he mentions that within a very few years, a small canal has been cut, to join the lake with the river. This is Tolly's Nullah, constructed in 1777 by Major Tolly, who utilised an old bed of the Ganges.

I have some suspicion that it is a Branch of this Creek that falls into the Hughly River at Betwallerah.[1]

The 17th. the Morning rainy, the middle of the day fresh Gales at SE, the Evening fine.

This Day surveyed 2½ miles of the Burrasaat, its Course nearly Southeast; the depth of Water from 13 to 41 Cubits.

The 18th. in the Morning the Assistant, whom I had sent to examine the Course of the NW Comer (or Westmost Branch of Custee Creek) returned & informed me that he had found it navigable 7 or 8 miles up, & that ye Countrey People informed 26
him that a few Coss farther up, a Creek ran out of it to ye Southwest. Upon this I left off surveying ye Burrasaat & proceeded up ye NW Branch of the Comer, in hopes that ye Creek above mentioned might communicate with Rangafulla, or ye Southern Lakes.

The place where we left off surveying the Burrasaat was named Maddepour, & lies on ye West Side.

This Evening proceeded one Mile up ye NW Comer, the Course NWBN; depths from 10 to 20 Cubits. The Creek is now 150 yards over.

The 19th. a hot Day, some slight Showers in ye Forenoon. Went 5 miles farther up the Creek, Course from NWBW to WBS. Five miles above the head of the Burrasaat a small Creek falls into this from the Northward, but is not navigable in the dry Season: the Water of it is quite black, as it runs out of the Jeels[2]; the Country being now entirely overflown in this neighbourhood; save only the Banks of the Creek, & the little mounds on which the Villages are built.[3]

About a mile above the Mouth of this Creek, & opposite to the Village of Away- 27
pour,[4] we found only 10½ Cubits Water, which with an allowance of 8 Cubits for the Rise, is only 2½ in ye dry Season. The People of Awaypour inform us that there is not quite 2 Cubits at some Seasons, so that it cannot be navigable for loaded Boats of 300 Maund. Farther up, the Creek deepens again to 4, 5 & 10 Cubits in ye dry Season. I proceeded farther up in order to get better Intelligence.

A mile & half above Awaypour a small Creek runs out to the S. & SW, but is not navigable 2 miles down in ye dry Season, although the Countrey People had informed the Assistant that it was navigable a long way.

The 20th. the Morning cool, the Afternoon very sultry. This Forenoon met a Boatman from Custee who seemed to be an intelligent Fellow. He tells me that the Creek near Awaypour will not allow a Passage for Boats of 200 Maund in the dry Season. He likewise informs me that this Creek is the Westmost Branch of Custee Creek & that 5 Coss to the Westw^d. of Awaypour a small Creek from Buxeypour falls into it from the Westward. This Buxeypour I imagine must be the Village of 28

[1] *Ante*, p. 10.

[2] Jeels—Jhils. The great marshes or lagoons so common in Eastern Bengal and Sylhet. Also called 'Bhils.' In Central India and Rajputana the name is applied to an artificial lake or reservoir (Hobson Jobson, p. 457).

[3] These mounds are artificial. The Chandals, a caste of Hinduized aborigines inhabiting this part of the country, habitually build their villages on artificially raised mounds. (Hunter, Imp. Gaz., Vol. iv, pp. 394, 396, 401).

[4] Abipur.

that name situated on ye Eastern Bank of the Jelenghee, tho' he says that it is only 18 Coss from Awaypour.[1]

It will now appear by our Observations that the Burrasaat is the Westmost of the navigable Creeks which run out of the Ganges to the Eastward of Jelenghee, & is therefore likely to afford the shortest Passage to Calcutta; but being at present destitute of Cash to pay ye People, or proper Boats to survey Sunderbound with; besides it being now nearly the height of the wett Season, we are very apt to be deceived in ye depths of Water, by the sudden swelling & falling of the Rivers; I have therefore judged it proper to go to Dacca to get a supply of Cash & larger Boats, before we proceed.

Being in the neighbourhood of Lettydoman Creek (or Eastmost Branch of Custee Creek) I thought it might be worth while to take a cursory Survey of it as far up as it is navigable, it being the common rout of the Boats from Jelenghee & Custee to Jaynagore, Hobbygunge, &c. when ye Rivers have rose enough to make it navigable, wch. commonly happens about ye latter end of May.

29 From the 20th. to the 26th. employed in tracing the Creeks of Lettydoman, Culsedaw & Bacout near 30 miles till we came to the Place where it is not navigable, which is at Columbery about 8 miles SW from Maudapour, & 5½ North from Awaypour. For ye particulars see the Maps of the Creeks. The Weather during this time was as follows:

The 21st Calm & Cloudy all Day, the 22nd. an excessive hot Forenoon; in ye Afternoon several heavy Showers. The 23rd. very fresh Gales from the Southward with heavy Rain all the Day. The 24th. all ye Forenoon heavy Rain with some Squalls, the Afternoon Cloudy. The 25th. the Forenoon dry, Afternoon & Night continual Rain. The 26th. a Cloudy Morning, in ye Afternoon some Rain; the Evening fine Weather.

This Morning having finished the Survey of the Creeks we dropt down the Comer for Dacca, & in ye Afternoon entered the Eastern Comer near Motrapour. The Water has rose 2 Cubits in this Creek since ye 10th. Inst. We passed three miles of the Creek this Evening. The Course of the Stream is to the Eastward: its Banks are now high out of the Water & we are informed will not be overflown the whole wet Season. The Country is pleasant & tolerably well cultivated.

30 The 27th. Cloudy Weather; the Morning & Evening cool & pleasant, but ye middle of ye Day excessive hot. This Day we passed by Estimation 25 miles of the Creek, & came to Jaynagore in ye Evening. This Village lies on ye South side of the Creek, & is distant from Motrapour only 8½ miles, altho' it is near 28 by Water. Fourteen miles NNE from Jaynagore a small Creek leads from this into ye Ganges, thereby allowing a short cut to Hadgygunge[2] & Dacca, but for want of proper Intelligence we passed it without knowing where it led to. The Burrashee Creek comes

[1] A Buxipour is shown on Rennell's map 15 miles SW of Kushtia, and 30 miles east of the Jalangi.

[2] This Hajiganj must have been an important place at this time, as it was the point where the main road from Calcutta to Dacca crossed the Ganges. It lay about 5 miles E. of the present town of Faridpur.

within a mile & half of Jaynagore, & afterwards winds off from ye neighbourhood of the Comer, taking a SSE & SE Course.

The 28th. in ye Morning some flying Showers, the middle of the Day Cloudy & cool, the latter part heavy Rain. Passed 17 miles of the Creek, which is rather streighter than yesterday, the Country on both sides is very pleasant. In ye Morning received a Letter from ye Governor by 2 Hircars. Lay this Night at Jadynundy.

The 29th. mostly clear Weather, but such fresh Gales of Wind from the Eastward, that we make but a slow progress. Proceeded 19 miles this Day, & came to Sadundy at Night. The Country here is mostly overflown.

The 30th. mostly fresh Breezes from the SE, with frequent Squalls of Rain. 31
The Country here is mostly overflown, & having the Wind right against us, we went only 8 miles this Day. Lay at Cassempour.

The 31st. the Weather nearly the same, tho' rather more Rain than yesterday. This Morning after going 3 miles the Creek divides into 2 Branches: we were directed thro' the Northmost for the nearest Passage to Hobbygunge & Dacca. Went only 7 miles this Day, & at Night lay at Commercandy about 4 miles from Hobbygunge.

August the 1st. fresh Gales from the Eastward with several Showers. In ye Morning passed by Hobbygunge[1] which lies on the South side of the Creek about 27 miles ESE½S from Jaynagore. About a mile below Hobbygunge this Creek joins with that from Budarashon: here the Countrey, being entirely overflown we had some difficulty to distinguish ye Creeks from the Jeels.

After proceeding 2 miles up Budarashon Creek we found that another large Creek joins it from the Northwest. From hence we proceeded to the NE 5 miles & then had a sight of the Ganges, which however we did not enter this Evening, it being late, & ye River excessive rapid.

From hence we saw the Pagodas of Rajanagur[2] bearing to the ESE, distant 6 or 7 miles.

The 2nd. the Weather nearly as yesterday. Early in the Morning entered the 32
great River, & were near 4 hours in crossing it, by reason of its breadth, and ye great Rapidity of the Stream. After gaining the Eastern Shoar we entered a Creek near Nullua in order to proceed across ye Country to Dacca, the Water being upwards of 4 Cubits above ye level of ye Country. Dacca bears from us NE distant 24 miles. This Evening came to Hautcola a Village situated 5 or 6 miles from ye Ganges. This Evening ye Wind came at ENE.

The 3rd. very fresh Gales of Wind from the East & ENE. This Evening

---

[1] Hobibgunge of Rennell's maps. None of the other villages mentioned are marked on his map. Habiganj has been superseded in importance by Madaripur, as Hajiganj has given place to Faridpur. Budarashon (Budrasan) lay 8 or 10 miles to the NE near the main river. There have evidently been great changes in the course of the river hereabouts, and most of these villages have disappeared.

[2] Rajanagur lay on the south side of the old channel of the Kirtinasa river, near the conflux of the Ganges Pudda and the Dhaleswari.

came to Daagdya, 4 miles from Hautcola. Here is an high white Pagoda. At Night a very hard Squall from ye Westwd.

The 4th. the Wind came from the South & SW, which being fair we made the best of our way for Dacca. At 10 in ye Forenoon came to Meergunge and Issamutey [1], & passed under ye Bridge [2], the Arch being just large enough to admit the Budgarow. From hence struck across to the Mouth of the Beurygonga [3] or Dacca River leaving Feringybazar [4] 3 miles to ye Eastward, & at ½ past 5 in ye Evening came to Dacca.

---

[1] Ichamati, a creek which flows out of the Ganges opposite Goalundo.

[2] The Taltala Bridge, standing upon the Taltala (formerly Meergunge) khal or creek. It is said to have been built by Raja Vallal Sen, before the conquest of Bengal by the Muhammadans, and if so is about 300 years old. It consisted of three arches, the central one of 30 ft. span. This arch was blown up by gunpowder during the first year of British rule, in order to secure direct communication for large boats between Calcutta and Dacca. (List of Ancient Mon. Beng., p. 220).

[3] The Buriganga.

[4] Firinghibazaar was the first Portuguese settlement in the Dacca district, and had been in existence for about 100 years at this time. The Portuguese settlers were originally soldiers, who had deserted from the service of the Raja of Arakan to that of Husain Beg, the Mughal general beseiging Chittagong. The village is now quite insignificant. It lies on a branch of the Ichamati, opposite Naraingani. (Hunter, Imp. Gaz. Vol. iv, p. 436).

SEPTEMBER 1764.

JOURNAL of the second Expedition for Surveying the Ganges from where we left it near Saatpour to its conflux with ye Megna, & the Megna &c. from thence to Dacca.

The 19th. of September 1764, being pretty well recovered from my Indisposition, I set out from Dacca in the forenoon in order to proceed with the Survey of the great River.

The Countrey being mostly under Water at this Time, our nearest Rout lies across ye Countrey to the Banks of the Ganges opposite Hadgygunge, after which (as the Country lies higher then) we must proceed up the great River. Hadgygunge or Hageagunge is about 31 English Miles WBS from Dacca.

From the 19th. to ye 21st. mostly fresh Breezes of Wind from SE to ESE & 2
dry Weather.

The Night after leaving Dacca, we lay at Tagerpour on the North Bank of the Isamutey or Dullasery River. Dacca in sight, bearing NE½E distant about 6 miles or more.

Ten miles to ye Westward of Dacca, the Countrey lies much higher than in ye neighbourhood of that City; The Banks of the Creeks here are mostly dry, whereas the Countrey round Dacca is from four to five Cubits* under Water.

*Cubits reckoned at 18 inches.

The 21st, at half past 11 AM came to the Banks of the Ganges opposite to Hageagunge, there being at this Season an outlet near Mousudabad. We crossed the River in less than a hour, tho' not without some risque, considering the crazyness of the Budgarow, & the monstrous swell occasioned by a fresh Breeze of Wind 3
against a Current of about five miles an hour. At 3 we came to Hageagunge, after going some Miles up a large Creek. The Countrey here is about a Cubit & half above the level of the Water but I find by the Village People that in the height of the wet Season, it was full as much under Water.

This Night (of ye 21st.) & the following Day very fresh Breezes of Wind with frequent heavy Squalls from S to SSE. This I presume may be looked on as an Equinoctial Gale; however the Wind is far from being veerable.

The 22nd. remained at Hageagunge, & repaired a Pulwar[1] that was stove in crossing the River yesterday.

From the 22nd. to ye 25th. the Weather more settled, the Wind mostly moderate & from the SE Quarter. The 23rd. in the Morning left Hageagunge & proceeded up a Creek that brought us into ye great River below Binetty Island.[2]

1 Or Pulwah. A native boat of 12 to 15 tons generally used as a cook boat by Europeans (Hobson Jobson, p. 737).

2 The topography of this part of the river is much altered since Rennell's time, no doubt on account of the incursion of the main stream of the Brahmaputra at Goalundo, at the head of this reach.

4 The River is fallen sufficiently for showing the exact bed of it, & ye farther we proceed up, the greater we find ye Fall.

The 25th. at 4 PM came to Saatpour, ye Place where we left off the Survey of the River in June last. There had been so much of the Bank carried away by the Freshes, that we hardly knew the place again; & could not have found the Mark out had it not been for a remarkable Tree which I formerly took ye bearings of.

Wednesday the 26th. in ye Morning began surveying the South side of the River from Saatpour. At noon a Pulwar arrived from Dacca with Letters.

From Saatpour the Course of the River is mostly East for near 11 miles,[2] & four miles below Saatpour it is not half a mile broad at this Time.

The 29th. PM the Weather threatning, we dropt down to a large Creek near
5 Kalkapour & secured the Boats there till ye next day, which proved quite Calm, & excessive hot. The Creek abovementioned runs out from ye South side of the Ganges about a mile from Kalkapour & falls into the River again at Hageagunge.[3] At this time it communicates with the Eastern Comer Creek by which it affords a passage to Boosna,[4] but in ye dry Season this Creek itself has not more than a Cubit & half water in it.

This day Septem^{r}, 30th. dispatched a Pulwar for Dacca, with a Letter for the Governor.

Octo^{r}. ye 1st. excessive hot Weather; came to the Mouth of Rottingunge[5] Creek this day. This Creek which falls into ye Great River on the North side, is the same which runs out at Pubna, & as it affords a safer Passage than ye great River for loaded Boats, it is mostly used by the Fleets which go up ye River from Sunderbound in ye dry Season. It is about 500 yards over near the outlet, the Eastern side of which is very flat, & must be avoided by large Boats.

* At ye mouth of Rottingunge Creek.

This Evening* found ye Var^{n}. by an Amp^{de}. 1-0° Westly.

6 From the 1st. to ye 6th. Octr. mostly calm, & ye Weather hotter than I have felt it before during the Season.

The 3rd. at Gondaely found the Magnetic Variation 1°-10′ Westly

The 3rd. came to the Head of a large Creek which runs out from ye North side near Jaffiergunge[6] & presently after receives a large Creek from Rungpour[7] &c. & then proceeds towards Dacca in two Branches which are the Beurygonga & Isamutey. The Creek which runs out of ye Ganges here, is commonly known by ye name of Jaffiergunge or Joupergunge[8] Creek, & is commonly used in ye Passage to Dacca. Jaffiergunge lies about two miles up the Creek which comes from Rungpour.

1 Before he turned down the Chandna Creek, *ante* p. 18.

2 Towards Goalundo, where it turns S.

3 The Mara or 'dead' Pudma, an old channel of the Ganges.

4 Bhusna. A large village and bazar west of Faridpur.

5 Ruttungunge of Rennell's map. This village seems to have disappeared.

6 Jafarganj. This village is now on the eastern bank of the Brahmaputra, 7 or 8 miles above Goalundo.

7 This is probably the channel down which the Brahmaputra subsequently found its way, the Jennai R. of Fergusson. Rungpur is a town and district far to the north in Rajshahi.

8 This name is somewhat illegible.

The River, opposite this Creek is full three Miles broad, having several Sand Islands in ye middle; from hence it runs with a due South Course near 15 miles, & is commonly narrow. The Ganges from this place downward is not near so much frequented as the parts above; by reason that most Boats that are bound to Dacca, 7
Luckypour, or Chittigong, proceed down the Creek near Jaffiergunge.

We have now surveyed about 22 miles from the place we began at last, & have passed upwards of 50 Villages, but all of them inconsiderable. 'Tis impossible to describe the face of the Countrey at this Season, because it is mostly under Water; however the Banks of the River are high, & in many places sown with Cotton, but there did not appear to be more Padda, than what the Inhabitants might very well consume.

The 4th. in ye afternoon a small Breeze of Wind from the North East, which is the first from that Quarter that I have perceived this Season.

The 7th. in ye morning perceiving the Weather to look threatning, the Wind also increasing from the Eastward, & it being near the time of the Monsoon's breaking, I judged it proper to lay the Boats in a secure Place, & for that purpose went into Diwaly Creek, which is situated opposite to Jaffiergunge Creek, & has now 8
four or five Cubits of Water in it. Lay there this Night, but the Weather cleared up again before Morning.

From the 7th. to ye 13th. variable Weather, but mostly fresh Breezes of Wind with some Squalls & Rain from the South East Quarter.

The 8th. finished the Survey of the long Southern Reach, at the turning of which we perceive a large Island, & the River afterwards proceeding with a SEBE Course towards Hageagunge.

The 12th. finished the Survey of the large Island abovementioned (v$^{t.}$ Binetty Island) & the Banks of the River opposite to it.

Binetty Island is about five miles long & near two over, & lies in a NWBN & SEBS direction; it has 11 small Villages on it, but scarce a single Tree. Being low it is mostly sown with Padda, of which I judge there is at least 3½ square Miles. The Channel of the River that runs by the North side of it, is the shortest & most commonly used by the Boats, it is about a Mile over & has a very rapid 9
Stream. The South Channel is about half a Mile over, & has several Sand Banks in it.

The Banks of the River opposite to this Island are mostly sown with Padda, & have a great number of Villages on them.

The 12th. at Ramcandapour near Binetty Island found the Magnetic Variation 1° – 0′ West^{ly}.

The 13th. the Weather began to settle, & from this time to the 26th. we had exceedingly fine Weather, the Winds from the Southern Quarter in small Breezes, the Atmosphere remarkably clear in general, the Morning of the 21st. only being foggy.

1 Now-a-days the expression 'break of the monsoon' is generally used to mean the *beginning* of the SW monsoon in May or June.

2 The channel of the river here has altered greatly since the time this was written owing to the incursion of the Brahmaputra, though the general direction is the same. The reach is still studded with large islands.

From the South East point of Binetty Island the River runs pretty streight to the SEBE for near 17 miles, & is from ¾ of a mile to a mile & half broad; from the end of Binetty Island a chain of small Islands & Sand Banks extends more than five miles; Boats should be careful not to cross the River at this Place.

10 The 13th. came to ye head of a small Creek which runs out from ye South side of the River at Ramcundapour & falling into the Creek from Kalkapour (see page 5th.) about 2½ miles down, proceeds to Hageagunge, & is navigable all the year round.[1] This Day mustered the People & exercised the Sepoys &c.

The 14th. at Ramcundapour the Variation of the Mag. Needle by a very good Amplde. 0°-15′ Eastly.

The 15th. surveyed to the Mouth of Hageagunge Creek, which I have mentioned before to be the same that runs out of the River at Kalkapour. Hageagunge[2] being a noted Village on account of its being a principal Stage on the Road from Calcutta to Dacca, I thought proper to survey the Creek in order to fix the true Situation of the Village.

It lies about 2 miles and half above the outlet of the Creek, & within a Mile overland from the South, or rather SW Bank of the great River.* It stands on a small extent of Ground on the West side of the Creek, & does not contain more than 80
11 Houses, & has a very paultry Bazar. The Creek is navigable in the dry Season for Boats of 600 Maund, & is about a quarter of a mile broad.

*Hageagunge lies about 31 miles WBS from Dacca.

The Southern Bank of the River from Binetty to this Place is by far the pleasantest Country I have seen since we left Jelenghee, it being made up of extensive Meadows towards the River, & scattering Groves of Trees within, & several Villages.

This Day found the Variation of the Needle to be 0°-31′ Westerly. At Night received a Letter from the Governor by 2 Hircars, & answered it immediately, inclosing a Sketch of the River from Saatpour to this Place. In Mr. VanSittart's Letter he approves of my Intentions of surveying the River on both sides, having before omitted to explain whether it was to be so surveyed, or only on one side, as from Jelenghee to Saatpour.

The 16th. at Coberpour[3] observed the Variation to be 1°-2′ Westly.

12 The 18th. came to the head of Nabobgunge[4] Creek, on the North side of the River, & about 9 miles below Hageagunge. This Creek is about 200 yards over, & is navigable all the year, affording the shortest Passage from Hageagunge to Dacca, Luckypour &. It joins the Isamutey or Dullasery above Feringybazar, & sends out several small Branches.

The Countrey (on the North side of the River) from Binetty Island to this Place is well inhabited & sown with Paddy & Cotton. Mousudabad[5] a very large Village & Purgana is situated in a pleasant Country opposite Hageagunge.

---

1 This creek is apparently not marked on Rennell's maps.

2 *Ante*, p. 22.

3 On the left bank of the Ganges, opposite to Hajiganj.

4 Nawabganj.

5 Mansurabad, now opposite Faridpur. A Pargana is a Fiscal division of a district.

From Nabobgunge Creek the River takes a more Southwardly Course, & is divided into several Channels by some large Islands, which are mostly covered with Jungle, & have many Tygers on them.

The 20th. came to ye mouth of a broad but shallow Creek, which is a branch of that from Nabobgunge, & falls into y^e River at Chorcumerdour about six miles below
the head of the former. The Country hereabout is mostly uncultivated. This Day 13
at Noon observed the Latitude at Jattapour [1] & found it to be in y^e Paralell of 23°-27′ North. At Sunset the variation of the Needle 0°-38′ $West^{ly}$.

The 21st. the Morning thick fog which continued about an Hour, soon after which from Gohulercandy we saw two of Rajanagore Pagodas [2] bearing in y^e South East Quarter distant near 14 miles.

Having left unsurveyed the South side of the River from Hageagunge which is about 20 miles, we put over to that side* in ye Forenoon, & began surveying up towards Hageagunge.

* near ye East end of Bunderculla Island.

The 25th. came back to ye mouth of Hageagunge Creek.

The Country between Hageagunge & Bunderculla (the South side of the River) is but thinly peopled or cultivated. Eight miles below Hageagunge begins a chain of Islands which divide ye River into several small Channells on the South side; these Islands of which there are three principal ones extend about 8 miles, & are covered with thick Jungles, being inhabited only by Tygers, which frequently make excursions to ye South side in quest of their Prey. Jallapour Island is the South-
most of the three; opposite to the Northwest point of it, a large Creek runs out to 14
the Southward and Southeast, making the shortest Passage to Hobbygunge from this part of the Country. This Creek is navigable all the year for large Boats. On the South point of its inlet is situated Saggaatpour, a large Village; this is distant from Hageagunge by land 12 English miles, & from Hobbygunge 17.

Near the South East point of Jallapour Island, begins the NW part of Bunderculla Island; This Island is not properly belonging to the Ganges, being divided by a very narrow shallow Creek. It is about 5½ miles in length & 1¼ in breadth, & has only one small Village on it, the rest being an entire Jungle. On the North part of this Island we perceived the fresh Track of a large Tyger, this being the first we have seen since we came out. Pulyculla and Bunderculla, two middling Villages are situated on the River Bank opposite to the NW part of the Island.

The 23d.[4] at Seneekondy, Variation p. Amplitude 0°-16′ W^t. 15

The 25th. at the time of finishing the Survey back from Bunderculla to Hageagunge, I found myself very ill of a Cold, which was followed by a Feaver; & being in the neighbourhood of Dacca, I thought it proper to go there for Assistance.

The 26th. in ye Morning dropped down to Nabobgunge Creek, & proceeded

1 On the left bank of the river. 2 *See below*, p. 39, also Appendix.

3 Mr. Ascoli tells me that the islands in the Padma between its junction with the Brahmaputra and Rajnagar are all now covered with sand, and contain no appreciable jungle. This change is probably due to the sand brought down by the Brahmaputra.

4 The date of the battle of Buxar, which placed the whole of Oudh and the north west of Bengal in the power of the English.

through it towards Dacca. At Sunset saw Dyatybalypour Pagoda to the NE distant 4 miles, & at the same time left the main Creek & proceeded through a very small Creek, which brought us into the Isamutey River about 9 at Night. We crossed the Isamutey again soon after & went through a small Creek to the NE'ward, & at 11 came within one Pour[1]* or Par of Dacca. Here we rested till Morning, & got to Dacca about 9 AM.

* Equal to 5 English miles or 6 Bengall Hours' travelling.

My Disorder increasing, I remained at Dacca till ye 2d. November when being tolerably recovered I set out from thence to proceed with the Survey.

16 During my stay at Dacca the Weather was remarkably fine & cool, the Mornings commonly Foggy till near 8 o'Clock.

Whilst at Dacca I wrote to Mr. VanSittart informing him of my illness, & of the late Progress of the Survey, inclosing a Sketch of it. At the same time I requested his Opinion of the utility of surveying the Baramputry or Megna from its conflux with the Ganges[2] to Dacca. He was pleased to express his Approbation of it, & ordered it to be carried into Execution when the present Service should be finished.

Novr. 2d. in the Afternoon left Dacca, & at 8 next Morning entered the Isamutey, leaving it again at 10, going back the same Road we came. At Noon ye 3d. set Dyatybalypour Pagoda bearing E 24° N dist. about 4 miles, & that of Barycally S 21°-30′ W. about 5 or 6 miles. We were at this Time half way down ye Creek, that runs from Nabobgunge Creek to ye Isamutey.

17 From Nabobgunge Creek we turned to ye Left & went through a very small Creek whose Course was from South to SBW; the inlet of it is near Churol distant from Nabobgunge 1½ pour or about 8 English Miles.

The 4th. following the Course of the small Creek came into Jeels which we were about 2 hours in crossing, & then entered a very small Creek, our Course mostly South. At Noon saw the Pagodas at Neurpour[3] bearing South distant 5 or 6 miles.

At 5 PM passed about ½ a mile to the Westward of the Pagodas & came very near our old Mark at Gohulercandy at Night. The Countrey here is mostly Swamp or Jeels.

The 5th. at 8 in the Morning came into the great River by Nullua Creek,[4] & coming to the place where we left off, proceeded with the Survey. We have now been absent from it 10 days.

From this time to the 17th. inclusive no remarkable Circumstance happened; the Weather being extremely fine, we have no other Obstacles to carrying on our

[1] Hobson Jobson has Puhur (Hind. pahar, pahr), a fourth part of the day or night, a 'watch' or space of 8 gharis. It is not mentioned in that work as a measure of distance. In the notes appended to this journal Rennell gives determinations of the Par or Pour (*see* p. 127.) The Bengal hour was the 'ghari', measured by a floating cup with a small hole in it, adjusted so that it would fill and sink within a certain time. This interval was 24 minutes, 8 of these intervals making a Puhur or Par.

[2] This was of course at that time to the south of Dacca, not to the west as it is now.

[3] Nurpur. None of these temples are mentioned in the List of Ancient Monuments.

[4] It is below this point, according to Mr. Ascoli, that the greatest changes in the course of the Padma have taken place since Rennell's time.

Business properly than the extensive Thickets with which the Countrey abounds, & 18
the constant dread of Tygers, whose Vicinity to us, their Tracks which we are constantly trampling over do fully demonstrate. The Weather now begins to grow cold, especially in the Mornings, but we have had very few Fogs as yet, which is a favorable Circumstance to us. The Winds have been mostly from the Northward, & if in a Morning it happened to blow fresh, the Air was very sharp.

From Gohulercandy, where we last began our Work, the Course of the River is mostly SBE (allowing the turnings) till it separates into two Branches near Tockya.

In the first Reach from Gohulercandy, there are four principal Creeks leading out of the River; & there being 2 large Islands in it, the River is at one place 3½ miles over.

The inlet of Budarashon Creek is on ye West side, 3 miles down the Reach, from
whence it is but 7 miles by Water to Hobbygunge. This Creek is navigable all the 19
year for large Boats, & is a good Track for Boats bound from Sunderbound to Jelenghee &c.

On the opposite side of the Reach, & within [1] Gonganagore Island, a small Creek runs out towards Rajanagore, & from thence to Loricul [2] & the Megna, affording a good Passage for large Boats from one River to the other; though Chycundy Creek which runs out four Miles farther down & joins with this within ye Country, affords the shortest Passage of the two.[3] In the dry Season they are neither of them navigable for large Boats at low Water, but the delay occasioned by that is of trifling consequence when compared with ye danger & risque of navigating the Megna; for unless this Creek existed, the Boats from Sunderbound to Dacca, Assam, &c. must have gone up that River.

Rajanagore,* formerly a place of consequence, lies about 3 miles in from ye East side of the River; there are 8 Pagodas in & near it, some of which may be seen a great way off.[4] From
Rajanagore to the Megna or Baramputrey is only 8½ miles, 20
so that the Peninsula formed by the 2 Rivers is not 12 miles over in this Place.

* Lat. 23°-20′ N. from Dacca SBW 27m.

At the bottom of the Reach close by Diggarypara a large Creek runs out to ye Southeast, but falls into the great River again after taking a Course of about 10 or 12 miles.

The 10th. at Pokera found the Variation of the Needle to be 1°·6′ Westerly.

Near the Village of Tockya,[5] about 16 miles S½W from Rajanagore, & in Latitude 23°-7′, the Ganges divides into two separate Branches, forming an Island of about 20 miles long, & in some Places 12 over, but of the Particulars hereafter.

---

[1] *i.e.* to the east of.

[2] Luricool of map, *see* p. 39 and Appendix A

[3] The position of these creeks is now mainly occupied by the united waters of the Ganges and Meghna. They were almost due west of Chandpur.

[4] *See* Appendix A.

[5] About 13 miles SE of Madaripur. The main stream of the Ganges now flows far to the North of this.

Of these Branches, the Eastmost is the largest, but afterwards divides into a number of small Branches forming 17 or 18 Islands before it unites again with the Western Branch. This Eastern one appearing to make the shortest Passage to Luckypour[1] I propose to make an exact Survey of it, & only a cursory one of the
21 other, one being sufficient to determine the distance.

The 16th. at Rypour found the Variation to be 0°-55′ Westerly.

I have not been able as yet to get any tolerable information concerning the Situation of Luckypour, & being informed that a little further on, the River divides into several Branches, I judge it prudent to take a cursory Survey of them at first, fearing lest we may take a wrong Rout, which may probably occasion the loss of more Time than what I have proposed, & to less Advantage.

On this Consideration I left off surveying at Tockya, & dropt down ye River the 17th. in the Evening.

The 18th. in the Morning fresh Breezes of Wind from the Northward, with several Showers, & the Air excessive cold. All day making the best of our Way down the River, keeping the Eastmost Channels, as their Course trends most towards Luckypour.

22 The 19th. at Noon after going from Tockya by Account 35 or 36 Miles, we entered the Megna or Baramputrey, coming into it by the Northmost Channel of the Ganges, known by the name of Mendygunge[2] River. The main Channel of the Ganges seems to fall in about 4 or 5 miles to the Southward.

We now proceeded along the Western Shoar of the Megna NBE & NNE, a confused cluster of uninhabited Islands forming the East side of the Passage. Between some of these Islands I could discover no Land at all, it appearing like an open Sea.

The 20th. in the Morning passed Doycally, & soon after had a view of Luckypour, the Factory being distinctly seen 13 or 14 miles. Before Noon we reached it. By a computation of the distances from Tockya to this Place, I judge that we have about 46 or 50 miles more to survey.

Being in daily expectation of receiving another Budgarow, I propose staying here another Day, & employ myself in copying the Surveys of the River for the public Use.

23 The 22nd in the Morning set out from Luckypour, on our return to the Survey, the Weather remarkably fine.

The 25th. in the Morning arrived at our old Mark at Gozarya,[3] & proceeded with the Survey. During the Passage from Luckypour, we have been employed in copying the drafts of the River. This Evening at Nagulpara[4] the Variation was 1°-10′ Westly.

From this time to the 16th. of December, the Weather continued to be remarkably serene; the Mornings (as is usual at this Season) very foggy till 9 or 10 o'clock,

---

1 Lakshmipur, a town on the left bank of the Meghna in Noakhali district.

2 Mehdiganj or Mehndiganj.

3 About 4 miles E of Tockya.

4 Nagerpara in Faridpur Dist.

& sometimes the Fog continued the whole Day in such a manner that no surveying Work could be performed. The Winds commonly blew in light Breezes from the North & NNE, with frequent intervals of Calms, at which Times ye Fogs continued. I remarked that the Fogs commonly came on immediately after Sunrising. The Morning Air seemed to me to have ye same degree of Cold, as that in England about the latter end of March.

The 28th. after surveying 3 Reaches from Tockya, came to Monerpour, where 24
the largest Channell of this Eastern River turns to ye SWt. We follow ye Course of the Eastmost Channell, as being ye nearest Rout, & best Countrey to survey in.

*The 27th. *Variation at Sunset near Monerpour 1°-0′ West.[2]

The 30th. received a new Budgarow from Calcutta. It has been 31 days on its Passage. Being a new one it will be rather safer than the one I had before, as that was old & ready to drop to pieces, but this seems one to be very crank & dangerous.

December ye 1st. came to Cusarya, opposite to which the great Southern Channell from Monerpour falls in. The Country here very full of Jungle & thinly inhabited. This day & the following employed in making a cursory Survey of the Southern Channells of this River, of which the best Idea will be formed by inspecting the Map No. III of the Ganges.

The 3rd. began the Survey of Mendygunge River, which is properly the north- 25
most Branch of the Ganges. I make choice of this Rout as being the shortest; proposing to make only a cursory Survey of the South Branch.

The 4th. dispatched the old Budgarow for Calcutta, by way of the great River.

The 5th. came into ye Western part of the Megna & proceeded to the Southward towards the main Channell of the Ganges. The Countrey here has a most unpromising appearance.

The 6th. proceeded with the Survey of the West side of the Megna, from the conflux of the two Rivers towards Luckypour. This part of the Countrey is full of thick Woods & Jungles, & has very few Inhabitants.

The 7th. came to Little Backergunge, which is situated at ye mouth of a large Creek, about halfway betwixt the conflux & Luckypour.

The 8th. all day thick Fog. The 9th. dropt down to the Mouth of the Ganges,
& began to survey the main Channell from thence towards the head of Mendygunge 26
River. The Tides are very strong here. The Floods about $1\frac{1}{2}'$ P hour at Springs.

The 10th. at Sunset Mag. Variation 1°-5′ Wt. near Loatto.

Ten miles above the conflux of the Rivers a large Creek runs out the South side of the River towards Backergunge & Sewtylewry,[3] & is used as a common Rout to those Places from Luckypour &c. The Boatmen call it Durgapour Creek. Its inlet

---

1 These fogs are still a great hindrance to the navigation of the water-ways of Bengal and Assam during the winter months.

2 Char Manpara, S.E. of Nagerpara. Mr. Ascoli says that to the South of this place the old course of the river is easily traceable by a series of 'char' lands (Char is a sandbank thrown up in the bed of a river), though it is now entirely dry to near Mehndiganj.

3 Sutylury on Rennell's maps, 12 miles west of Barisal. It is apparently the same place as the modern Jhalakati or Mahrajganj, one of the largest timber markets in Bengal.

is near the Village of Jaggatdul. Three miles above this, is the Mouth of the Western Branch of the great River whose head is near Tockya. I propose leaving this River unfinished till I can receive further information of the Courses of the different Branches of it, lest I may take a wrong Rout & lose much Time by it.

The 13th. having finished the Survey of the River from the head of Mendygunge Creek to the conflux, we proceeded about six miles along the Western Shoar below the Mouth of the Megna, in order to observe the face of the Countrey &c. It is
27 mostly covered with Jungle, & I could discover only one Village the whole Way.

By an Observation of Latitude taken this day about four miles below the Mouth of the Megna, I find myself in 22°-40′ North, & being now at least 20 miles from the Sea, it appears that the old Maps have laid down the Latitude of the Mouth of the Ganges much too far Northerly; for instance M. d'Anville places it in 22°-36′[1] or thereabouts, whereas if the least dependance can be placed on the distance of Backergunge from the Sea, as estimated by the Boatmen, the Latitude of the Ganges Mouth must be about 22°-20′ North.[2]

The 14th. passed Doycalley, & the 15th. at Noon came to the Point opposite Luckypour from whence we crossed over in the Afternoon. The Megna seems to be about five Miles over.

From the 15th. to the 23rd. inclusive, the Weather generally foggy in the Mornings & commonly continued till 10 or 11 o'Clock, sometimes it was not clear enough all day to see the opposite side of the Megna from Luckypour. The Winds variable & in light Breezes.

28 The 16th. began to make an exact Survey of the Nulla, Fort & Village of Luckypour, chiefly with a design to show the present Situation of the Factory with respect to the Bank of the River, which is continually wearing away by reason of the high Surges of the River in ye time of ye Southwardly Winds.[3]

The 20th. having finished the Plan, took ye Latitude of the Place by Hadley's Quadrant, but the Horizon was not good enough to place any dependance on the Observation. The Latitude found was 22°-57′ North.[4]

From this time to ye 23rd. employed in finishing ye Original Maps, copying

1 Evidently a slip of the pen for 23 36′.

2 The conflux of the Ganges and Meghna is now in about 23°-20′ N or a degree further north than it was in Rennell's time. The old channel, now known as the Arial Khan, enters the Meghna at Mirzaganj in about Lat 22°-40′.

3 In 1756 a cloth Factory was established here by the East India Co. A report to the Council, probably furnished by Mr. Bartholomew Plaisted (*see note* p. 38), and entered in the Proceedings for Octr 1st 1767, states:—"No longer since than 1761, it '(the Factory)' might have been said to have stood a mile up a creek, locked in and secure both from the strong freshes and the impulse of bores and the SW Monsoon, but within this short space the cover it had from the monsoon has been washed away, and it is now entirely laid open The factory was at first built 200 yards from the water side, but when I arrived the SW corner was scarcely two yards from the bank, and it would certainly have got into the ditch, if a boat of 1,000 maunds had not been sunk, that keeps by way of a break-water, and bamboos, etc., been drove in by way of further precaution; this I am in hopes may secure it till the monsoon is broke up, but no art can secure it against another" (Rev. J. Long, Selections, No. 914, p. 481). In 1761 the district was overrun by thieves and Mr. Billers the Chief of the Factory wrote to Nawab Kasim Ali, asking him to give orders to the Phousdar (Native Governor) "to fire off the mouth of a cannon the leader of the thieves, who was made prisoner, that others may be deterred" (*Ibid.*, No. 557, p 259).

4 This is the exact latitude of Lakshimpur, according to the Imperial Gazetteer.

others, & making a small Map of the Ganges which was immediately dispatched to the Governor. Began likewise a compleat Sett of Maps of the Ganges on a scale of 2 miles to an Inch.

The 23rd. having received further Information concerning the Course &c. of the 29
Western Branch of the Ganges, set out from Luckyp^r. in order to survey it. The same day had an Observation of Latitude tho' not very exact. By this the Latitude of Luckypour appears to be 22°-54′. This Evening put ashore at Doycalley Point.

The 24th. employed in surveying the Western Shoars of the Jungle Islands opposite Luckypour.

The 25th. arrived at ye Mouth of the Western River & next day proceeded up it. After going 4 miles up found it divided into 2 Branches, we kept the Northmost imagining that the other led to the Woods.[1] At Night after having traced it to the North & Northwest 6 or 7 miles it decreased from a large River to a very small Creek, but finding the Tide to ebb & flow pretty strong I thought it best to proceed the next day, & after going about 3½ miles to the South & West, we came into the Western River near Kiddarpour. The South side of this Creek is mostly Jungle, the North is well cultivated, & produces Sugar Canes, Tobacco, & Betel nut. The principal Village is named Azimpour.

From this time to ye 29th. employed in tracing ye Western River from Kiddar- 30
pour to Tockya. Its breadth is from ½ to ¾ of a mile. There are few particulars about it worth remarking. Four miles below its separation from the great Ganges a large Creek from Hobbygunge falls in; nine miles below that lies Goanuddy or Gurnuddy,[2] a large Village. There is a high Pagoda by which the place may be known at 9 miles distant. Many Boats are built in the neighbourhood, & here are abundance of Betel Trees, which seem to be the chief Produce of the Countrey.

Twelve miles below Gurnuddy a large Creek or River falls in from the Westward; as this Creek is seldom used by Boats, I could get but little information regarding its Source, however I am well persuaded that it must be the Burrashee Creek from Jaynagore.[3]

Immediately below the mouth of this Creek, the Western River divides into
two principal Branches, & those again soon after into others, so that it would be a 31
laborious & difficult work to attempt describing them. We took our Rout through the Eastmost of them, which brought us again into the great Ganges by the Southmost of the two Branches mentioned ye 25th.

Being now in the neighbourhood of Backergunge, I thought it might not be altogether useless to describe the Situation of that place by tracing some Creek which should afford ye shortest Passage. I fixed on a branch of the Western River for this purpose, & the 31st. in the Morning proceeded to the Southwest, Backergunge being distant about 2 days by Water.

[1] *i.e.* the Sundarbans.

[2] Gaurnadi. The pagoda has disappeared.

[3] This creek is probably the 'Lolcherra creek,' mentioned below, p. 94. It is not connected with the Barasia, which is a branch of the Madhumati or Baleswar river, and enters the Bay of Bengal by a separate mouth, the Haringhata.

The Countrey from Gurnuddy to Sastenagor is mostly Jungle, & consequently very thinly inhabited. Below Sastenagore it begins to be more open. Sastenagore is about 16 miles below Gurnuddy.

32 The 31st. in ye Evening passed Burryshel,[1] a Bazar Village a little below Sastenagore; opposite Burryshel a large Creek runs out to ye Eastward, & is known to the Boatmen by the name of Durgapour Creek; through it lies ye common Rout from Luckypour to Backergunge.[2]

The 28th at Kessepour Varn. of the needle 1°-14′ Westly.

Four miles below Burryshel, the River divides into four Branches, the Eastmost to Gobindapour & ye Sea, the Southmost to Backergunge, & ye two Western ones to Sewtylewry, which is situated two Par from thence.

January 1st. 1765, at 3 PM arrived at Backergunge, which lies on a very small Creek about 14 miles below the four Creeks. It lies in Latitude 22°-36′ or 37′ North, about 16 miles from the Great Ganges, 74 from Dacca & 116 from Calcutta. The Inhabitants report that the Sea is about 20 miles to the SSEt.

Having now compleated the survey of the Ganges &c. I proceeded to construct a Set of Maps of it, on a Scale proper for common Use,* to be divided into 3 parts, each on a Sheet of Royal Paper, & a fourth Sheet to contain the whole on a Scale of 10 English Miles to an Inch, & a Plan of Luckypour.

* 2 miles to an inch.

33 The 2nd. in the Morning set out for Luckypour in our way to Dacca, where I must proceed in order to get a supply of Money. Nothing remarkable happened in our Passage, save that we took our Rout through Durgapour Creek,[3] & that the 5th. in the Morning a fresh Gale of Wind drove all the Boats ashore on ye Jungle Islands off of Luckypour; the Budgarow was got off again without Damage, by carrying out a Grapnel. That Morning the Air was very sharp, (occasioned by a Northerly Wind).

The 6th in ye Morning one of the Sepoys was taken off by a Tyger from ye Northwest part of Daokytya Island, he having stept ashore out of a Pulwar.

The 8th. at Night arrived at Dacca. Still employed on the Maps. Weather mostly Calm since the 5th.

From the 8th. to ye 12th. at Dacca. Hired some new Boats &c. One of my European Assistants having cut a Dandy's[4] Ear off, I delivered him prisoner to the Chief,[5] agreeable to his Desire.

1 Barisal, the head quarters of Bakarganj district, now a town of over 18,000 inhabitants. The Imperial Gazetteer states that in the middle of the eighteenth century it was an important salt *chauki* or place where salt-tax was paid, but on Rennell's map it is shown as a very small village.

2 Bakarganj. The head-quarters of the district were transferred from here to Barisal in 1801. It is described in correspondence of about this period as "the last place in India on which anyone would wish to build" (Ascoli). The southern part of the district was much subject to ravages by Magh pirates from Arakan in the seventeenth and eighteenth centuries. On one of Rennell's maps, Bengal Atlas No. XX, it is marked "country depopulated by the Muggs."

3 The creek E of Barisal.

4 Dandy, a boatman, a term peculiar to the Gangetic rivers, from Hind. & Beng. dand, a staff or oar (Hobson Jobson, p. 296).

5 The Resident in charge of the Factory. This was probably Mr. Leycester, who was certainly Chief of the Factory

The Weather in general hot since ye 8th., Winds variable.

The 12th. at Noon left Dacca, & proceeded down the Rivers towards Luckypour, 34
in order to continue ye Survey from thence towards Dacca.

The 14th. at Night arrived at ye old Mark near Doycalley Point,[1] & prepared for surveying ye next Morning.

From the 14th to ye 24th. employed in surveying the Western side of the Megna from the Point opposite Luckypour to Rajabarry[2] being upwards of 38 miles. The best Idea of the Course of ye River may be obtained by a view of the Map; the Islands & Sands in it are almost innumerable. The Ganges & Megna near their conflux form a Peninsula, the Isthmus of which is not four miles over; this Isthmus lies between the villages of Soylerhaut & Serampour (the latter of which lies on the Megna) about 20 miles above ye Point of ye Conflux.

The Countrey between Doycalley & Rajabarry is full of Betel Trees, but has little
cultivated Land, & is but thinly inhabited towards ye River side, this must be owing 35
to the number of Tygers which have their haunts thereabouts.[3]

Five or six Miles below Rajabarry is the Mouth of Chiddypour or Luricule Creek; this Creek affords a short & safe Passage from the Megna to the Ganges going by way of Luricule & Rajanagore, & entering ye Ganges either at Gonganagore or Chycundy. The distance overland from Chiddypour to Chycundy is not 11 miles, so near do these Rivers approach each other, though they afterwards run upwards of 40 miles before they unite. It must be observed that Luricule Creek runs from the Ganges to ye Megna, & that the flood Tide from the Megna has not strength enough to keep back ye current of Chycundy Creek, which always runs to the Eastward.

The Village of Rajabarry is situated on ye Western side of the Megna in Lat. 23°-21′ N distant from Dacca 22 miles & from Luckypour 34. An old Pagoda stands about ¾ of a mile to the Southwest of it.[4] The Village has formerly been large, but
is now reduced to a small Bazar only. An extensive cluster of Islands divides ye 36
River into a number of Channels opposite Rajabarry, & forms several commodious Harbours for Boats.

From the 12th. to ye 24th. January the Winds & Weather variable, the former mostly from the Northward, though but in light Breezes. The Mornings in general

when Dacca was taken by body of rebellious 'Fakirs' in 1763. His conduct on that occasion drew down the wrath of Lord Clive, when Leycester was a member of Council, in 1766 (Long, Selections, No. 839, p. 429; *see* also Bengal, Past and Present, Vol. V, p. 2 9). Two Leycesters are mentioned among the lists of those who were in Calcutta in 1756, of whom one, Ralph, escaped in the ships with Governor Drake before the tragedy of the Black Hole.

1 Opposite Lakshmipur.

2 Rajabari, now quite a small village, on the left bank of the Meghna below Narainganj and just above the conflux of the Ganges & Meghna

3 Great changes have taken place in this area since Rennell's time. A vast series of 'chars' or sandbanks now extends southwards, and a large river, the Nayabhangani, has broken through the isthmus Serampur has disappeared into the bed of the Meghna, and Mr. Ascoli remarks that "there are no 'Tygers' now."

4 This is the Rajabari *math*, a monumental tower built, it is said, over the funeral pyre of the mother of Chand Rayya and Kedar Rayya, independent princes of the locality, about 200 years before this. It is built of brick about 30 feet square at base and 80 feet in height, and still forms a conspicuous landmark. (List of Ancient Mon. Beng., p. 218). A view of the 'math' is given in the Journ. As. Soc. Beng., Vol. XLIII, Pl. XI.

foggy till near 11 o'clock, & the rest of the day close & sultry. The 23rd. some Squalls from the NNW & a few flying Showers; the 24th. much Thunder & Lightning with Squalls & Rain from the NW & SW.

The 21st. at Daadpour Island found y[e] Variation 1 -7 W[t].

The 25th. the Weather clearing up, left Rajabarry, & surveyed to y[e] North end of Amidabad Island (the Northmost of y[e] cluster) & afterwards proceeded to survey y[e] Islands.

The 28th. finished y[e] survey of the Rajabarry Islands & put over to the North end of Mohunp[r]. Island, in order to survey the East side of the River from thence to Luckypour.

The Islands abovementioned are in number 18 great & small, out of which
37 number 8 only are inhabited. The length of the whole Range is about 13 miles, & the main Channell of the River (which is near a mile over) runs on the east side. It is worth remarking that the whole breadth of the River at & opposite Chiddypour is 7½ miles in y[e] dry Season. There are two good Channells for crossing the River between the Islands, one between Amidabad & Pomomarra, the other round y[e] north end of Shukypoura.

The 29th. began the survey from Mohunpour downwards, & the next Evening came to the North side of the Niagonga or Panghia Riyer. This River appears to be a branch of the Baramputrey, & near its conflux with y[e] Megna is more than ¾ of a mile over. The Countrey on the North side of it consists mostly of clear Meadows which are entirely overflown in y[e] wet Season.

Chaundpour[1] a small but remarkable Village lies on the South Bank of the Niagonga near the point of its conflux with the Megna. It is situated about 31 miles from Dacca, 11 from Rajabarry, & 23 or 24 from Luckypour. Here the Country begins to be full of Betel Trees again, & continues so almost to Luckypour.

38 February y[e] 2nd. surveyed to Havatya Creek about 11 miles below Chandpour, when hearing that Mr. Plaisted[2] was at Luckypour, I set out for that Place in hopes of getting from him some Materials for making a general Map of Bengall. Arrived at Luckypour in y[e] Evening.

[1] Chandpur, now the terminus on the Meghna of the Assam-Bengal Railway.

[2] Through the kindness of my friend the Rev[d] W. K. Firminger, Editor of 'Bengal, Past and Present', I have been able to learn some particulars of the career of Mr. Bartholomew Plaisted In 1743, being then Captain and Supercargo of the ship Kent, he was appointed 'Engineer and Surveyor' by the Council, and in 1747 prepared plans for the improvement of the defences of Old Fort William, his connection with which is fully set out in the late Dr. C. R. Wilson's work 'Old Fort William in Bengal.' In a small book published by Plaisted in 1758, a Journal of his voyages from Calcutta to Bussora and thence across the desert to Aleppo and home (which Mr. Firminger has kindly placed at my disposal), is included his Map of Bengal, with an "Account of the countries, cities, and towns adjacent to Bengal" by "a gentleman who resided there many years" This map, which he states in the legend attached was "collected from the best authorities," is not, it must be confessed, much if at all superior to Van den Broucke's map of 1660 in point of accuracy or detail, and he is not referred to by Rennell in the 'Memoir' as one of the authorities for his map of Hindoostan. From 1761 to 1765 Plaisted was employed in surveying the river and coasts near Chittagong, with a salary of Rs. 1,800 a year, increased in 1765 to the emoluments of a member of Council (Wilson. *op. cit*, Vol. II., pp. 162. 164. 165, 172, 174). In July 1767 he was surveying at 'Luckypore' but died at Calcutta in October of the same year.

From ye 2nd. to ye 9th. at Luckypour; employed in reducing & copying ye particular Maps of ye Ganges, surveying Daokytya Nulla,[1] the Sand Banks below Luckypour, &c. & taking ye Latitude of the Place which by an exact observation appears to be 22°-55′ North.

*The 9th. found ye Variation at Solacally Creek 1°-30′ West.

*The 9th. left Luckypour without having seen Mr. Plaisted, & proceeded with the Survey from that place towards Havatya Creek.[2]

The 12th finished the Survey to Havatya, & now all that part of the Megna lying to ye Southward of Rajabarry being surveyed, I propose in ye next place to survey Chiddypour Creek.[3]

The 13th. in ye Afternoon arrived at Chiddypour & proceeded up ye Creek passing 39
by Mulputgunge. The 14th. in ye forenoon passed Luricule which is situated on the South side of the Creek. Luricule, once a remarkable Village lies almost half way betwixt ye Ganges & Megna, is about 28 miles S½W from Dacca, & 3 ESE from Rajanagore. Here are ye ruins of a Portuguese Church, & of many Brick Houses.[4]

Jaopsa Pagoda[5] (which is very high & may be distinctly seen in both Rivers) is situated ¾ of a mile SE from Luricule. The Countrey hereabouts is pleasant & well cultivated; there are likewise many Groves of Betel Trees.

The 15th. finnished the Survey of the Creek, having traced it almost to Gonganagore on ye east side of the Ganges

Rajanagore[6] is situated about a mile & half from ye east Bank of Gonganagore Creek, on a small Rivulet which falls into ye said Creek but is navigable for Boats only at half Flood.

Chycundy Creek joins that from Gonganagore about 3 miles below Rajanagore. 40

The 16th. returned to Berackondy near Rajabarry where we left off surveying the 24th January last.

From the 16th. to ye 19th. employed in surveying from Berackondy to Iddyracpour, & having now finished all the Western side of the Megna, we put over to ye other side in order to finish that before the Northwest Squalls begin.

---

1 A stream entering the Meghna a short distance above Lakshmipur

2 On the same side of the river, about 15 miles up stream.

3 The creek below Rajabari referred to on p. 37, connecting the Meghna with the Ganges. It afterwards became the main channel of the latter river, but is now a small creek again.

4 Perhaps the relics of the Portuguese who were in the employ of the Raja of Arakan at the beginning of the 17th century, and on being expelled from his dominions, took to piracy at the mouths of the Ganges. Under their leader Sebastian Gonzales, they were constantly at war with the Mughals. They were finally overcome by Shaista Khan, the Governor of Bengal under Aurangzib, and their families were settled near Dacca, where they gradually sunk to the level of the natives.

The name of this place may perhaps be connected with the title of the Marquis of Louriçal, who was in 1741 Viceroy of Goa, and defeated the Marathas at Bardez (Hunter, Imp. Gaz., 2nd Ed, Vol. v, p 104). In the Atlas of India, sheet 126, SW, it is marked 'Noreekole.' No mention is made of these ruins or of the pagodas at Raja nagar in the List of Ancient Monuments, Bengal (*see* Appendix A).

5 This pagoda was swept away by the Kirtinasa River in 1881-2 (Ascoli).

6 The main branch of the Ganges or Kirtinasa river now passes 5 or 6 miles to the north of the site of this place.

From ye 19th. to ye 22nd. inclusive employed in surveying ye eastern Shoar from Kallagutchy to the North End of Mohunpour Island, & likewise the eastern sides of ye intermediate Islands, ye western sides of them being done before. The Baramputrey or River from Assam seems to be about 2 miles broad; its conflux with ye Issamutey is in Latitude 23°-28′ or nearly under the Tropic of Cancer.

41 The 23rd. made an exact Plan of Iddyracpour Kella[1]: this lies about 2 miles SE from Feringybazar & near 14 from Dacca.

From that Time to the 3rd. March employed in surveying the Rivers & Creeks in ye nearest Rout from Iddyracpour to Dacca.

Feringybazar[2] a large Village extending 2 miles along ye Southern Bank of ye Issamutey River is situate about 11 miles SEBS from Dacca, but the Passage by Water in ye dry Season is full 15 miles. This Village lies on ye highest spot of Ground in the whole neighbourhood, & is some feet above ye level of ye Water during ye wet Season. Luckya River,[3] the Water of which is so remarkable for its clearness & sweetness, falls into ye Issamutey opposite to Feringybazar.

Five miles above Feringybazar, the Beurygonga[4] or Dacca River falls into the Issamutey. The Countrey here is well cultivated, & sown with Paddy Cotton &c.

42 The Beurygonga or River on which Dacca is situated, is the Eastmost Branch of the River Ganges. Its breadth in general is about 250 yards, & its Course in the neighbourhood of Dacca pretty streight from NW to SE. It is navigable in the dry Season for the largest Boats.

The City of Dacca lies on the Northeast side of this River & extends near 4 miles along ye Bank. The British Factory[5] is nearly in Latitude 23°-40′ North, & stands near a quarter of a mile above high Water Mark; Its figure approaches nearest that of a Square, whose sides are a little less than 100 yards. The French & Dutch Factories are smaller & lie further up ye River. Dacca is situated with respect to ye head of Jelenghee River EBS$\frac{1}{4}$S* 109 Statute Miles, & from Calcutta according to a Map constructed from ye best Authorities that I can procure E 27° N or ENE$\frac{1}{2}$N dist. 142 Miles.†

* Mr. D'anville places it on ye North Bank of ye Ganges & only 64 Miles from ye head of Jelenghee River.

† 22$\frac{1}{2}$ from the Banks of ye Ganges.

43 The Weather during the latter end of January (vt.) from ye 24th. to ye 31st. was as follows: The 25th. & 26 clear Weather with fresh Breezes of Wind from ye N. &

1 Idrakpur Kil'a or fort. Hunter says that the remains of a circular fort, built by Mir Jumla, one of the Governors of Bengal during the reign of Aurangzib, were visible at Idrakpur, S of Firinghi Bazar, in 1839 (Stat. Acc. Beng., Vol. V, p. 72). The town of Munshiganj now stands on the site of Idrakpur, and the Sub divisional Officer's house is built on one of the bastions.

2 *Ante*, p. 24.

3 The Lakhmia river, the waters of which are still remarkable for their purity and sweetness.

4 The Buriganga, a branch of the Dhaleswari river.

5 The English, French, and Dutch factories were established in Dacca about the middle of the 17th century, when the city was visited by Tavernier. After 1801, the trade of the place declined considerably, and the Commercial Residency was discontinued in 1817. The position of the factories is shown in the map of the Environs of Dacca, Rennell's Bengal Atlas No. XII.

NNET the remaining days mostly Calm: the Air in general was moderately warm, the Mornings foggy till 8 or 9 o'clock.

The 1st. of February I perceived the first Breeze of Southerly Wind for ye Season, the next day we had another more fresh about 9 in ye Morning but after this we had commonly Northerly Breezes in ye Morning & Southerly ones in ye Afternoon though both of them light.

The Morning Fogs continued till ye latter end of ye Month & were the cause of much trouble & hindrance in surveying so broad a River as the Megna, where I was frequently obliged to look out for Flags at the distance of 7 & 8 miles.

By the middle of the Month the Air began to be very warm, & in ye middle of the day excessive hot, as but little Wind was stirring; & I think that we had more Calms in this Month than in any other that I have observed since I have 44
been out.

The Month of March began with clear Weather, & very variable Winds though mostly from ye South & West; the Air very warm.

The Fogs are now almost over, there being only a foggy Morning now & then, & seldom continuing after 8 o'clock.

The 15th. threatning Weather all day; the 16th. in ye Evening we perceived the first Northwester for the Season. A heavy Shower of Hail fell in the beginning of it, & afterwards Rain;* the Wind was violent only for a few Minutes.

* Thus far copied.[1]

The 17th. close Weather all day, & some Rain; the Wind mostly from the Westward in fresh Breezes.

The 18th. fine Weather. The 19th. at Night several heavy Squalls of Wind from ye SW & SSE & much Rain. The bad Weather continued from 7 to ½ past 9 PM.

The 20th. the Morning fair, The Evening rainy, Wind variable. 45

The 21st. in ye morning some very fresh Gales from the Northward, & Rain the remainder of the Day; the next Day ye Weather cleared up.

From the 21st. to ye 31st. little remarkable in the Weather, the Winds mostly from ye SWt. & West, the Air very warm.

The 28th. March sent the Governor a general Map of the Megna on a scale of 2 Miles to an Inch, & the 4th. April sent ye remaining 8 Maps of the Ganges: there has now been sent a compleat sett of Maps of the Ganges, both general and particular.[2]

1 Probably transcribed from the journals he was in the habit of sending to the Governor, and from the entries in his Field Books.

2 Regarding the fate of these maps see p. 93.

The 5th. April received Orders from the Governor to survey the Megna or Baramputrey from its conflux with the Issamutey to Gaulpara,[1] or as high as it can be done without offending the Natives.

46 The Month of April began with fine Weather: the Winds in general from the Westward till ye 7th. the Air moderately cool. The 6th. very fresh Breezes.

The 7th. Winds West & WSW the Morning Rainy, the remainder of the day very fresh Breezes the Wind rather more Southwardly.

The 8th. Winds West & SW very fresh in ye Morning: very lowering Sky all ye Afternoon.

The 9th. Wind vad. from N. to E. The Afternoon squally, Thunder, Lightning, & Rain: the next day fair Weather.

The 11th. variable Winds & much Rain; the 12th. Winds S. & SW. Weather very cool & pleasant: the 13th. & 14th. nearly the same.

The 15th. in ye Night squally with Rain, the Wind from the Northwest. The 16th. all day lowring, the Night windy, some Rain towd. Morning.

The 17th. at 1 Afternoon a Squall from the Northwest & from thence variable to S. & SE. Rain for several Hours.

47 The 10th. April sent the Governor a Sketch of the Rivers, with my Idea of the situation of Gaulpara.

The 19th. in ye Evening a Squall of Wind from the North & NNW but no Rain. A small Shower in the Night.

From 19th. to 22nd. inclusive the Winds mostly from the SE & SSE, the Weather excessive hot & sultry.

From ye 22nd. to ye 25th. Winds mostly from the South & Southwest, the mornings & evenings fresh Breezes, but ye middle of ye day Calm & very hot.

The 25th. in ye Evening a very hard Squall from ye WNW & Rain for about an hour. This Squall was by much ye severest we had felt for the Season, & it gave but little warning.

The 26th. in ye Evening much Thunder, & Lightning with a heavy Shower of Rain; a small Breeze of Wind from ye Northward.

The 27th. ye Morning very cool, Wind from ye SW. Evening cloudy & threatning.

48 The 28th. Morning fair, Wind from ye Westward. At 3 PM a heavy Squall from the Northward & Rain till near 7. The Night clear.

The 29th. in ye Morning fresh Gales from ye NE and very cold. The Afternoon cloudy, Wind West. I observe that the Wind is commonly Westerly in ye Night. A Shower in the Night.

The 30th. a close Morning, & the forenoon excessive hot, the Wind variable. The Afternoon Wind from the Northward & a great deal of Rain. The Evening drizling Rain, Night cloudy.

[1] Goalpara, in Assam.

May 1st. fine Weather all day, the Evening very close & some Rain in ye Night.

The 2nd. 3rd. & 4th. remarkable fine Weather, ye Wind in the Morning from the NE & the remainder of ye day from ye W & SW.

The 5th. Weather all day excessive hot the Wind from the Westward.

The 6th. the Morning very hot, at Noon a Squall from the Westward with 49
heavy Ra'n for about an Hour, ye Evening Cloudy & cool.

The 7th. at Sunrise began heavy Rain, wch continued till near 11 in ye Morning, ye remaining part of ye day cool & cloudy.

The 5th. dispatched ye remaining Maps, (vt.) those containing a Copy of ye late Survey on a scale of 2 In. to a mile, a Map of Luricule Creek on 1 In. to a mile, & Plans of Iddyracpour & Daapeka [1] Killas.

The 6th. received Intelligence of Lord Clive's arrival at Calcutta.[2]

The 8th. having all the Boats & People ready, I proposed setting out on ye survey of ye Baramputrey, but we had bad Weather all the day, & the following Night. At Noon that Day began heavy Rain ; the Wind in fresh Breezes from the South & SSE. The Afternoon mostly rainy, but little Wind. At 10 at Night it began to grow squally & from 11 to ½ past 1 next Morning we had a hard Gale from the South East, the Weather dry. We sheltered the Boats near the French Factory.

[1] A small fort on the Buriganga, 7 miles from Dacca on the road to Naraingunj: probably one of the numerous forts built in the neighbourhood by the Mogul Viceroys, to check the incursions of the Maghs and Portuguese. All traces of it have now disappeared.

[2] Lord Clive arrived at Calcutta on the 3rd May 1765, to take up his second term of administration.

JOURNAL of the third Expedition for surveying the Megna & Baramputrey from its Conflux with ye Issamutey towards Gwalpara; as likewise the Rivers & Creeks leading out of it towards the Province of Bengall.

Thursday May 9th. set out from Dacca in order to survey the Baramputrey, & proceeded by way of the Issamutey River The Weather being remarkably bad we were employed from this time to the 11th. in making a Passage of 22 miles with ye Current in our favour.

The 11th. in the Afternoon began surveying at Doarsanny a small Village situated on ye South Point of the Conflux of the Megna & Issamutey. Opposite to this Place lies a very large Sand Bank which divides the River into two unequal Channells, of which the Northmost is the safest & best. The Countrey here is mostly covered with Jungle.

2 From the 11th. to the 14th. employed in surveying from Doarsanny to Allynya in distance about 9 miles; the course of the River is about WSW, & its breadth in general about a mile & quarter. The Countrey on the S. side is quite flat & destitute of Trees, the North side is a continued Jungle.

At Allynya[2] a branch of the Megna turns off to the SE & falls into the great Megna again at Chandpour after taking a Course of about 24 miles. This Branch is named the Panghia River, & is navigable all the year for the largest Boats. Two Miles above Allynya a large Creek or River falls into the Megna on ye East side; this is commonly called the little Megna, & affords the shortest Passage from thence to Silet & Azmarygunge.[3]

From the 13th. to ye 17th. employed surveying between Allynya & Nauldee[4]; the River being very crooked between those Places I shall refer to the Map. No. 1 from which the best Idea of its Course may be obtained. The Countrey on both sides is but thinly cultivated or inhabited, & there is scarce a Tree to be seen for many Miles. The Winds & Weather have been variable during this time, as will appear by the Journal annexed.[5]

3 This River altho' it be in general (& especially by Europeans) named the Baramputrey; yet the Countrey People call it the Megna, & this Name it preserves upwards of 50 miles above its conflux with the Issamuty; when it takes the name of Baramputrey or Barram-pcut.[6]

1 This name is given in Rennell's Atlas to the combined waters of the Ichhamati, Dhaleswari, Buriganga, and Lakhmia rivers. Doarsanny lay on the eastern bank of the Meghna, opposite the conflux.

2 A small village close to Daud Kandi, where the road from Dacca to Comillah leaves the river.

3 Azmeriganj, a large village on the Surma in the Sylhet district, about 80 miles NE of Dacca.

4 Probably Nawadee, now an important mart on the right bank of the Meghna about 7 miles above Sonargaon, the ancient Muhammadan capital of Eastern Bengal.

5 See p. 112.

6 Hobson Jobson does not give this mode of spelling the name. Buchanan Hamilton writes it 'Brohmoputro.'

Few particulars worth remarking happened between the 17th & 23rd. except that we had in general excessive turbulent weather, & much Rain; & that on ye 21st. we had a very hard Gale from the Southward. During this Time we were employed in surveying the West side of the River from Nauldee to Nursingdy. The River within this space is very broad, rapid, & dangerous, it being full of Islands & Shoals: its breadth is in many places 2½ miles; its Course in general SWBS. The Pagoda of Sultansuddy[1] lies about 1¾ mile within ye Western Bank, & is situated EBN distant about 16½ miles from Dacca. The Countrey here is mostly sown with Padda.

Nursingdee a Bazar Village is situated on the Western Bank of the Megna & bears ENE½N dis^{t} 23 miles from Dacca. Near this Village a large Branch of the Baramputrey falls into the Megna, after forming (by means also of that River) an Island of about 18 miles long & 7 over. The nearest Passage to Chilmary & Gwalpara 4
lying through this Westmost Branch, I judged proper to make an exact Survey of it first, & to leave the Eastern River, till I could inform myself of more particulars concerning its Course; for even the Countrey People themselves are not acquainted with all the Channells, & they are but little frequented by Trading Boats.

At Nursingdy likewise another small River or Creek falls into the Megna; this Creek as I am informed affords a short Passage to the Luckya River, but my Orders directing me to leave the Western Branches of this River unsurveyed, till ye great River is described, I cannot give any account whether it is all ye year navigable for large Boats, but I suspect that it is. The Tides are almost imperceptible at this Place.

From the 23rd. May to ye 2nd. June, employed in surveying the Western River* 5
whose length is near 40 miles, the windings & turnings included. It frequently separates into smaller Channells forming many pleasant & well cultivated Islands; the Western side, the soil is of a red Colour & very firm, & in several places there are very steep Cliffs by the River side. The Country here is likewise Woody, but none of the Trees are fit for Timber.[2] Here are many Villages whose situations are all particularly described in the Map.

*This River is called the little Baramputrey or Poggolah.

The Current of this River is very rapid; the Tide rises at Pikerchoar about 8 or 9 inches, but farther up I could not perceive any Tide. The Western Bank of this River harbours a great number of Snakes, amongst which there are some of an enormous Size.

June 3d. came into the great Baramputrey, whose Course is from the WNW. I still omitted to survey the Eastern River, for want of a proper Person to inform me of the Courses of the several Branches that lead out of it.

---

[1] Sultan Shahadee. Marked on map No. XVII in Rennell's atlas, but not mentioned in the List of Ancient Monuments.

[2] This tract of country is described in Hunter's Statistical Account of Bengal (Vol. v, pp. 18, 19). The soil consists of red ferruginous clay. The whole tract is known as the Madhupur jungle or 'Garh Gazali,' so called after the 'Sal' (*Shorea robusta*), the principal timber tree (*see* p. 60), and lies comparatively high, rising to 100 feet above flood level. It is still but little cultivated and infested by wild animals.

6 From the 3d. to the 9th. of June inclusive employed in surveying from the head of the Western River to the head of the Luckia River. The Course of the River within this space is nearly SEBE & is divided into a number of Channells by an extensive Cluster of Islands. The Countrey on both sides has very few particulars worth remarking; it is very flat & mostly covered with Jungle toward ye River; in the neighbourhood of Adampour, & the head of the Luckya River the Countrey abounds with Betel or Areca Trees. The Islands are mostly uninhabited.

The Luckya River is the Westmost Branch of the Baramputrey, & falls into ye Issamutey a few Miles below Dacca,[1] after sending out a navigable Creek which leads to Dacca, & thereby allows a much shorter Passage from that City to Chilmary & Gwalpara than any of the Branches of the Megna.

7 The 9th. of June having procured a Pilot for the Megna, I proceeded to make a cursory survey of that part of it which lies betwixt Nursingdy & the head of the Western River, & set out on that Service in ye Morning.

From the 9th. to the 16th. employed on the above Service. This part of the Megna is in some places upwards of three miles broad & has near 21 Islands within ye space of 25 Miles. All of them are covered with Jungle & entirely uninhabited.

The Banks of this River also are mostly covered with Jungle, insomuch that there are only 3 considerable Villages within ye abovementioned space About 8 miles above Nursingdy, a large Creek runs out to the Southeast; this Creek, the Countrey People informed me, is the same which falls into the Megna near Allynya, & is included in Mr. Plaisted's Surveys of the Silet Rivers. Three miles further up the Silet River,[2] joins wth. the Megna from the North East. This River is more
8 than half a mile broad, & as I am informed, has its Source near the Province of Silet. This River is likewise included in Mr. Plaisted's Surveys. The Water of this River is clearer than that of the Megna.

Opposite to the Village of Paragarahandy another River or large Creek falls into the Megna on ye Et. side[3]: I could not learn from the Countrey People any particulars concerning its Course; it was near half a mile broad at that time, but it must be much smaller in ye dry Season on account of the flatness of the neighbouring Countrey. I imagine that it must be some Branch of the Baramputrey which separates from that River a great way to the Northward.

The 16th. proceeded with the Survey of the Baramputrey, from the head of the Luckya River, northward.

Near this Place the Baramputrey is scarce half a mile broad, but excessive deep
9 & rapid. The Rains had swelled the River very considerably, so that the Water was in many places even with the top of the Banks.

A few Miles above the head of the Luckya River we discovered one of the Northern Hills[4] which was then distant from us upwards of 70 Miles.

[1] Where the large town of Naraingani is situated.

[2] The Surma. The clearness of the water is due to the numerous jhils through which it flows, where the silt carried by the river is to a great extent deposited.

[3] On map XVII of Rennell's Atlas this creek is shown as a branch of the Surma.

[4] The Garo Hills.

The 22nd. came to the Village of Ossunpour,[1] at which Place are the Ruins of a Portuguese Chapel. This Village is about 50 Miles NBE½E from Dacca. Immediately below this Village a navigable Creek runs out of the Baramputrey to ye Eastward, & communicates with Silet River. This part of the Country abounds with Betel Trees. The Variation of the Magnetic Needle was 0°-38′ Westerly at this Place.

The 23d. saw another Range of Mountains to the Northw^d^. dis^t^. at least 80 Miles These are said to be the Boundary of the Kingdom of Bengall.[2]

From ye 22d. June to ye 14th. July employed in surveying from Ossunpour to Coustya a small Village on the West side of the River. This Day we were obliged
to leave off surveying, by reason of the Rivers suddenly overflowing the Banks, & 10
rendering it impossible either to measure Station Lines, or note the exact bed of the River.

The Course of the Baramputrey between the head of the Luckya River & Coustya is about SEBS notwithstanding that the old Maps have made it nearly South The breadth of the River is very unequal, it being from half a Mile to three Miles. The Country on both sides is full of Villages, & has a great deal of Padda sown in it, & there are many Groves of Betel Trees. There is not a Tree fit for Timber to be met with, the trunks being very short & crooked.

Baganbarry a large Bazar Village is situated on ye West side of the River, & near the Place where we left off surveying. From this Village a small Creek leads into the Luckya River during the wet Season, & allows a much safer Passage for Boats than ye great River.

It being but a short Passage from Baganbarry to Chilmary,[4] I imagined that a 11
few days would be usefully employed in tracing the River to that Place & making a cursory Survey of it, in order to render the general Map more compleat to this Time, & to get some Information from ye Countrey People concerning the Situation of Gwalpara, & the Course of the Creeks that lead out of the Baramputrey towards Muxadavat.[5]

From the 14th. to ye 19th. of July, employed in tracing ye Baramputrey from Baganbarry to Chilmary. The Course of the River between these two Places is nearly the same as between the Luckya River & Baganbarry (v^t^.) SEBS. The distance by

[1] Hoseinpur. The Portuguese chapel here is not mentioned either by Hunter or in the List of Ancient Monuments. 'Ossumpur' is mentioned in a letter of Père Barbier, dated 15th January 1723, included in the Lettres Edifiantes et Curieuses (Tome XIII. p. 272), as one of the places where the 'gens à chapeau, or Portuguese in the service of the Great Mogul, were especially numerous He visited the place himself in company with Bishop Laynez in 1714, and describes it as 'une bourgade toute chrétienne, nommée Ossampur' This letter will shortly be published by the Rev. W. K. Firminger in Bengal, Past and Present.

[2] *See below*, p. 130.

[3] Baganbarry—spelt Bygonbarry on Rennell's map=Maimansingh or Nasirabad, the head-quarters of the Maimansingh district. Baigunbari is mentioned by Hunter as a village with a large indigo factory near Gobindganj, about 5 m. NW of Maimansingh. It is a place of pilgrimage for Hindus (Stat Acc. Beng, Vol. V. p. 415).

[4] Chilmari, a town on the west bank of the Brahmaputra, a short distance above the point where the present river leaves the old channel.

[5] A corruption of Maksudabad, the old name of Murshidabad. Rennell uses both forms, and in the Bengal Atlas always Moorshedabad.

Estimation is near 70 Miles, & as I was assisted in ascertaining it both by the bearings of the Mountains & the Latitude of Chilmary, there can arise no very considerable Error. The Latitude of Chilmary by an Observation taken by Hadley's Quadrant was 25°-27′ N.[1]*

* The Lat^de^. has since been taken in a truer Manner 25 -24′.

12 The Countrey betwixt Baganbarry & Chilmary is quite flat all ye way on ye West side of ye River, & is mostly Padda Fields; the Eastern Side likewise is flat till within 20 miles of Chilmary, & then the hilly Countrey begins. Some of the hills lie close to the River side, & are of a very moderate height, & covered with Jungle.

The Chain of high Mountains beforementioned that are said to be the Eastern Boundary of Bengall begin about the Latitude of 25°-10′ N & run in a curve Line to the Northwestward. Part of this Chain comes within 30 miles of Chilmary. I have not yet had an Opportunity of taking their exact Altitude, but judge that they are near a mile & half in perpendicular Height.[2]

In the accompanying General Map only one of the Mountains is placed in its
13 true Situation (v^t^. Mount Sosong[3]), the others by reason of the very frequent thick Weather were not seen from the South end of the Base, & therefore their Situation must be left undetermined till ye dry Season.

There are no Creeks leading out of the Baramputrey towards Jelenghee betwixt Chilmary & Dacca, but I am informed that betwixt Chilmary & Gwalpara there is one which affords a Passage for small Boats all ye year round to Surda & Jaffiergunge Rungpour & Gorrygatt are situated on ye Banks of this Creek.[4]

By the best Information that I can procure concerning the Situation of Gwalpara, it must lie near ye Latitude of 26° N[5] & about 70 miles NWBW from Chilmary. However there is little dependence to be placed on ye Countrey People's Intelligence.

The Curreut of the Baramputrey is remarkably rapid, near Chilmary in some places it runs at the rate of 6 miles an Hour.

14 From the 19th. to ye 25th. of July staid at Chilmary, during which time we were employed in taking ye Latitude, getting Information from ye Countrey People, & constructing a Sett of General Maps of the late Survey.

The 25th. left Chilmary, & ye 29th. at Night entered the Luckya River, the frequent Gales of Wind preventing our making any greater Progress. In proceeding down the Luckya River we made a Sketch of it, which is inserted in ye general Map. The first of August arrived at Dacca.

---

1 25°-27′-20″, according to Hunter.

2 This is the Tura range, the backbone of the Garo hills. The highest point is Nokrek, 4,652 ft.

3 This is the peak 3,375 ft. high overhanging the Someswari R. about 14 miles NNE of Susang Durgapur, the residence of the Raja of Susang. The hill is known to the Bengalis as Kailas and to the Garos as Chikmang, and is considered sacred by them, as the place which the spirits of the Garos inhabit after death. (Playfair, 'The Garos,' p. 102.) I ascended this hill in 1882, and was surprised to find that my Garo guides showed no reluctance to accompany me. One of them, indeed, caught and eat *à l'huitre*, an unfortunate crayfish that he caught in a stream near the crest of the hill, a circumstance that did not indicate much awe, or reverence for the spirits of his ancestors supposed to inhabit it!

4 This information was incorrect. The Jennai river, which afterwards became the main channel of the Brahmaputra, now known as the Jamuna, left the latter below Chilmari. Rangpur and the ruined city of Ghoraghat lie well to the west.

5 Goalpara lies in Lat. 26°-11′ N., but to the NE of Chilmari, not to the WNW as stated by Rennell's informant. The distance in a direct line is about 70 miles.

NOTE.

Having no Colours to distinguish the Data for the Construction of the general 16
Map, an account of it is here given in Writing.

The Hughly & Jelenghee Rivers, together with that part of the Ganges wch lies to ye Westw^{d}. of Jelenghee is taken from a Map of Capt. Polier's.

The great Ganges from Jelenghee to its conflux with ye Megna, & likewise the Megna & Baramputrey from thence to Baganbarry, is laid down by exact Surveys. Dacca likewise is placed in its true Situation by means of a Survey from the mouth of the Issamuty to that Place.

The Chunnunah & Comer Creeks are laid down from Surveys, but the Burrashee, Najapour, Beurygonga, Issamuty & Panghia Rivers are chiefly from the report of the Pilots.

The Luckya River is from a Sketch taken lately, as likewise the Baramputrey from Baganbarry to Chilmary.

The Latitudes of the Southern Places are reckoned from an Observation of Latitude taken at Luckypour in 1764.[1]

---

[1] *See* p. 34.

17 Measured the height of a Mark on ye Poostah[1] 22d April at New Moon. High Water.

		Foot.	In.
The Height was then	.. ..	14	3
do 7th. June	.. ..	11	7½
22nd. do.	.. ..	10	6½
27th.	.. ..	9	11
July 7th.	.. ..	7	4
9th.	.. ..	7	5
19th.	.. ..	5	2½
August 2d.	.. ..	1	10½
3d. Morn.	.. ..	1	7
4th. Morning	.. ..	1	2½
5th. do.	.. ..	0	10¾
7th. do.	.. ..	0	7
8th. Low Water	.. ..	0	9¼
9th. at 11 am ½ flood	..	0	12½
10th.	.. .	—	—
11th. at ½ past 9 ¼ flood	..	0	9¾
12th.	.. ..	—	—
13th. { 9 Morn.	.. ..	0	8½
13th. { 6 Evg.	.. ..	0	8½
14th. 6 Evg.	.. ..	0	9
15th.	.. ..	0	0
16th. Morn. HW	.. ..	0	9½
17th. 10 AM	.. ..	0	10¼
19th. 10 AM	.. ..	0	10½
20th.	.. ..	—	—
21st. HW	.. ..	0	13
23d.	.. ..	0	12½
25th.	.. ..	0	15¼
29th.	.. ..	0	20
Sept. 3d.	.. ..	0	26½
4th.	.. ..	0	29½
7th	.. ..	0	36
10th.	.. ..	3	7

[1] Poostah. *Hind.* Pushta, a quay or masonry terrace along the river bank (Cal. Rev., Vol. xciv, p. 320). A place named 'Postagolah' (Gola=Warehouse) is marked on Rennell's map of Dacca (Beng. Atlas No. XII) close to the city.

JOURNAL of the fourth Expedition for making a general Map of the Bengall Provinces, beginning with that of Bengall, & continuing the Survey of the Baramputrey & the Countries bordering on it.

The 10th. of October whilst at Dacca I received Lord Clive's Orders to set about forming a general Map of Bengall with all Expedition; & as it appeared to be a very tedious Work should all the Distances be exactly ascertained, his Lordship gave Directions that they should be taken in a cursory Manner only, correcting them by Latitudes or any other eligible Means.[1]

As his Lordship was pleased to leave it to my Discretion where to begin my Surveys, I judged it most proper to proceed with the Survey of the River Baramputrey, & the Countries that lie contiguous to it.

Sunday 13th. set out from Dacca. The Rainy Season not broke up but ex- 2
pected to break[2] at the new Moon which was to happen ye next day. Being to go by way of Naranda Creek[3] I judged that no ill Consequences could happen to the Boats by the Monsoons breaking, whilst they continued in so narrow a Creek: the Weather also appeared to be settled.

In the afternoon we had a slight Squall from the NNE, & at 5 perceiving that the Clouds began to rise very quick from that Quarter, we returned back to Diagunge & secured the Boats near the Bridge.[4] Very heavy Rain from 5 till Midnight, the Wind in moderate Gales from the Northward.

The 14th. at ½ an hour past Midnight the Wind increased, and at one blew a stiff Gale: from that Time till 6 in the Morning several heavy Squalls, with much Rain, the Wind veering gradually from N^d. to ENE. At 9 the Wind came at East & blew much stronger than before, & from 9 to 5 PM it veered gradually to SWBW, its violence increasing till it had settled in that Quarter near two Hours. The Rain continued without Intermission. At 7 PM the Wind veered to West, & grew 3
moderate, the remainder of the Night moderate Gales from WNW to West, with flying Showers The Moon changed at 11 at this Night.

The 15th. moderate Gales from WSW to NNW, the Weather cloudy & threatning, but before Night it cleared up. The Water of the River rose a Cubit & half during the Storm, but fell again this Day.[5]

[1] The historian Orme had written to Lord Clive (21st Novr. 1764), imploring him to "make a vast map of Bengal, in which not only the outlines of the province, but also the different subdivisions of Burdwan, Beerboom etc. may be justly marked. * * * * * Take astronomical observations of longitude, if you have anybody capable of doing it * * * *." These instructions to Rennell were no doubt the outcome of this appeal (Malcolm, Life of Clive, Vol. II, p. 253). On the 29th Sept 1765 Clive wrote to Orme promising to let him have the maps (*Ibid.*, Vol. III, p. 132).

[2] The expression "break of the monsoon" is now generally used to denote its beginning: *ante* p. 27.

[3] The Dolai or Naranda creek is a branch of the Balu, a tributary of the Lakhmia (Luckya) river, and intersects the city of Dacca.

[4] The Narandia bridge, built (together with a mosque) in the year 1664 A.D. The creek is now crossed by an iron suspension bridge (Rankin).

[5] These cyclones often occur during October in the Bay of Bengal and the surrounding countries, and frequently

The 16th. the Weather appearing to be settled, we set out from Diagunge & got to Demra[1] in the Evening, when the Wind settled in the NE Quarter.

The 17th. a thick foggy Morning, being the first for the Season, & I remarked that the first Morning of this kind last year happened the 21st. of October. For the remainder of the Weather see the last Pages of the Journal.[2]

The 19th. in the Morning came to the outlet of Bermya Creek, which is a Branch of the Baramputrey falling into the Luckya River near Simulya. As this Creek had not been surveyed, I struck thro' it in order to trace it to the Baramputrey.

4 The 22nd. in the Afternoon came into the Baramputrey near Toak & opposite to the Village of Akarasonda, having traced the Bermya Creek whose Course is very crooked, & the Banks everywhere covered with Jungles & Woods. We saw but one Village the whole way, which is that of Bermya, situated on the Western Bank of the Creek, & about 8½ miles WSW from Akarasonda. Four miles NE from this Village the Creek receives another small Creek from Bagunbary, but it is not navigable all the Year.

The Current of the Baramputrey appeared to be much stronger this Time than when we passed through it before; occasioned I imagine by the Waters falling off.

The 23d. at Noon took an Observation of Lat^{d}. at Ossunpour,[4] by which that Place lies in 24°-26′ N^{d}.

The 25th. in the Evening arrived at the Place where we left off surveying in July last, near Baganbary, & prepared for surveying next day. Found the Magnetic Variation at this Place 0°-32′ Westerly.

In coming up the River we have been employed in copying the original Survey of the Baramputrey & Luckya River for the Governor.

5 The 26th. continued the Survey of the Baramputrey from the old Mark, towards Chilmary & Gwalpara, & from this Time to ye 10th. November (15 days) employed in tracing it by a cursory Survey from Sunacalley[5] to the Mouth of the Dherla River[6] which is upwards of 76 miles. The Western Bank betwixt Baganbary & Dewangunge being laid down in July last by a cursory Survey, I omitted going over it again; but from Dewangunge to Chilmary the Countrey was too much overflown at that Time to lay down the River Bank with any tolerable exactness, so that that part was surveyed again, & accordingly appears very different in particulars from the Map which was sent in August last.

cause much damage. As I write these notes (19th Octr 1909) one has devastated the E.B S. Railway station at Goalundo, caused some loss of life, and destroyed a number of steamers anchored there.

[1] At the junction of the Naranda creek with the Lakhmia.

[2] *See* pp. 63 to 65

[3] A large village at the head of the Lakhmia river, the Egarasindhur of history. It was a seat of the famous Isa Khan, the founder of the Maimansingh family, who is mentioned by Ralph Fitch in 1586 as "Isacan the chiefe of all the other kings, and a great friend to all Christians" (Ryley, Ralph Fitch, p. 119). A battle is said to have taken place here between Isa Khan and Raja Man Singh, Akbar's famous Hindu General (Rankin). The Lakhmia and the Bermya creek run through the heart of the Madhupur Jungle, the elevated tract of country extending from the Meghna to the Brahmaputra, already referred to (p. 45).

[4] *Ante*, p. 47.

[5] A village on the left bank of the Brahmaputra opposite Maimansingh.

[6] The Dharla river joins the Brahmaputra at Bagwa, above Chilmari.

The Courses of the River are various, being from SW to East; however the whole distance is chiefly meridional, & therefore easy to be corrected by the Latitudes. By this Base I was enabled to fix the Situations of several of the Sosong Mountains[1] which in clear Weather will serve as Marks 80 miles off.

I mentioned in the former Journal that the Hilly Countrey began on the East side a few miles below Chilmary: the Hills continue afterwards in scattering Ranges along the Eastern Bank of the River. The Sosong & Rungjulee[2] Mountains lie near 6
30 miles within & bound the Garrow Provinces.

The Baramputrey within the above mentioned Space is from ¾ of a mile to 7 miles over within its bed; but during the Months of July & August it overflows all the Low Lands, few spots of Ground having less than a Cubit or a Cubit & half water on them.

The Countrey on both sides of the River, between Baganbary & Mobagunge, is mostly Padda Fields, interspersed with Groves of Betel & other Trees; between Mobagunge & the Dherla River the Countrey is mostly jungly near the River; & the opposite side is one entire Jungle. There are no Timber Trees to be found near the River.

I reckoned upwards of 80 Villages between Baganbarry & the Mouth of the Dherla River, but there are no Bazars save at Buzerapour, Dewangunge & Chilmary. & these are very paltry ones. The Countrey abounds with Cattle, Rice, & Poultry, & there are prodigious numbers of Tygers & wild Buffalos in the Jungles, particularly
in the neighbourhood of Baggooa.[3] 7

I had several Observations of the Variation of the Magnetic Needle, the quantity from 0°-46′ to 0°-58′ Westerly; & some Observations of Latitude, by which I place Chilmary in 25°-24′ N. That Place is now 1½ mile distant from the Western Bank of the River. The Teesta Creek[4] from Boutan falls into the River 11 miles above Chilmary, & 5 miles below the Mouth of the Dherla River.

Being entirely ignorant of the Situation of Rungpour,[5] & the adjacent Countries; the knowledge of which would enable me to regulate my Route after the Survey of the

---

1 The Tura range of the Garo Hills.

2 The northern portion of the Garo Hills (*see* map No. V in Rennell's Atlas) Buchanan Hamilton remarks concerning this name, "In the nomenclature of these hills there is great confusion. The names given to the same hill by the different tribes who inhabit near are not only different, but it is usual for the Bengalese to call whatever hill you point out to them by the village that lies nearest it in the direction from whence you are then looking; so that for every hill you may find as many names as it has villages near, and not one of these may be its proper name. It seems to have been owing to this custom not having been understood, that Major Rennell has given the name of Rungjula to the Garo mountains. As he was endeavouring from the riverside to find out the name of this elevated region, he probably pointed out to the natives the highest peak, Gorokhyonath; and Ronggojuli village being in the direction, the natives called it the Ronggojuli hill" (Martin, History, Vol. III, p. 475). The northern range of the Garo Hills is now commonly known as the Arbela range, after one of the villages situated upon it.

3 Bagwa, at the mouth of the Dharla.

4 This was not the main channel of the Teesta, which in those days flowed due south. It now joins the Brahmaputra below Chilmari The change in its course took place in 1787 (Hunter, Stat. Acc. Beng., Vol. VII, p. 165, p. 296).

5 Rangpur, the head-quarters of a District, on the Ghaghat River. It had only just been taken over from the Muhammadans, and was in a very unsettled state. Buchanan Hamilton spells the name Ronggopoor (Martin, History, Vol. III, p. 351). Regarding the changes in the courses of the rivers of this district he writes, about 1809:—"Since the survey was made by Major Rennell, the rivers of this district have undergone such changes, that I find the utmost difficulty in tracing them. The soil is so light, and the rivers in descending the mountains have acquired such force, that

Baramputrey was finished, I judged it proper to trace the Roads to that Place & then to return to the Baramputrey by way of Coorygong & the Dherla River; at the same time describing the Courses of the Dherla & Teesta Rivers, which intersect the Roads.

The 10th of November entered the Teesta Creek & proceeded up it towards Olyapour which lies in the Rungpour Road. The 12th. in the Forenoon came to
8 Olyapour after going 22½ miles thro' the Creek, altho' the distance by Land is only 10¼ miles. The Teesta Creek is not above 100 yards over, & very shallow in some Places, so that it cannot be navigable during the dry Months.

Olyapour [2] is a large Village situated on the North Bank of the Teesta, but the Bazar is small & ill supplied. The Countrey round it is pleasant & well cultivated, every spot of Ground being either sown with Padda or planted with Betel Trees. But within 5 miles of the great River's Bank there is but little cultivated Land. Rannygunge a middling Village lies 3 miles SE from Olyapour & on ye north Bank of the Teesta.

The Countrey round Olyapour belongs to Baharbund Purgannah.[3]

From Olyapour we proceeded towards Rungpour by Land, there being no Water Passage at this Season. We passed the Teesta [4] about 6 miles WNW of Olyapour at a small Village named Tytari; after this its Course is more to the NW^t. About a mile & half West from Tytari crossed the Monaash Creek,[5] which is now fordable: its Course is to the ESE, joining the Teesta at Callygunge. The Countrey from Olyapour to this Place is full of Padda Fields & Betel Trees, but here it is uncultivated
9 for several Miles, owing I suppose to its lying too high to be overflown during the rainy Season.

After crossing the Monaash Creek we proceeded 3½ miles along the southern Bank of it, having a pleasant Plain to ye Southward, & thick Woods to the Northward. After leaving this Plain we entered a well cultivated Countrey, being full of Padda fields & Betel Groves, & having a very good Road through it. At Dammo-Choculo 6 miles ESE from Rungpour, crossed the Allykury Creek, which is another Branch of the Teesta, & about 2 foot deep at this Time. The whole Countrey appears to be very well watered, being everywhere intersected by small Creeks. The Allykurey

frequent and great changes are unavoidable; so that whole channels have been swept away by others, and new ones are constantly forming. The nomenclature therefore is exceedingly difficult. After tracing the name of a river from some distance you all of a sudden lose it, and perhaps recover the same name at a distance of 20 miles, while many large rivers intervene, and no channel remains to assist in discovering the former connection. * * * * The confusion that has arisen from these circumstances is so great, that Major Rennell seems to have been overpowered, or unwilling to waste time on the investigation: and owing to the contradictory accounts given by the natives, he seems to have altogether avoided giving names to many of the rivers. * * * *" An account of the rivers as they were in Buchanan Hamilton's time follows (*op. cit.*, Vol. III, p. 358 *seq.*).

1 Kurigram, on the right bank of the Dhar'a, which is now bridged here by the E.B.S. Railway.

2 Ulipur, a village about half-way between the Dharla and the present channel of the Teesta, due south of Kurigram.

3 Pargana, a fiscal division of a district. The two parganas of Bhitarband (Bittrebund of Rennell's Atlas), or 'inner,' and Baharbund, 'outer', boundaries (? *band*) or frontiers, lay along the Brahmaputra and were two of the former divisions of the ancient Hindu kingdom of Kamarupa, which extended westwards to Rangpur.

4 *i.e.* the Teesta creek above mentioned, not the main river at that time. This was the channel taken possession of by the river in 1787.

5 The Manas, one of the numerous branches of the Teesta, not the larger Manas, or Banas, of Assam.

runs by y[e] side of the Road for near 4 miles to the Westward of the place where we crossed it.

Rungpour is situated with respect to Olyapour W[t]. 12°-20′ North, distant 22¼ British Miles,* tho' by the Road it is upwards of 24 Miles. The Goggot Creek [1] comes within ¾ of a mile of the west part of the Town: it is navigable for Boats of 150 Maund till the Month of January. This Creek is said to be a Branch of the Purnabubah River,[2] which has its Source in the Kingdom of Boutan,[3] & runs by way of Raajgunge, 10
Denospour[4] & Bulloa; afterwards joining the Ganges by several Branches, the chief of which are those of Mahanada, Surda, & Jaffiergunge.

* Latitude 25°-43′ N. Lon. from Dacca 1°-6′ West.

There is but little worth remarking about Rungpour, it being only a principal Gunge,[5] & like most of the others, the Houses are built of Matts & Bamboos, there being but one Brick house in the Town.

The British Factory is now at Nabobgunge, a Bazar Village lying about 3 miles NWBW from Rungpour.

We arrived at Rungpour the 14th. & the two following Days were employed in collecting some particulars concerning the Situation of the neighbouring Countries, the Course of the Rivers, &c.

From the 16th. to the 19th. employed in tracing the Roads from Rungpour to Gurygong.[6] This is a middling Village belonging to Baharbund, situated on the South Bank of the Dherla or Durla River & about 12 miles N 37°-30′ West from the Place of its Conflux with the Baramputrey. The Dherla is from 350 yards to a ¼ of a mile broad & is navigable all the Year for Boats of 2000 Maund between Gurygong & y[e] great River. This River has likewise its Source from Boutan, & in the wet 11
Season has a communication with the Purnabubah. It separates the Purgannahs of Baharbund & Vittrebund.[7]

The Roads between Rungpour & Gurygong are in general very rough & Jungly, especially in the neighbourhood of the latter. In our Route we crossed the Monaash & Teesta Creeks, besides several Jeels which render the Roads impassable 6 months of the Year.

The 20th. & 21st. employed in tracing the Dherla River from Gurygong to Baggooa (the place of its Conflux with the Baramputrey): the distance by the River is near 18 miles; the Current is in general excessive rapid.

From the 21st. November to y[e] 2d. December employed in laying down the Western Bank of the Baramputrey from the Mouth of the Dherla River to Jugygupa:[8]

1 The Ghagat, formerly a branch of the Teesta, but now silted up at its head. It is a very sluggish and tortuous river. In the lower part of its course it receives the name of the Alai, and afterwards of the Bengali River.

2 The Purnabhaba R. lies considerably to the West in Dinajpur District, and was at that time one of the main branches of the Teesta.

3 Bhutan

4 Dinajpur.

5 A Bazar village or Market. There were 42 brick houses in Buchanan Hamilton's time (1809).

6 Kuriganj or Kurigram.

7 Bhitarband. Bittrebund in Rennell's Bengal Atlas, No. V.

8 Jogighopa, a village on the north bank of the Brahmaputra opposite Goalpara, Yogighopa of Buchanan Hamilton. The Ahoms had a fort here, taken by Mir Jumla in 1662 (Gait, Hist. of Assam, p. 127). The name appears to be

the distance is 71 miles, & the Courses various. Between Baggoa & Rangamatty the Course of the River is in general S 31°-30′ Wt. 36½ miles; the Countrey within this space is quite flat & destitute of Trees, & the Soil sandy & barren near the River; there are very few Villages & no Bazars or Haats.[1]

12 The Rangamatty Countrey begins about 10 miles above Baggoa, & continues to the Frontiers of Boutan & Assam. Ten miles below Rangamatty the Sunecoss[2] River from Boutan falls into the Baramputrey at Dubarye.[3] The Sunecoss River is about 200 yards broad & 12 or 14 Cubits deep for upwards of 40 miles above the Conflux.

Rangamatty is at present a small illbuilt Village situated on a Range of small Hills which form the Western Bank of the Sunecoss River, & about 2½ miles NW from the Baramputrey, with which it has a communication by means of the Sunecoss. It has a small mud Fort with some few Guns mounted in it, & I observed about 50 Guns from 2 to 4 pounders lying without.[4] The Latitude of this Place is 26°-6′ North & Longitude from Dacca 0°-20′ West.

The Course of the Baramputrey between Rangamatty & Gwalpara is from EBN to WBS 35 miles, the breadth irregular, & a great number of Islands in it. Between these Places four Rivers from Boutan empty themselves into the Baramputrey on the North side; Three of them (vt.) the Gowrong, Champomattey, & Hāārypaany are fordable; but however serve to float down Timbers from Boutan & the Forests of
13 Bisnee.[5] The fourth of these Rivers is named the Bonaash,[6] whose Course is from the Boutan Mountains, to the SW, first separating the Low Countries of Assam & Boutan, & afterwards those of Bengall & Assam; emptying itself into the Baram-

derived from that of a Garo princess, Jugé Silché, who was hidden by her people in a cave here to protect her from a rapacious chief of Assam (Playfair, The Garos, p. 9).

1 Hind. Hāt, a market held on certain days.

2 The Sankos, formerly the boundary between Bengal and Assam.

3 Dhubri, for many years the terminus of the Railway on the Brahmaputra, and the head-quarters station of Goalpara district.

4 Rangamati, signifying 'Red earth,' is a common village name in Bengal and Assam, such villages being built on patches of the older alluvium, which is usually of a red colour. This particular village is not shown in the Atlas of India, but is marked conspicuously on Rennell's maps (Bengal Atlas Nos. V and XVIII) on the bank of the Sunecoss (Sankos) near the Brahmaputra. It is also marked in the same position, on the north bank of the Brahmaputra, not far beyond Dhubri, in the map attached to Mr. Gait's History of Assam. But in Hunter's Imp. Gazetteer of India (Vol. XI, p. 470) and in the latest edition of the same work the position is given as in Lat. 26°-19′ N., Long. 90°-48′ E.; that is to say, the site of a small village of the same name on the Manas, 38 miles further to the east. It is also stated that the village was an important outpost of the Muhammadans at the beginning of the 18th century. As, however, the Rangamati of the Gazetteer lies on the eastern bank of the Manas, which was then the boundary, and therefore within the dominions of the king of Assam, it is not likely to have been in Muhammadan hands. Moreover Rennell's description shows that his Rangamati had not long before been a fort of importance, and it is much more likely therefore to have been the Muhammadan outpost in that direction. It was one of the places visited by Bishop Laynez in 1714, as recorded in the Lettres Édifiantes et Curieuses (Tom. XIII, p. 288), and was considered to be very unhealthy, as Père Barbier says:—"On nous faisoit appréhender ce voyage, car c'est un proverbe commun à Bengale, que de deux personnes qui vont à Rangamati, il y en a toujours une qui y reste. Mais le courage de notre Prélat étoit à toute épreuve."

5 Bijni, an estate in the Goalpara district.

6 The Manas R., called the Banas in the Muhammadan records (Gait, History of Assam, p. 113 *note*). It joins the Brahmaputra opposite Goalpara.

putrey at Jugygupa, a few miles below Gwalpara. The Bed of this River is in general 200 yards broad, but its Waters are not navigable even for Pulwars during the driest part of the Year. As this River affords so short a Passage to the Boutan Mountains (it being less than 60 miles on a streight Line from the foot of the Mountains to Jugygupa), there is no doubt but that any Number of Firr Trees may be brought down by it, if a right understanding subsisted between our People & the Assamers; as I have myself seen a large Firr Tree which floated down the River, after being washed down the Mountains by the Land Floods.[1]

Between Rangamatty & Gwalpara the Countrey is Hilly on both sides the River, & so full of Woods & Jungles that it is scarce penetrable, & I could see but two or three Villages the whole way.

Gwalpara[2] is a small Village belonging to Measpara Purgana, & is situated on
the South side of the great River in Latitude 26°-7′ North & Longitude from Dacca
0°-16′ East. The Factory lies on the side of a small woody Hill immediately to the 14
Eastward of which the Keestrey, a small River from the Garrow Provinces, falls into
the Baramputrey.

The Assam Countrey begins from the Bonaash River on the North side the Baramputrey & one of their Chokeys[3] is placed directly opposite Gwalpara; but on the South side the Bengall Provinces continue for upwards of 21 miles. The Countrey is very little cultivated in the neighbourhood of Gwalpara and Jugygupa.[4] The Woods abound with several kinds of wild Animals, as Tygers, Rhinoceros, Buffalos, Elephants, &c., the tracks of which may be seen everywhere.

I could not perceive that the Current of the Baramputrey was more rapid near Gwalpara &c. than it was 200 miles farther down, altho' it is commonly reported otherwise: it is indeed rocky in some places, particularly between Rangamatty & Gwalpara; but in other respects the Navigation of this River appears to me to be full as easy as that of the Ganges.

From the 2nd. to ye 6th. December employed in tracing the Baramputrey from 15
Gwalpara to the Frontier of Assam on the Southern side. The distance by y^e^

---

1 The timber trade has assumed large proportions since the Eastern Duars were taken over by the Government of India in 1866.

2 Goalpara. Formerly one of the frontier outposts of the Muhammadans in Assam. The true latitude is 26°-11′. A French Factory was established here in 1754 or 1755 by M. Chevalier, and on the fall of Chandernagore in 1757 he remained in the employ of some English gentlemen. In 1767 a Mr Laval was appointed agent of the English in partnership with M. Chevalier (Bengal Past & Present, Vol. III, No. 2, p. 366). Buchanan Hamilton describes 'Goyalpara' in 1809 as containing "some good thatched houses, and a street of shops, which in such a country is considered as a kind of miracle, and the place is looked upon as a city of the utmost elegance. It is only, however, in its containing many distressed objects, and many profligate and vicious persons, that it resembles an European city; and, in proportion to its size, in these points it probably far excels any place west from the Cape of Good Hope" (Martin, History, Vol. III, p. 477).

3 Chokey. Hind. Chauki, a police station. Assam was an independent kingdom until 1825, when it was conquered by the British.

4 One of the duties of the Muhammadan military officers in charge of the posts of Rangamati and Goalpara was to encourage the growth of jungle and reeds as a protection against the inroads of the Assamese (Hunter, Imp. Gaz., Vol. V, p. 113).

River is 22 miles, the Course of which is from West to WNW, very different from the description given of it in the Maps.[2] We were not permitted to land on the Northern or Assam side, all the way, there being several Chokeys placed; however we found means to lay down about 10 miles beyond the Bengall Frontiers, & in returning we coasted the Assam side near enough to inform ourselves of all the particulars which we wanted.

This River must needs have a very long Course before it enters the Bengall Provinces, since 400 miles from the sea it is twice as big as the Thames. By measuring the Banks &c. I find that the Rains swell this River 32 or 33 foot.

The Bengall Country extends 18 or 20 miles to the Eastward of Commerputa (the Frontier Town on the River) & afterwards as I am informed the Boundary runs in a Southerly direction towards Silet & Bermas.[3] However, that must be the Object of a future Survey, as we are now surveying the Countries to the Westwd. of the Baramputrey.

16 The Garrow Provinces begin about 12 miles south of the Baramputrey, & are bounded by the Rungjulee & Sosong Mountains[4]; some of them are independent of Bengall.

The 6th. returned to Gwalpara; the next day employed in reducing & compiling the Surveys, & procuring Pilots & Hircaras for the Bisnee Countrey.

From the 8th. to the 11th. employed in tracing the Bonaash & Birally Rivers from Jugygupa to the Frontiers of Assam & Boutan. I have mentioned some particulars concerning the Bonaash in page 12 & 13; the Birally or Barrally is a small River from Boutan which joins the Bonaash 12 miles above Jugygupa & has a Course from NW to SE.

1 To the present boundary with the Kamrup district. The northern side is now part of the latter district, Kamrup marking the western extension of the Assam kingdom in the 18th century

2 In his 'Memoir of Hindoostan' (p. 356) Rennell says:—"On tracing this river in 1765, I was no less surprised at finding it rather larger than the Ganges, than at its course previous to its entering Bengal. This I found to be from the east: although all the former accounts represented it as from the north; and this unexpected discovery soon led to inquiries, which furnished me with an account of its general course, to within 100 miles of the place where Du Halde left the Sanpoo. I could no longer doubt, that the Burrampooter and the Sanpoo were one and the same river: and to this was added the positive assurance of the Assamers, 'That *their* river came from the north-west, through the Bootan mountains.' And to place it beyond a doubt, that the Sanpoo river is not the same with the river of Ava, but that this last is the great *Nou Kian* of Yunan; I have in my possession a manuscript draught of the Ava river, to within 150 miles of the place where Du Halde leaves the Nou Kian, in its course towards Ava; together with very authentic information that this river (named *Irabatty* by the people of Ava) is navigable from the city of Ava into the province of Yunan in China."

I have quoted this passage at length, because it shows the acuteness of Rennell's reasoning, and that he was the first to recognise the identity of the Brahmaputra with the Tsan-po of Tibet. The controversy has not even yet been settled by actual exploration, but Mr. Needham in 1885-6 proved that the river that flows past Sama, in the Zayul valley, is not a tributary of the Tsan-po as had been supposed, but is continuous with the Brahmaputra at Sudiya, and as it had already been shown that the Tsanpo does not flow to the east of Sama, there is no doubt that it breaks through the Himalayas by the channel of the Dihang, the largest river falling into the Brahmaputra from the north. This passage, however, shows that even Rennell was liable to be misled by hearsay information, for the Nou Kian or Lu Kiang of Yunnan is the Salween, and not the Irrawaddy or 'river of Ava.'

For an account of the changes in the course of the river between the time of Rennell's Survey and 1809 *see* Buchanan Hamilton (Martin, History, Vol. III, p. 387 *seq.*).

3 Burma. This boundary coincides with the eastern limits of the Garo Hills disrict.

4 *i.e.* on the north and south sides respectively. The Garo Hills were not entirely brought under control till 1873.

The Luhêet River, a Branch of the Baramputrey, which separates from the great River 3 days above Gwalpara, joins the Bonaash by two Branches; one above, the other below the Mouth of the Barrally. This River is navigable for Pulwars all the Year.[1]

The Boutan or Thibet Countrey begins immediately on the North side of the Barally, & to the Westward of the Bonaash; which is about the Latitude of 26°-20′: but those Lands are held by the Rajah of Bisnee,[2] as Tributary to the King of 17
Boutan. The Boutan Mountains begin in the Latitude of 26°-50′, & form a Curve Line whose ends are turned to the ENE & WNW. The Boundary of Assam is formed by the Bonaash River to the Westward, & the foot of the Boutan Mountains to the Northward. The Bisnee Countrey has the Bonaash for its Eastern, & the Mountains for its Northern Boundary.

The 11th. Ensign Richards[3] with a Detachment of a Jametdaar[4] and 10 Sepoys joined me on my return to Jugygupa, & on the 12th. we set out by Land to survey the Countries between the Bonaash River & Rangamatty.

We first proceeded to the NNE through the Beesnee Province, the South part of which is full of Hills & thick Jungles; the Roads are scarce broad enough for a Palankeen to pass, & the Countrey is everywhere intersected by Creeks & frightful Gullies overgrown with Jungles. Ten miles NNE from Jugygupa we entered Dawaaty Valley which is pleasant & well cultivated, having a small River named the Kongeea winding through it in its Course to the Bonaash. There are several Villages situated in this Valley but all of them inconsiderable. Seven miles to the NE of Dawaaty we crossed the Birally River, & entered the Boutan Countrey, but this Province of it is (as I have before mentioned) held by the Bisnee Rajah. The 18
Barally is now 4½ foot deep, & from 150 to 200 yards broad, & runs rather too rapid to be forded. The Hilly Countrey ends on the South side of this River: the North side is a continued Jungle.

Three miles & Half NE of the Barally we crossed the Dulelly[5] Creek; this Creek has its Source from Boutan, & empties itself into the Bonaash; it is not above 3 foot deep in December, & must consequently be dry some part of the Year.

Bisnee, the Residence of the Rajah of Bisnee & Howargott,[6] lies about 3 miles NNE from the Dulelly in a very Jungly Countrey. This Place lies in Lat^{d} 26°-29′ North, & Longitude 0°-23′ East from Dacca: with respect to Jugygupa it lies N 26° E^{t} distant 33 miles. Bisnee is but a small Village, & has no Bazar, so that we

1 The Lohit is the name given to a branch of the Brahmaputra much further to the east, separating the districts of Sibsagar and Lakhimpur. It is interesting to find the name applied to a branch lower down the river and suggests that these branches represent an old course of the river.

2 Bijni. The Raja claims descent from the royal family of Kuch Behar. The territory is one of the Eastern Duars, attached to Goalpara district. This tract, with the Western Duars, was annexed in 1865 as a result of the aggresions of the Bhutan Government, but the Rajas of Bijni and Sidli were left in possession of their estates.

3 Afterwards appointed as a permanent Assistant Surveyor, *see* p. 86.

4 Jama'dar, a native officer. Rennell's spelling of the word is not given in Hobson Jobson.

5 ? the Dalani, a tributary of the Manas.

6 Habraghat, a pargana in Goalpara district of which the Raja of Bijni is Zemindar. In Rennell's Bengal Atlas 'Howeragot' is shown as lying on the south side of the Brahmaputra south of Goalpara.

had very much difficulty in procuring Provisions. The present Rajah (who is a Youth) resides in a very paultry House surrounded by a small Ditch & high Pallisadoes of Bamboo, which they dignify with the name of a Killa. We halted at this Place one day to procure Provisions & Hircars for the Western Roads, & then struck to the Westward after recrossing the Dulelly & Barally Rivers.

19 After recrossing the Kongeea Creek 4 miles North of Dawaaty we entered a pleasant & well cultivated Valley running from SE to NW: this Valley is formed by the Batyamarry & Seepansilla Hills, & has in it several Villages, the chief of which are Maahgong & Beejura, the latter lying on the Frontier of Great Thibet. The Hilly Countrey in these parts ends near Beejura, in Latitude 26°-25′ N., the Countrey Northward of it being flatt till you approach the Boutan Mountains.

We entered the Boutan Countrey between Beejura & Tanjygong, & crossed about 7 miles of it between Tanjygong & Bassagong: this part is flat, open, & well cultivated, & has two Creeks flowing through it which afterwards fall into the Champamutty River. This part of Boutan belongs to Siddylee Purgannah,[1] & is subject to the Rajah of Cutchubary, a principal Village 2 days' Journey to the Northwest & close to the foot of the Mountains.

I had some thoughts of proceeding as far as Catchubary, in order to take a view of the Countrey, as well as to be informed of the Situation of the Firr Forests, but finding the Natives very averse to it, & that they withdrew into the Countrey in order that we should not be able to procure Provisions, I judged it prudent to desist without further orders, as being foreign to the Service now in execution.

20 After re-entering the Bengall & Bisnee Provinces at Bassagong, we proceeded to the Southwest for Rangamatty, that being the only road that is passable in these Parts. Two miles SW from Bassagong, we crossed the Champamuttey River which falls into the Baramputrey 19 or 20 Miles below. The Eastern Banks of this River are covered with thick Jungle or Sedges, & the Western with thick Woods of Guzzally Trees,[2] which are felled in great numbers & brought down the River in Floats. However there are but few large Trees, the generality of them being fit for no other use than Boat building.

These Woods continue for many miles to the NNW, & to the Southward within a few Miles of the Baramputrey; but Westward scarce four Miles. The Village of Chowtakee lies near ye Road on the West side of the Wood, & within 2½ miles of the Boutan Countrey. There is a small extent of cultivated Land in the neighbouhood of this Village, but from thence Southwestward, we found nothing but thick Jungle for 7 miles; the Guzzally Woods lay about a mile on our left. The Tarang Creek passes within 2 miles of the West side of Chowtaakee.

[1] Sidh, one of the Eastern Duars, now included in Goalpara District.

[2] The *gujali* or *sal* tree, *Shorea robusta*, the most valuable timber tree in N.E. India. The wood so heavy that it sinks in water and has to be supported by bamboo floats or rafts. These forests are enumerated by Buchanan Hamilton (Martin, History, Vol. III., p. 474) and are still of great importance. The Government Reserves in 1903-04 covered an area of 787 square miles in the Goalpara District, of which about 163 square miles are stocked with pure *Sal*. Most of the timber is still used for boat-building (Imp. Gaz., E. Bengal and Assam, p. 518).

From the end of Chowtakee Jungle we entered a pleasant & cultivated Countrey 21
at the Western foot of the Damaderpour Hills; Botagong is situated in this Countrey & affords Rice & other Provisions. The Gowrong River[1] passes to the Westward of this Village in its Course from Boutan to the Baramputrey: it is now 3 foot deep. The Western Bank of the Gowrong is covered with thick Woods. After crossing it near Boutagong our Road lay along the West side of it for upwards of 3 miles, when we turned off to ye SW & came to the Sunecoss River which in this place approaches within 3 miles of the Gowrong, but afterwards turns off short to ye SW & WSW to Rangamatty.

The Bisnee Provinces end at Coresacattee on the Sunecoss River, & Pharlee is the first Village in the Rangamatty Country independent of Bisnee.

We crossed the Sunecoss on Rafts at Goga, a mile & half below Pharlee, after which our way to Rangamatty lay thro' a very thick Jungle for upwards of 7 miles; several small Creeks run through this Jungle in their Course to the Sunecoss. There is a Range of low, woody Hills extending several miles to the NNE of Rangamatty, & the Countrey appears to be woody a long way to the Northward.

The 23rd. came to Rangamatty, & the next day began surveying the Eastern 22
Shoar of the Baramputrey from opposite that Place towards Curybarry.[2] We finished that Business ye 28th & entered the Dherla River in ye Evening.

The Current of the Dherla River opposite & a little above Baggoa is so rapid that it is with much difficulty Boats can pull up. The River is likewise very full of Sands at that Place. The Current I judge to run at the rate of 7 miles p. Hour, so that Boats must be very careful not to get aground there. Between that Place & Gurygong the Current runs at a Moderate Rate, & the Water is sufficiently deep for any Boats.

We arrived at Gurygong the 30th. in the Afternoon, & the next day being the last of the Month I discharged all the Boats, except the Budgarow & Pulwars, having now no farther Occasion for them.

From the 1st. January to the 9th. inclusive, employed on a Sett of particular Maps of the Baramputrey, & a general one of the late Survey. The particular Map is in 3 Sheets of Imperial Paper & on a Scale of 2 miles to an Inch: the general Map is in one Sheet Imp. Paper & on 10′ to an Inch.

During the above Time I sent all round the Baharbund Countrey to hire Coolies 23
& Bearers, but was not able to procure a single one, although I offered a sufficient Price. The Countrey People likewise refused to supply my People with Provisions, & upon enquiry I found it was all owing to the Villiany of the Dewan of Olyapour who had threatned to punish any Person who should supply me with Men or Provisions. Upon this I wrote to the Dewan [3] (Ramsinker) to know the Truth of it, threatning to make him a Prisoner if he did not immediately order me to be supplied with Provisions & Coolies. His Answer was that the People might sell me Provisions

[1] The Gaurang, Gauranggo of Buchanan Hamilton.

[2] Kuribari, a village at the S.W. end of the Garo Hills.

[3] The native manager of the estate.

if they chose it, but dared me to take any Coolies. I forbore making him any farther Answer that Time, intending to visit him the first Opportunity.

I immediately applied to the Resident at Rungpour requesting his Assistance in procuring Bearers & Coolies. He sent me a considerable Number from Rungpour,
24 but as they deserted on the Road I received no more than 18.

The 10th. in the morning we left Curygong, having prest what Coolies we could at that Place, & proceeded by way of Olyapour in order to explain Matters with the Dewan. We arrived at Olyapour late in the Night.

I sent a Message to the Dewan this Night & another in ye morning of ye 11th. requiring him to make his Appearance, but he treated them both with great Indifference About 8 next morning I went with Mr. Richards & 16 Sepoys towards his Countrey House under cover of a thick Fog, but he had got intelligence of our March, & was gone before we entered the House. I informed the Servants that if they did not produce their Master I should set fire to the House, which was accordingly done soon after & we retired to our Baggage on the South side of the Teesta.[2]

The fire was extinguished immediately after we left the House.

25 Although the Dewan had not Resolution enough to defend his House, yet he followed us immediately with 150 Burgundasses[3] & 300 Villagers some of which came close to our Rear & began to fire at us, which Fire we returned in single Shots for upwards of 6 miles they being afraid to close with us & retreating whenever we made a Stand. When we arrived at a Jungle opposite Tytari we turned & cleared the Village & adjacent Jungles of them, & by that Means got through the thick Jungle without Damage, nor did they follow us any farther.

The Dewan sent two threatning Messages to me whilst I stayed in Tytari, but soon after he retired & we set out for Rungpour.[4]

We arrived at Rungpour the 12th. in the Evening, after meeting a Detachment of Sepoys which were sent at my request from Rungpour. Here we remained till ye 22nd. being detained for want of Bullocks & Coolies.

[1] Probably the Chief of the Factory at Nawabganj (*ante* p. 55).

[2] This somewhat high-handed proceeding is related as though it were quite an ordinary occurrence, and it was not the only occasion on which Major Rennell had any serious trouble of this kind with the natives (*see* Appendix B). As the following passage shows, the Dewan had a quite sufficient force to defend his house had he the resolution to do so.

[3] More commonly written 'Burkundauze', derived from 'barkandaz' a 'lightning darter' and signifying an armed retainer or policeman. Hobson Jobson quotes an extract from a letter of Rennell's dated August 5th 1776 (sic.) describing this affair. He says:- "The Country Jemit lars" (Zemindars or land owners) "remote from Calcutta, treat us frequently with great Insolence, and I was obliged to retreat with only an officer and 17 Sepoys near 6 miles in the face of 3 or 400 Burgundasses, who lined the woods and kept a straggling Fire all ye way" (p. 980).

[4] This appears to have been the end of the 'incident.' No mention is made of it elsewhere in the Journal.

OCTOBER 1765.

	Wind.	Weather.		Wind.	Weather.
1	S. SSW. N.	Some Rain.	18	Var^{r}.	Fine Weather.
2	Variable	Flying Showers.	19	NE. to NNW.	Light Winds & very fine Weather.
3	S. NE.	Clear Weather.	20	NE. N^{o}.	Foggy Morning & a fine Day.
4	Var^{e}. & Calm	Hot Weather. Light Winds.	21	Calm	Clear Weather.
5	N^{o}. W^{t}.	Some Rain.	22	SE.ENE.	Most part of the Day fine W^{r}. a Shower in ye Morning.
6	Var^{e}, NE	Flying Showers.	23	ENE. SE.	Foggy Morning. Hot Day.
7	Var^{e}.	do. Light Wind.	24	N^{o}. WNW.	Cold Morning. A fine pleasant Day.
8	E. N.	Fair Weather.	25	NW. N.	Foggy Morn^{g}. middle of the Day hot, ye rem^{r}. fine W^{r}.
9	E. N. NW.	Clear Weather.	26	N. NW.	Fine Weather.
10	N. Var.	Fine Weather.	27	N^{o}. WSW.	Fine Weather.
11	N^{d}.	Dry W^{r}.	28	Calm	Morning & Ev. cool. mid. of the Day hot.
12	N. NW.	Hot Weather. Thunder & Lightning.	29	E. N.	Very fine Weather.
13	N^{o}.	Much Rain.	30	E. NNE.	do. Weather.
14	N. to W.	Storm at y breaking of the Monsoon.	31	SE. ESE.	Fresh Breezes. Weather pleasant & cool.
15	W. NW.	Tolerable W^{r}. Some R.			
16	SW. to N.	Fine Weather.			
17	NE.	The first Foggy Morn^{g}. A fine Day.			

NOVEMBER 1765.

	Wind.	Weather.		Wind.	Weather.
1	N. NE.	Very cold Morning. Fine Weather.	16	NE. E.	Foggy Morn. the rest of the Day fine W^{r}.
2	N. E.	Hot Weather.	17	ENE. E.	Foggy most part of the Day.
3	N. NNE.	Very fine Weather.	18	E. Calm	Variable Weather.
4	NNE NNW.	Clear fine Weather.	19	E. EBN.	Fair Weather.
5	N.	Fresh Wind. Pleas^{t}. W^{r}.	20	NNE. ENE.	Fair Weather.
6	NE.	Fresh Gales & Clear W^{r}.	21	N. ENE.	Clear W^{r}.
7	NE. NNE.	Very fresh Breezes of Wind.	22	SE. NE.	Foggy Weather.
8	NE.	Very fresh Breezes & cold.	23	SE.	Very thick Weather.
9	NE. E.	Light Breezes & fair W^{r}.	24	NE. ENE.	Thick Weather.
10	N. Calm	Calm & hot Weather.	25	NNE. fresh	Tolerable clear W^{r}.
11	NW. N.	Foggy all Day.	26	NNE.	Clear Weather.
12	N. Calm	Foggy Morn^{g}. rest of the Day fair W^{r}.	27	NE. NNE.	Clear W^{r}. Wind fresh.
13	ENE.	Fine Weather.	28	NE.	Fresh B eezes & Clear W^{r}.
14	E. ENE.	Fair Weather.	29	NE. NNE.	Very clear Weather.
15	E.	Fresh Wind & fine W^{r}.	30	NE. NNE.	Very foggy all Day.

DECEMBER 1765.

	Wind.		Weather.
1	NE. E.	..	Foggy Weather.
2	E. SE.	..	Foggy Weather.
3	ENE.	.	Thick Weather.
4	EBN.	..	Mostly foggy Weather.
5	East	.	do. W^{r}.
6	ENE.	..	Clear Weather.
7	Calm	..	Calm & pleasant W .
8	E.	..	Fresh Breezes. Clear W^{r}.
9	E. ENE.		Clear Weather.
10	E.	..	Mostly Foggy W .
11	EBN.	..	Very fine Weather.
12	ENE. N.	.	do. Weather.
13	East	.	Clear & fine Weather.
14	NE. E.		Cold & Foggy Weather.
15	NE.	..	Pleasant W^{r}.
16	Var.	..	Foggy W^{r}.
17	N. NNE.	..	Fine Weather.
18	NE.	..	Foggy Weather.
19	E. NE.	..	Hazey W^{r}.
20	NE. N.	..	Remarkable thick W . & very cold.
21	NE.	..	Tolerably clear.
22	ENE. NE.	..	Clear Weather. Fresh B.
23	NE.	.	Fresh Breezes & cold W .
24	ENE.	..	Fresh B. &c. as Yest^{d}.
25	East	.	Clear Weather.
26	ENE.	..	Hazey all day.
27	NE.	..	Clear W .
28	Var.	..	do. W .
29	....		Calm & clear W^{r}.
30	NE.	..	A cold foggy day.
31	N. E.	..	Pleasant W^{r}.

JANUARY 1766.

	Wind.		Weather.
1	Var^{r}.	..	Foggy W^{r}.
2	N^{d}.	..	Morn^{g}. foggy. Fresh Wind.
3	NE.	..	Weather as Yesterday.
4	Var^{r}.	..	do.
5, 6, 7	EBS. to NBW.		The Mornings rem^{ke}. Foggy the middle of ye days tolerably clear.
8	N .	..	The Air remk. cold.
9	Calm	..	Thick fog all day.
10	N .	..	Foggy.
11	Calm N .	..	Fine W^{r}. all day.
12	NE. E.		Fresh B. & fine Weather.
13	N. NNW. S.		Very thick fog in ye Morn. the Air very cold.
14	NNW.	..	do. W^{r}.
15	NE. S.	..	do. W^{r}.
16, 17, 18	Var^{r}. Wind & Calms.		Foggy Mornings & in general very Cold.
19, 20, 21	N . to SE.	..	Foggy Mornings, the Air in gen. Cold.
22	E. ENE.	..	Fresh B. of Wind. ye Air rem. thick.
23	SE. to N .	..	Light B. & thick foggy Weather.
24	ESE. SE.	..	Clear Morning. Wind moderate.
25	SE. SSE.	..	Wea^{r}. as yesterday.
26	NE. to SE.	..	Fresh Wind, & very hazey all day.
27	NE. E.	..	Very foggy Morning.
28	NE. SE.	..	Very hazey all day.
29	E. to SE.	..	Very fresh Winds, the Morning Foggy.
30	E.	.	Hazey Weather.
31	N^{o}. NE.	..	Very thick cloudy W^{r}. threatning Rain.

FEBRUARY 1766.

	Wind.	Weather.		Wind.	Weather.
1	SE. to NNE.	Thick cloudy Wea^{r}. as yesterday.	15	SW. W. WNW.	Morning cloudy & threatning, the Wind fresh.
2	E. to N. ..	Cloudy & threatning all day.	16	W. to SW. ..	Fresh Wind. Foggy Morning.
3	SE. ESE. ..	Cloudy Wea^{r}. Wind fresh.	17	E. Calm ..	Clear W^{r}. Saw the Mount. (of Boutan).
4	Calm SW. ..	The Morning foggy, ye rest of ye day clear.	18	NW. SW. .	Foggy Morn. Fresh Wind.
5	S. to SE. ..	do. W^{r}.	19	S. NE. ..	Foggy till 9 a.m.
6	SE. fresh ..	Hazey all day.	20	NE. S. SE. ..	Morning foggy, the rem^{r}. Clear W^{r}.
7	West ..	Very fresh Gales of Wind.	21	Calm SE. ..	in fresh Breezes.
8	West WBS. ..	A pleasant Morning. Wind very fresh.	22		
9	Calm W. N. ..	Morning calm & foggy The Aft. fresh B.	23		
10	N. to W. ..	Foggy Morning.	24		
11	NE. to SE. ..	do. Morning.	25		
12	NE. ESE. ..	do. W^{r}.	26		
13	NE. ESE. ..	do. W^{r}.	27		
14	N. NNE. NE.	Fresh Breezes of Wind & much Rain this day.	28		

JANUARY 1766.

From Rungpour to the Northwest.

33 The 22nd. of January left Rungpour & proceeded to the Northwest. Our Road lay along the NE Bank of the Goggot or Rungpour River for upwards of 5½ Miles; we then crossed it, it being but 3 foot deep. This Ford lies opposite to the Village of little Jaffiergunge.

On the West side of the Goggot & opposite to Jaffiergunge are the remains of an old Intrenchment: it is of a circular figure & more than half a mile in diamater: the Parapet (Rampart) is 16 or 18 foot high.[2] The Sanashygotta Road lies thro' the Intrenchment. The Countrey here is not so well cultivated as on the east side of the Goggot.

Gungepour is the next Village to little Jaffiergunge & is distant from thence about 5 miles to the WNW. The Roads here are bad, & the Countrey but little cultivated. Great Jaffiergunge a Bazar lies near 8 miles from Gungepour & on the Jabbunseray Creek. This Creek is not above 2 foot deep at this Time: its Course is from NNE to SSW.

34 Five miles & half NNW from Jaffiergunge we crossed the Sannalkotta River which is about 60 yds. broad & about 2½ foot deep: the Water of it is remarkably clear. The Countrey on the Eastern Bank of this R. lies high & is mostly uncultivated. After crossing this River we passed Cochymeda a large Village & Gunge: here the Countrey begins to be better cultivated & is planted with Tobacco[3] in many places. The Road from Cochymeda lies along the SW Bank of the Sannalkotta for near 7 miles when we crossed it again near a small Village named Luckypour. The Roads here are mostly thro' Paddy Fields.

Banchdaw a middling Village lies 2½ miles N. from the crossing place of the Sanalkotta; & about 4 miles NW from this place is Meergheer Hāāt where the Sanalkotta must be crossed a third Time. This River is a Branch of the Teesta, & comes out of that River above Allygunge & as we are informed runs into the Coretya.[4]

Dammo-Choculo a Hāāt is 2½ miles WNW from Meergheer Hāāt. The Countrey
35 between these Places is cultivated. Four miles NNW from Dammo-Choculo is Dewangunge a large Village & the limit of Rungpour towards Baär[5] or Ajora. There is much Tobacco planted in this Neighbourhood.

---

1 The Ghaghat R.

2 This entrenchment is not mentioned in the List of Ancient Monuments.

3 Tobacco is one of the chief exports from Rangpur District. The leaf is bought up by Mughs from Chittagong and Arakan for the purpose of being manufactured in Burma (Hunter, Imp. Gaz., Vol. XI, p. 496).

4 The Karatoya, formerly the boundary between Kamrup and Bengal. For an account of the changes in the courses of these rivers, since the Teesta broke away from its old channel in 1787, *see* Hunter, Stat. Acc. Beng., Vol. X, p. 226, *seq.*

5 Cooch Bahar. Vihar of Buchanan Hamilton. He says that in his time the addition of ' Koch ' to the name was considered ' exceedingly uncourtly ' (Martin, History, Vol. III, p. 418).

About 3 miles NWBW from Dewangunge, we came to the Eastern Bank of the Teesta, a large River from Boutan.[1] The bed of this River is from a mile to a mile & quarter in breadth, but the Channell at this Time is not more than 300 yards over & from 3 to 7 Cubits deep; the Stream not very rapid & the Water extremely clear. The bottom is Sand & Pebbles. Its Course is here from N. to S. running as we are informed by Raage Gunge & Denospour,[2] & emptying itself into the Ganges by several Channells. · Near the Place of crossing are the remains of two small Intrenchments, one on the West side thrown up by M. Courtin,[3] & ye other on the East side by the Nabob of Rungpour.

The Rungpour Countrey begins again on the West side of the Teesta; this being 36
the Province of Bodaw [4] ceded to Rungpour some years ago by an independent Rajah.

1 Now the upper portion of the channel of the Atrai, from which the Teesta broke away in 1787-88 (Martin, History. Vol. III, p. 361).

2 Dinajpur.

3 M. Courtin was chief of the French Factory at Dacca in 1756, and on the capture of Calcutta by Siraj-ud daula took under his protection the Company's servants in the English Factory; but, after the breaking out of war between the English and French in 1757 and the fall of Chandernagore, M. Courtin found himself in a very precarious position, and the day before the battle of Plassey was fought (*i.e.* on June 22nd 1757) he left Dacca in order to join Siraj-ud-daula at Murshidabad. On the way he heard of the battle and of the death of the Nawab, but not relying on the report, pushed on to the mouth of the Bhagirathi, where the news was confirmed, and he also learned that M. Law, the chief of the French Factory at Cossimbazaar, who had come down from Patna to join the Nawab, but had not been in time to do so, was being pursued by the English. He accordingly turned northwards (though at the time it was supposed that he had taken refuge "in the east of the Province of Dacca, in the kingdom of Assam which borders on Cochin China" [Hill Bengal in 1756-57, Vol. III, p. 262]), and proceeded to Dinajpur, where the Raja attempted to oppose his passage up the Atrai, at that time the main channel of the Teesta. Having however made the passage in spite of the Raja, M. Courtin proceeded up the river, intending as he says to take refuge in the mountains of Tibet, and advanced to within two or three days' journey from the foot of the Hills. But his boatmen objecting and beginning to desert, he accepted an offer from the Raja of Sahibganj, in Kuch Behar, to give him a site for a fort, which he built on the side of a creek flowing into the Teesta about 15 miles south of Jalpaiguri. The fort was triangular, with a bastion at each angle, on elevated ground, protected on one side by a marsh. Two Swedish guns were mounted on the ramparts. The fort was named 'Fort Bourgogne' and took rather more than a month to build. Before it was quite finished, M. Courtin received news of the arrival of a French force at the mouth of the Hughly, and of an insurrection against Mir Jafar, and determined to return. After considerable difficulty in extricating his boats from the marsh, the creek having almost dried up, and to add to his misfortunes, an outbreak of sickness among his men, he left the fort in the middle of December 1757. Not long afterwards, while still in the Rangpur district, he heard that the rumours of succour by the French were unfounded, but as the river was too low for him to return to his fort, he remained where he was, and was attacked in the middle of January 1758 by Kasim Ali Khan, the Faujdar or Military Governor of Rangpur. Having entrenched himself on the bank of the river (this is the small entrenchment referred to in the text), he held out till the beginning of February, when he was compelled to abandon his position, and started again down the river closely pursued by the enemy. At the same time he wrote to Mr. Scrafton, the Resident at Murshidabad, whom he had befriended at Dacca, offering to surrender. After many adventures, constantly harassed by the enemy, and having had to abandon all his boats, he reached Dinajpur. Here he remained, in considerable peril on account of the timidity of the Raja, who would he feared deliver him to the Faujdar of Rangpur, until the beginning of March, when orders were received from Lord Clive that he should be sent to Murshidabad. He arrived there on the 12th March, not without further adventures and after some time his boats and so much of his goods as could be recovered were restored to him by the English. He subsequently went to Chandernagore, whence he wrote to Lord Clive in 1759 protesting against the proposed demolition of that place, and from thence to Pondicherry, and was present at the capitulation of that place by Lally in January 1761 He afterwards returned to France, and, it is supposed, was elected to the Conseil des Indes in that country.

These particulars are taken from a letter from M. Courtin to his wife, quoted at p. 137 of Mr. S. C. Hill's work, "Three Frenchmen in Bengal, or the Commercial Ruin of the French Settlements in 1757"—London, 1903.

4 Boda, one of the six *chaklas* or divisions of the old Province of Rangpur, part of the Zemindari of the Raja of Kuch Behar.

It is a fine Countrey, & well cultivated, the Produce, Wheat, Sugar Canes & Tobacco. We proceeded about 3½ miles along the West Bank of the Teesta & then struck off to the NW, & within a mile of the Teesta crossed the Curume or Ponjah River which is deep & rapid. Four miles NWBN from hence we crossed the Guramarra another deep & rapid River which joins the Corto[1] & Curume some Miles to the Southward & all fall into the Teesta. Nabobgunge lies on the West side of the Guramarra & is the limit of the Bateese-Hazary Province[2] to the Southward. We found Saringas[3] or Canous in both these Rivers.

Five miles N ½ E from Nabobgunge is Taledāār Hāāt situated on a small Lake
37 named the Jabbonau. This Village is just within the Limits of Bateese-Hazary; the Teesta River is about 3 miles to the Eastward.

From Taledar we struck to the NNE out of the Sanashygotta Road in order to have a view of the Limits of the Countries, & of the Course of the Teesta. After crossing the Jabbonau & Ponga two shallow Rivers we came to Farsydunga, a Bazar Village lying on the Teesta & about 6 miles NNE from Taledāār. The Countrey here is open & well cultivated on the West side of the River, but the East side (which is part of Boutan) is Jungly & desart. We perceived pieces of different kinds of Trees lying on the Sands in the River: these the Countrey People informed me are brought down from the Boutan Mountains by the Freshes: amongst many other kinds of fine Timber I perceived the stump of a Firr Tree of which I brought away several pieces.

38 From Farsydunga we proceeded to the NNW along the Western Bank of the Teesta, & noted the Limits of the Rungpour district about 3 miles above Farsydunga. Here the Bateese-Hazary Province begins, & to the Northward of that Boutan, so that this is the utmost Limits of the Bengall Territories to the Northward.

After going about 9 miles along the R. side above Farsydunga we struck away to the Westward across the Bateese-Hazary Province for Sanashygotta. About 8 miles from the Teesta we came to another old Intrenchment but much larger than

[1] The Corto and Curume are old channels of the Teesta. Corto is a corruption of the name Karatoya. For a legend regarding the origin of the Ghoramara *see* Martin. History, Vol. III, p. 361.

[2] Now known as Baikunthpur, an estate included in the Jalpaiguri district. *See note* 7, p 69.

[3] This word is not given in Hobson Jobson. My friend Mr. B. L. Chaudhuri, Asst. Supdt. of the Indian Museum, a native of N. Bengal, informs me that it is "a common local name in Northern and Eastern Bengal for a long boat used in daily work and generally managed by two men. It is not a dug-out, which is called a 'Kunda' in East Bengal.

I have received an interesting letter on this subject from the Dept. Collector, of Rangpur. He writes:—The name of the kind of boat is not 'Sharingha,' but the correct name is 'Shad'anga,' pronounced as 'Sharanga.' * * In some of the police reports the term is spelt as Sharanga. * * The Kaligunge Outpost man has spelt it as 'Sadanga.' From these mistakes in spelling some have thought the term is derived from 'Sarang'—a musical instrument, to which it may be said to bear some resemblance. * * * The Shadanga (Saranga) boats very largely in use in the District consist of a large straight tree hollowed out. On the top of the upper side of this hollow tree, there are in every case six crosspieces of timber scantling fixed to give rigidity to the sides and to provide seats. These six pieces of cross timber forming the seats of the passengers give these dug-outs their name, shat=six and anga= limbs (Sansc). * * * This to my thinking is the correct derivation of the term Shadanga (Sharanga) * * * "

Buchanan Hamilton says that 150 or 160 canoes were made annually by the people of Battris-Hazari worth from Rs. 12 to Rs. 18 each. They were used for floating down logs of *sal* timber.

the former one, this being near 2 miles broad, the River Talmang running thro' the middle of it.[1]

Dubonee[2] a large Village & Bazar is 3 miles from this Intrenchment having the Chowery a Rivulet running by the West side of it. The Limit of Bodaw is within a mile & half SW from Dubonee so that only a narrow slip of Bateese-Hazary runs
into the Bodaw Province from hence to Nabobgunge From Dubonee proceeded to 39
the NWBN for Gaatra-Hāāt, leaving the limits of Bodaw about a mile & half or two miles on our left. Gaatra-Hāāt is 9 miles from Dubonee, & between those places are 3 small Rivers; namely the Corto, Saön, and Doank, neither of them is more than 90 yards broad or more than 2 foot deep at this Time. The Countrey here is mostly uncultivated Plains, & thinly inhabited.

Sanashygotta[3] is 4½ miles NWBN from Gaatra-Hāāt. This Place is remarkable by having a Fort in it belonging to the Rungpour Phousdar,[4] who collects a Tribute in Bateese-Hazary. The Sanashy Facquirs[5] had once a Mud Fort in this Place & the remains of it are now to be seen. The Phousdar's Fort is very small, & capable of mounting only six or eight guns.

The Mahanada[6] another Boutan River runs by Sanashygotta, seperating Bateese-Hazary from Boutan in this Place.

The Latitude of Sanashygotta is 26°-33′ N. The Countrey round it is tolerably 40
well cultivated. The Bateese-Hazary Province[7] extends about 7 or 8 miles farther to

---

1 These are the ruins of Bhitargarh, believed to be the city of Prithvu Raja, one of the kings of the earliest Kamrup dynasty. A full account of the ruins is given in Hunter's Statistical Account of Bengal, Vol. X, p. 265, quoted from Dr. Buchanan Hamilton's MS. account of Rangpur, written in 1809 The city consists of four concentric enclosures, each surrounded by a rampart and ditch. The innermost is said to have been the abode of the Raja, and contains a deep tank, which is still held sacred by the natives. It is said that the Raja, being attacked by an impure tribe of Kichaks or gypsies, and afraid of having his purity sullied by contact with them, threw himself into this tank and was drowned with his guards, who followed him. The outer rampart is said to be six miles in length from north to south. There are no remains of any considerable buildings. Buchanan Hamilton gives a plan of the place in Martin's History, Vol. III, p. 443 (also *see* List of Ancient Mon. Beng., p. 176).

2 Dhubni. Buchanan Hamilton mentions a tank here where Prithvu Raja's washerman is said to have dwelt, and a square mound, containing some bricks, is pointed out as the foundation of his house (*op. cit.*, p. 446).

3 Sanyasikata, a thana or police circle in Jalpaiguri district. The place derives its name from a Hindu temple, concerning which tradition has it that "when the first of the Raikats or Rajas of Baikuntpur, Sira Kumar, was building a fort, the workmen in digging the foundations came upon a religious ascetic (Sanyasi) who was passing his time underground in devout retirement. This person was wounded by the diggers before they were aware of his presence: but he made no complaint, and only requested to be covered up again This was accordingly done and a monastery (akhra for persons of his order was built on the spot." The ascetic is now worshipped as a god, and the village has become a place of pilgrimage (Hunter, Stat. Acc. Beng., Vol. X, p. 265).

4 Phousdar=Faujdar, commander of a military force, or the military governor of a province.

5 Sanashy=Sanyasi, a Hindu religious mendicant, Fakir has the same meaning. The name was applied in Bengal to a body of banditti claiming to belong to a religious fraternity, who had their headquarters in the forest tracts at the foot of the Himalaya; Buchanan Hamilton says at Nidantora, in the dominions of 'Gorkha' or Nepal (Martin, History, Vol. III, p. 517). Not long before this (1760) they had penetrated to and plundered the city of Dacca. An account of a skirmish with these bandits, in which Rennell was wounded and nearly killed, will be found below.

6 The Mahananda, one of the principal rivers of Bhutan. It traverses the Darjiling, Jalpaiguri, Purniah and Maldah Districts and joins the Ganges near Godagiri.

7 Bateese-Hazary. Hind. Battis- or Battris-hazari, signifying thirty-two thousand. The name of the province is of high antiquity, having been given to it in the time of Biswa Singh, the founder of the Kuch Behar family. This portion of the country was bestowed upon the descendants of his cousin Sib Sinh, and as it produced an annual revenue of Rs. 32,000 it was called Battris-hazari (Hunter, Stat. Acc. Bengal, Vol. X, p. 404). The royal family formerly lived

the Northward, & then the Boutan Countrey begins. The Revenues of the Province are said to be 32,000 Rupees annually ; out of which they pay a Tribute of 13,000 to the Phousdar of Rungpour. The Rajah or Chief lives at Parpour a large Village situated on the Western side of the Teesta.

That part of Boutan which fronts Sanashygotta on the West side the Mahanada appears to be very woody & thinly inhabited.

A mile & half below Sanashygotta on the West side of the River, the Parranya[1]
Country begins. We took our route from Sanashygotta along the East side of the
Mahanada (whose Course is here SSW) for about 4½ miles, & then crossed it at Maha-
Raage-Gunge a small Bazar Village. The River is here about 120 yards broad, &
41 from 2 to 3 foot deep. The Purranya Limits begin on the East side of the River just
below Maha-Raage-Gunge, joining Bodaw on the West.

After crossing the Mahanada, we proceeded about 4 miles to the Westward & came to the Balasun River,[2] which is nearly the size of the Mahanada. This River seperates Morung & Purranya, the former lying on the West side, the Course of the River being from North to South. The Purranya district extends from hence in an Angle to the NW for about 6 or 7 miles, where the Village of Gosepuckarya forms the Limits of that & Boutan.

The Balasun River joins the Mahanada about 12 miles SW from Sanashygotta. The Peninsula formed by these two Rivers is composed of little Hills & rising Grounds which afford a pleasant Prospect. We perceived some Hills likewise in the Morung Countrey, & that Countrey seems in general to lie very high & to be thinly cultivated, & scarce of Wood.

We recrossed the Mahanada about a mile & half above the conflux of the two
42 Rivers, & proceeded to the SW to have a view of the Course of the Mahanada & the
Limits of Purranya & Morung.

The Course of the Mahanada is in general about SW & it is increased very considerably by several small Rivers that fall into it between Sanashygotta & Maha-Raage-Gunge.[4] We passed several Bazar Villages, namely Sonapour, Haldubarry, Jaffiery-gunge, Dergyeygunge, & Maha-Raage-Gunge, the last of which is a very large Village, & the limit of our Survey to the Westward. All those Places above mentioned lie near the River.

at Baikunthpur, but on the decay of the Moghul power they settled at Jalpaiguri (the Parpour of Rennell). Their residence here is known as the Baikanthpur Garh (house), and is surrounded on three sides by double moats. There are the ruins of a fine brick building, but of no great age (List of Ancient Mon. Beng., p. 178).

[1] Purniah. One of the Mughul Provinces, and now a British District. Buchanan Hamilton spells it Puraniya.

The Balasan. This is the old Balasan. The new Balasan joins the Mahananda higher up, just below Siliguri. It is not marked on Rennell's map, and probably did not exist at that time.

Now one of the administrative divisions of Nepal. In Rennell's time and before this the name was apparently applied to the whole of Nepal. In Van den Broucke's map of Bengal, 1660, the territory is marked 'T. Ryk Van Morang. At the time of Rennell's visit in 1766, the Gurkhas had not conquered the whole of Nepal. It was not till 1768 that Ranjit Mall, the last of the Surya-bansi race, was defeated by the Gurkhas. (Hunter, Imp. Gaz. Vol. X, p. 285). Buchanan Hamilton calls the district 'Gorkha.'

[4] Now Krishnaganj, the headquarters of a subdivision and police circle.

Four miles & half above Maha-Raage-Gunge we crossed the Doank[1] River just above the place of its conflux with the Mahanada. The Doank is near half the size of the Mahanada : I am not acquainted with the place of its Source.

The Morung Countrey is about 10 miles N from Maha-Raage-Gunge & extends a considerable way to the Westward; bordering on the Purranya Countrey which extends as far West as the River Cosa.[2]

The Purranya Province appears to lie high & is a fine Wheat Countrey, & exceeding well stocked with Cattle. Near Maha-Raage-Gunge are several thick Groves of Trees, but I saw none fit for Timber, they having all very short Trunks.

From Maha-Raage-Gunge we proceeded back to the Eastward, for Nabobgunge & the River Teesta.

Twenty-one miles EBN from Maha-Raage-Gunge crossed the Nagoor River[3] near Seebgunge a large Bazar Village. The Nagoor River seperates the Provinces of Purranya & Denospour. The River is small & fordable. Its Course is from the NNE & must of course be one of the Rivers that we crossed between the Teesta & Mahanada, tho' called there by a diffeient Name. The Countrey here is well cultivated & has a pleasant Appearance. Thirteen mi'es East from Seebgunge crossed the Tangally River[4] near Currumka; This River is small & fordable & has its 44
Course from the Northward. The Countrey on both sides of it is pleasant & well cultivated.

Six miles farther to the Eastward crossed the Patraage Nulla[5] at Canerykotta, a mud Fort belonging to Rungpour. The Patrāāge Nulla seperates the Provinces of Denospour[6] & Bodaw; the Bodaw Province ends a few Miles farther to the Southward. Eight Miles more ENE crossed the Corto or Coretya[7] River. This River is 150 yards broad & very rapid tho' fordable in most places. It receives the Guramarra & Curume Rivers a little farther down & afterwards falls into the Teesta. Nabobgunge lies about 2 miles NE from the Place where we crossed the Corto. The Countrey is here mostly waste interspersed with Groves of Betel Trees.

From Nabobgunge we proceeded to re-cross the Teesta & trace the Northern Boundaries of Rungpour towards Baär.[8] We left Nabobgunge the 14th. February, & had that day much Rain, it being the first we had seen since the Month of October 45
last. We found the Curume fordable between Nabobgunge & the Teesta, & coming to Ammerconna prepared to cross the Teesta. We had much difficulty in procuring Saringas or Canous to cross over; & the River being a quarter of a mile broad, & very deep & rapid, we did not cross without difficulty, & hazard of losing some of the Baggage. The Wind blowing from the Southward we could plainly hear the noise of the Falls which are near Allygunge, & interrupt the navigation of the River during the dry Season. An Armenian who was with me informed me that M. Courtin dropt his Boats down the Falls when he quitted his Fort in 1757, & lost but two of

1 The Dank. It rises in the Terai a short distance West of Jalpaiguri.

2 The Kusi or Kosi, the principal river of Nepal.

3 The Nagar, one of the tributaries of the Mahananda. Both this river and the Dank are shown on Rennell's map as flowing out of the Mahananda below Siliguri.

4 The Tangan, another tributary of the Mahananda, which it joins near Maldah.

5 Patrad on Rennell's map. 6 Dinajpur. 7 The Karatoya. 8 Kuch Behar.

them out of upwards of twenty.[1] The Fall is said to be 4 foot & the breadth of the Cascade 100 yards.

On the East side of the Teesta nearly opposite Nabobgunge is the remains of a small Fort[2] built by M. Courtin when he retreated from Dacca in 1757. M. Courtin
46 contrived to have it just without the Limits of the Bengall Countrey, in order to have the Protection of the Baär Rajah.

From the side of the Teesta we proceeded directly to the Eastward, sometimes crossing the Limits of the two Provinces. Seven miles East from the Teesta came to Sibegunge,[3] a large Village belonging to Baär & situated on the same River[4] as Rungpour, it being a Branch of the Teesta. Santashgunge a Killa belonging to Baär lies 3 miles N. from this Place. The Countrey here is very thinly cultivated. Four miles from Sibegunge we came on the Northern Skirts of Singaseer Wood.[5] This Wood extends many Miles to the SE, & belongs partly to Rungpour & partly to Baär. The Daddoi Nulla runs on the North side of it.

Nine Miles East from Sibegunge came to Chowar-Raja-Hāāt, a Village situate on a small spot of Land belonging to Baär, tho' lying in the heart of Rungpour. The
47 Teesta or Saunyajan Nulla runs by this Village in its way to Calpauny Olyapour &c. It is very small & fordable. The Countrey to the Northward near Chowar-Raja-Hāāt appears very woody. It belongs to Patgong,[6] a Purganna of Rungpour. The Durla River runs within 4 miles NE of this Place.

From Chowar-Raja-Hāāt proceeded to Kochabarry, a Hāāt 8 miles ESE from the last Place. From thence the limits of Rungpour runs to the SSE & SE. Here we learnt by means of a Baär Soubedar[7] that the Sanashy Facquirs had made War in Baär & that they were at this Time in possession of Bullerampour[8] the Capital of the Province. This Place is said to be 15 Coss to the NE.

---

[1] M. Courtin mentions this episode in the letter to his wife quoted at p. 67 above (S C. Hill, "Three Frenchmen in Bengal," p. 146). "The second day after my departure" (from Fort Bourgogne) "was marked by a very annoying accident, namely the loss of one of my largest boats, on which was my library and a quantity of my effects. These were quickly drawn out of the water, but were none the less ruined for the company and for me. From that moment commence my misfortunes. The sixth day—I had passed three in the salvage of the effects on my boat—I received a *pattamar* (messenger), who informed me that the English and the troops of Jafar Ali Khan were at Purneah, from which they had chased Huzir Ali Khan and wholly destroyed his faction." M. Courtin does not mention the loss of a second boat at this place. The Armenian was killed a few days later (*see note*, p. 74 below)

[2] This was 'Fort Bourgogne,' the account of the building of which has already been given (*ante*, p 67). M. Courtin says that it was about two leagues from the river, but Rennell in his map places it within two British miles of the bank.

[3] Saibgunge on Rennell's map.

[4] The Ghaghat.

[5] This forest is mentioned by Buchanan Hamilton under the name of 'Singheswor Jhar' "a considerable forest, which extends far into Vihar proper, where indeed the greater part is situated" (Martin, History, Vol. III, p. 438).

[6] Patgram, now a pargana of Jalpaiguri District.

[7] Subhadar, a native Captain.

[8] Balrampur is a trading village in Kuch Behar situated on the Kaljani, a tributary of the Sankos, and is about 11 miles SE from Kuch Behar town. Balrampur was the residence of the Nazir Deo, or hereditary Commander-in-Chief, who belonged to the same family as the reigning prince In 1766 the affairs of the state were in great confusion. The infant Raja, who was under the protection of the Bhutias was assassinated at the instigation of Ramanand Gosain, and a conflict arose between the Nazir Deo, Khagendra Narayan, and the Bhutias, concerning the succession, which resulted in the defeat of the Nazir Deo, who was driven out of the country and appealed to the English for assistance. The Bhutias were finally driven out of the country in 1773 (Hunter, Stat. Acc. Bengal, Vol. X, p. 412 *seq.*). The history makes no mention of the Sunyasis, who had probably taken advantage of the disturbances to overrun the country.

From Kochabarry Hāāt proceeded to the SE for Lol Bazar[1] 12 miles, keeping the Limits of Rungpour close on our Right & the Durla River about 4 miles on our left. The Countrey is tolerably cultivated, & produces Wheat & Opium. Two Miles below Lol Bazar crossed the Gaddari or Rotany Creek wch. falls into the Durla.

Thirteen Miles SEBE from Lol Bazar came to the SW Bank of the Durla which 48
here seperates the two Provinces. We proceeded 3½ miles along the Bank & crossed it at Giddildow nearly opposit Mongolhāāt.[2] The River is here from 100 to 150 yds broad & fordable in many Places. We received Intelligence that a Detachment of English Sepoys were sent in quest of the Sanashys, & that they crossed the Durla the day before us. The Villages were every where deserted.

From Giddildow we left the Durla on our right & proceeded 6 miles to the SE, passing the Durgah[3] & Grove of Nodunga. We now found ourselves on the Western Bank of the Neelcomer or Curesa[4] River which is a Boutan River passing near Bullerampour. The bed of this River is from 600 to 800 yards over, the Water at this Time 400 & very deep tho' not rapid. It joins the Durla near Curygong & from thence proceeds by Baggoa to the Baramputrey.

We found that the English Detachment crossed this River during the Night 49
before our arrival & that the Rear had not crossed over many Hours. The Sanashys were reported to be marching towards us, & had several Detachments posted in different Villages to the Northward & North East. On receiving this Intelligence I judged it prudent to join our Detachment & continue with them till the Countrey should be a little settled.

We accordingly crossed the River Neelcomer & marched for Curesa,[5] a large Village belonging to Baär & situated on the Neelcomer about 2 miles NNE from the crossing Place. At Curesa I learnt that a Party of the Sanashy's Horse had been routed that Morning near the Town & that the Detachment were gone to the NE to meet the main Body of the Enemy. I stopt at Curesa to refresh my People & during that Time (the Forenoon) heard a firing of Cannon & Musquetrey to the NE.

We set out in the Afternoon & marched 6 miles to the NNE, & found the 50
Detachment under the Command of Lieut. Morrison[6] encamped at Bouter Hāāt,[7] having that Forenoon defeated the Main Body of the Sanashys who retired to the SE towards Paradanga. Morrison had 90 Sepoys Rank & file ; & the Sanashys were

1 Lal Bazar, the site of the ancient city of Kamatapur, the capital of the kingdom of Kamrup. It is the original of the name Comotah, capital of the Reino de Comotah of Barros, Portuguese map of Bengal (1540), and the Comotay of Blaev's map of 1650, published in Journ. As. Soc. Beng., Vol. XLII. Pt. 1, p. 310, by H. Blochmann. A full account of the ruins, by Dr. Buchanan Hamilton (1809), is given in Hunter's Stat. Acc. Bengal, Vol. X, p. 362 *seq.* (List of Ancient Mon. Beng., p. 182).

2 Mughulhat, a large trading village on the Dharla, formerly the terminus of the Kuch Behar branch of the N. Bengal State Railway.

3 Durgah—the shrine of a Mahomedan saint.

4 Probably the the Toresha or Torsha is meant, one of the tributaries of the Dharla. This is now the main channel of that river.

5 Coorsah of Rennell's map.

6 Lieut. Morrison had been a midshipman on board the *Medway* while Rennell was on the *America*, and they had gone out to India in company. (Sir C. Markham, James Rennell, &c., p. 47).

7 Boothaut of map.

700 strong & near 150 of them armed with English Musquets. We halted with
Morrison this Night (of the 20th February).

The next Morning early Morrison set out in quest of the Enemy, & my Sepoys
being joined with his, I acted as a Voluntier under him. We marched 8 miles this
Forenoon, & then halted at Santashpour to refresh the Troops. About ½ past Noon
set forward again, but saw no Appearance of the Enemy. We continued marching
all the Afternoon to the S & SE, till we came in sight of the River Baramputrey, &
51 were then assured that the Enemy were hemmed in between the forks of that River
and the Durla. About 4 we entered the Village of Deenhotta,[1] where a Party of the
Enemy had posted themselves or rather as I am inclined to think had sat down to
rest themselves. The sudden Approach of our People however roused them & they
made a desperate Effort to defend themselves, at the same Time that they might
have run off, & probably escaped. In this Skirmish I had the misfortune to be
surrounded by the Enemy, & received several Cuts from their broad Swords, one of
which threatned my Death.[2] Morrison pursued his Course towards the Durla the
following two days, the second of which at ten in the Morning he came to the Banks
52 of that River & found difficulty in getting Boats to cross over, the River at the Place
he crossed it (vt. Baggoa) being excessive rapid & very deep.

The Sanashys had separated themselves into small Parties & scattered themselves over the Countrey, so that scarce 50 of them had crossed the Durla with their Commander; who as Morrison was informed had retired towards Olyapour.

I followed the Detachment in my Palankeen & was embarked on a small Boat for Dacca the 23rd. The 26th. I arrived at that Place & for the first time got Assistance from a Surgeon, having been near 6 days without the least Assistance.

I staid at Dacca till the beginning of June for the recovery of my Health & then
set out to survey the Countrey between Luckypour & the Fenny,[3] in order to join on
53 Mr. Verelst's[4] March to Cospour[5] to the general Map of Bengall. Ensign Richards

1 Deenhotta is marked on Rennell's map as 15 miles due north of Baggoa or Baqwa at the mouth of the Dharla.

2 The following account of this skirmish is quoted in Hobson Jobson, 2nd Ed., p. 872, from a MS. letter of Major Renneil's dated August 30th 1766, six months after the event. 'The Sanashy Faquirs (part of the same Tribe which plundered Dacca in Cossim Ally's Time) were in arms to the number of 7 or 800 at the Time I was surveying Báár (a small province near Boutan), and had taken and plundered the Capital of that name within a few coss of my route . . . . . I came up with Morrison immediately after he had defeated the Sanashys in a pitched Battle . . . . . Our Escorte, which were a few Horse, rode off, and the Enemy with drawn Sabres immediately surrounded us. Morrison escaped unhurt. Richards, my Brother officer, received only a slight Wound, and fought his way off; my Armenian Assistant was killed, and the Sepoy Adjutant much wounded . . . . . I was put in a Palankeen, and Morrison made an attack on the Enemy and cut most of them to Pieces. I was now in a most shocking Condition indeed, being deprived of the use of both my Arms, ... a cut of a Sable (*sic*) had cut through my right Shoulder Bone, and laid me open for nearly a Foot down the Back, cutting thro' and wounding some of my Ribs. I had besides a Cut on the left Elbow wh took off the Muscular part of the breadth of a Hand, a Stab in the Arm, and a large Cut on the Head. . . . . .

3 A tributary of the Meghna separating the Noakhali and Chittagong districts in E. Bengal. It rises in Hill Tipperah.

4 Henry Verelst, in charge of the Factory at Chittagong from 1761 to 1765; succeeded Lord Clive as Governor of Bengal 1767 to 1769.

5 Khaspur, now an unimportant village in Kachar, but capital of the Rajas of Kachar during the eighteenth century. Rennell refers to this journey of Mr. Verelst's in his 'Memoir of Hindoostan,' p. 298, in the following words:—"Mr. Verelst, who meditated an expedition into Meckley from Bengal and actually advanced as far as

was sent in the beginning of May to finish the survey of the Curesa River & the Ragamatty Countrey.

The 1st. of June I set out from Dacca for Luckypour, & the 3d. at Night arrived there. The 4th. employed in procuring Coolys &c. for the Baggage & the 5th. began to measure the Roads from Luckypour towards the Fenny River.

The Course from Luckypour to the Fenny is almost East. Four miles & a quarter from Luckypour we crossed a Nulla named Rummutcally which runs from thence to the Westward & falls into the Megna. This Nulla is the limit of the Company's Lands to the Eastward: the Countrey is open & cultivated, and quite destitute of Trees.[1] The Revenues of the Company's Lands here are said to be 8,000 Rupees P. Annum. The Rummutcally Nulla is 50 yds. broad & too deep to be forded.

From the Nulla the Countrey begins to be rather more close, & the Roads 54
broken; the Countrey lies excessive low & must be several Feet under Water during great part of the Rains.

The first Village of any Note from Luckypour is Chandergunge distant 15 miles from the former; this Village is situated in the Purganna of Amidabad,[2] which is an extensive & fertile Province. The Countrey about Chandergunge is very full of Betel Trees; the Roads are in general broken.

Colinda or Koilindy is the next Village of any Note & situated E $\frac{1}{4}$ N from Chandergunge distant by the roads 14$\frac{3}{4}$ miles. The Roads between those two places are in general very bad, & the Countrey excessive low & at this Time overflown near a foot, but it is notwithstanding extremly fertile, & produces great Quantities of Padda, & some Betel Nut. I saw but little Cotton growing, so that the immense quantitiet of Cotton used in the Manufacture of their Cloths must be brought from distant Places.[3]

There is a small Factory at Colinda[4] for collecting coarse Cloths, of which a 55
prodigious Quantity are manufactured in these Parts. The whole Countrey hereabouts appears to be very scarce of Bamboos.

From Colinda the Roads are still worse & worse as you proceed towards the Fenny. The Course inclines to the ESE. About 6 miles from Colinda we crossed the Daddanacherra Creek thro' which the Tides flow almost up to Colinda. This Creek is only passable at half Tide. Two miles beyond this we crossed a River named the little Fenny thro' which the Tide flows regularly all the Year. The

---

Cospour on his way to it, in 1763, was informed by his Meckley guides, that after passing the first ridge of mountains beyond Cachar, he would find a fertile and well inhabited country all the way to Ava. He, however, went no further than Cospour," on account of the difficulties of the country (Imp. Gaz., Vol. IX, p. 251). The journey was undertaken in response to "an invitation made by the Raja of Meckley to assist him in obtaining redress for some grievance he complained to have suffered from the Burmas, and enclosing a paper of articles of alliance which the Raja had tendered to be executed between him and us for this purpose" (Consultation in Council 4th Oct[r] 1762. Wheeler. Early Records, p. 291).

The 'Meckley' of Rennell is the State of Manipur, a corruption of the Assamese (*Makli*) or Kachari (*Mogli*) name of the State (Hobson Jobson, p. 597). One of the subdivisions of Cooch Behar State, a relic of the old Koch Kingdom of Assam, is called Mekhliganj.

[1] In 1754 the country about 'Luckepur' was "almost entirely uncultivated" (Long. Selections, No. 127, p. 48).

[2] Ahmirabads of the 'Bengal Atlas.'

[3] The cotton is grown in Hill Tipperah and the Chittagong Hill Tracts.

[4] Kaliyandi. Hunter says (Stat. Acc. Beng, Vol. VI, p. 288): "At the end of the last century Kaliyandi must have been a place of considerable importance, as its name appears in all the old maps. At the present day, however, it has completely relapsed into jungle." The trade in cotton cloths is said to have amounted to £120,000 a year

Course of this River is from NBE to SBW, it has its Source in the Tipera Province & runs by Kundal. From the crossing Place its Course is to the SW to Jugdya,[1] which Place is situated about 4 miles from hence. The Countrey here is close & but thinly cultivated.

56 Kossidya or Cassidya a Bazar Village lies about half a mile to the SE of the little Fenny, & is surrounded by Betel Groves & Thickets. Meerjapour or Assaropgunge is the next Village & lies 5 miles from Cossidya. The whole Countrey hereabouts is so low that it is quite overflown during 5 Months of the Year. The Countrey does not seem to be well inhabited.

From Assaropgunge to the Banks of the Fenny is near three Miles; the Roads in general excessive bad.

The Fenny River at the crossing Place is more than a mile & quarter broad at present, & continues widening daily, several Sand Banks gathering in the middle. This River has its Source in the Chittigong Province, & is very narrow a few miles up, & so shallow that I am informed it is fordable at low Water. It empties itself into the Bay of Bengall about five miles below the crossing Place. You have a view
57 of part of the Island of Babnee[2] (or Baminy) from the SE point of the River, & if I mistake not, of part of Sunedeep[3] likewise (those are two of the Islands lying in the head of the Bay).

The Sea Coast from the Mouth of the Fenny to Islamabad River[4] runs in general about SEBS without any considerable Bays or inlets. As Mr. Plaisted is said to have surveyed all the Coasts & Islands betwixt Luckypour & Islamabad,[5] I forbore setting about surveying them, as well to prevent double Trouble & loss of Time, as that the Season of the Year was improper for it. Being however in the neighbourhood of Islamabad I judged it proper to go there in order to collect what Maps I could, & to inform myself what remained to be surveyed of the Province.

The Roads between the Fenny & Islamabad are intersected by a great number
58 of Nullas, & as most of these want Bridges, the Roads are almost impassable during the rainy Season. The whole Road is skirted by a Range of small Hills to the Eastward which sometimes come within half a mile of the Road. The Sea is from 4 to 6 miles distant & frequently in view: the low Lands between the Hills & the Sea are very fertile, & are by much the best part of the Province.

[1] Jugdia. Both the English and the French had factories here. The English Factory appears to have been transferred to Lakshmipur in 1754 Long, Selections, No. 128, p 48). After the fall of Chandernagore the French Factory was taken over by a Mr. Cree (Bengal. Past & Present. Vol. III, No. 2, p. 364).

[2] Bamni Island.

[3] Sandwip Island. These islands were the scene of the depredations of the Portuguese pirates in the seventeenth century, and it was on Sandwip that Sebastian Gonzales, their leader, after defeating the Mughul Governor Fathi Khan, established a settlement in 1609. They were finally subdued by the Nawab Shaista Khan in 1666, and their descendants are still settled near Dacca.

[4] The Karnaphuli on Chittagong R.

[5] Chittagong. The name Islamabad was given to it by the Mughals, who besieged and captured it in 1666 under Shaista Khan.

The surveys, plans, and drawings attributed to Plaisted are: a plan and survey of the coast of Chittagong and Khaut Colley in 1761; sketch of the coast of Chittagong in 1761; instructions for the coast of Chittagong, January 1, 1762; and plan and survey of the Chittagong River in 1764 (Wilson, Old Fort William, Vol. II, p. 164 *note*).

None of the Hills exceed the height of 240 yards, & of these Sittacoon [1] is the highest & situated about half way between the Fenny & Chittagong. On the top of this Hill is built a small Pagoda which is much resorted to by the religious Gentoos,[2] who very zealously venture their Necks to go up to worship; for the sides of the Hill are in some places quite perpendicular.[3]

Near Barracoon [4] (a Village 3 miles to the Southward of Sittacoon) is the famous
burning Well. It lies within the first ridge of Hills, & thro' a narrow, bad road. 59
The Spring rises at the foot of a Hill, & has a small House or Pagoda built over it,
from whence you decend by six or seven stone Steps to the level of the Spring. The
Water bubbles up on one side of an artificial Bason or Tank of about 6 foot square &
5 deep; from whence it is carried off by a subterraneous Passage into the Valley.
On that side of the Tank where the Water rises is built a Brick Wall of about 4
foot high as a kind of facing to the Rock from whence the Water issues. This Wall
by being built very loose, & without Cement, allows the Water a free Passage thro'
the lower part of it into the Tank; & with it a pure flame is continually issuing forth
for near the breadth of 4 foot, & commonly it rises near 3 foot high, so that the
Wall itself does not ill represent the back of a large Kitchen Chimney in England. 60
The Flames are seen to spread near a foot from the Wall, over the surface of the
Tank when the Water continues its bubbling motion to that distance; but over the
still parts of it there is not ye least appearance of Flame.

I observed that when the Water of the Tank rose, or was much disturbed by the People that went in to bathe, the Flame went out for some Seconds, but afterwards broke out with much greater violence than ever.[5]

The Flames are seen very distinctly in the day Time occasioned by the darkness of the House. Altho' I stood very near them I did not perceive the least sulphureous

[1] Sitakund, the highest hill in the Chittagong District. 1155 ft. above sea level.

[2] Gentoo, a term applied to the Hindus, to distinguish them from the Moghuls or 'Moors.'

[3] The principal gathering is the Siva Chaturdasi festival on the 14th day of the moon sacred to Siva (usually in February). Minor gatherings take place in or near the months of March and November and at eclipses of the sun and moon. The ascent of the hill is said to redeem the pilgrim from the misery of a future birth. There was formerly a sacred spring in the mountain, said to be bituminous, which dried up in the latter part of the 18th century (Hunter, Imp. Gaz., 2nd Ed., Vol. XIII, p. 25). Major Rennell makes no mention of this spring.

[4] Bharatkund. The springs of Sitakund are enumerated in Dr. Oldham's list of the Thermal Springs of India (Memoirs, Geol. Sur. Ind., Vol XIX, Pt. 2, p. 52). The description given is Pogson's, who visited them in 1778. The one called Barracoon by Rennell appears to be Pogson's Babu Kund, which is "at the end of a valley surrounded by hills; the water is always cold; springs covered by brick work. Flames in successive flashes were playing on the surface of the water which, though cold, had the appearance of being boiling, from the volume of perpetually rising bubbles of gas; water is brackish, sulphureous, and chalybeate. There are seven other springs within a circle of 6 miles." Rennell's account of the phenomenon agrees very well with this except that he says he could perceive no sulphurous smell.

Sir J. Hooker visited the locality in 1851, but was disappointed with the phenomenon. He writes:—"The mountain (Seetakoond) is very sacred, and there is a large Brahmin temple on its flank; and near the base a perpetual flame bursts out of the rock. This we were anxious to examine, and were extremely disappointed to find it a small vertical hole in a slaty rock, with a lateral one below for a draught, and that it is daily supplied by pious pilgrims and Brahmins with such enormous quantities of ghee (liquid butter) that it is to all intents and purposes an artificial lamp; no trace of natural phenomena being discoverable' (Himalayan Journals, Vol. II, p. 352). He does not mention the spring, and it is doubtful whether he saw the place described by Rennell and Pogson.

[5] From this the gas would appear to take fire spontaneously.

smell; the House itself is very hot & disagreeable for want of a proper Circulation of Air, besides the Bramins make a Cook Room of it, there being a little Hole left in
61 ye top of the Wall for placing the Pots.

The Water of the Well is very cool & moderately clear. 'Twas hard for me to distinguish whether the oily Substance on its Surface rose with the Water, or was the consequence of so many People's bathing in it.[1]

The City of Islamabad is 49½ miles from the Fenny, and in Latitude 22°-20′ North. It is a large stragling Place, built like the rest of the Bengall Towns, the Houses mean, & the streets laid out without the least design. It is surrounded by little Hills to the West & North & by the River to the East.[2] I had a view of a range of very high Mountains named the Muggs which are said to be the boundary of the Province to the East & SE;[3] the Fenny being the Northern Boundary towards Tipera. The Mugg Mountains appear to be from 50 to 70 miles distant & run in
62 several Chains from the NNE to SSW. There are several Ranges of small Hills between Islamabad & the Mugg Mountains, the nearer of which seems to be within 20 miles. I am informed that the River[4] is navigable for near 50 miles up, but that the Fenny has no communication with it. The Chittigong Province extends to the Southward as far as 21°-28′ N. where Cruzcolly[5] is the Boundary between that & Aracan.

On my return from Islamabad towards Dacca, I was seized with a Fever & Ague the 27th. & continued very ill till near the middle of July. I recrossed the Fenny the 1st. July, & the 5th. arrived at Luckypour where I continued for the recovery of my Health till the middle of the Month.

63 By the apparent Situation of the Islands of Sunedeep, Hattiah, Babnee[6] &c. it seems probable that they must afford Shelter for Ships during both Monsoons, but especially during the SW or Southwardly Monsoon when the Passages must be of easy Access. If the Water is so deep as reported between Sunedeep, Babnee, & the Main, a competent knowledge of the Place might be a means of saving those Ships which are drove to the Eastward of Balasore Road,[7] & may not be able to enter Chittigong River for want of a Pilot, depth of Water, or other Accident. There is likewise an Advantage attending the making of this Coast, which that between Balasore Road & the Megna is entirely destitute of; I mean Land Marks. Seetacoon Hill is said to be an excellent Mark for the Chittigong River; besides the Flagstaffs, Hills & Houses of Chittigong must afford sure Marks for the Coast.

---

1 This may have been a thin film of petroleum.

2 The modern European quarter of Chittagong is built on these hills, most of the houses occupying separate knolls.

3 The Lushai Hills, inhabited by non-Hindu aboriginal tribes. The lower ranges are now comprised in the district of the Chittagong Hill Tracts, inhabited for the most part by Maghs or Arakanese.

4 The Karnaphuli, navigable by shallow draught steamers as far as Rangamati, about 50 miles above Chittagong.

5 Cruz-cool R. on Rennell's map. Opposite Maiskhal I. and just north of Cox's Bazar.

6 Bominy I. of Rennell's map.

7 On the Orissa coast, where before the days of steam ships were accustomed to anchor till wind and tide served for the passage up the Hugli (Bengal Atlas No. XIX).

NOVEMBER 1766.

The 4th. of November set out from Dacca to survey the Northern Branches of * the Ganges. The Dullaserry was surveyed in 1765 from its conflux with the Megna to the Beurygonga & we now proposed to go on with the Survey of that & its principal Branches first.

The Dollasery River runs out from the North side of the River Ganges at Jaffiergunge,[1] & soon after loses itself in a number of Jeels for the space of 11 or 12 miles, afterwards passing by Pyelapour & Saapour. A few Miles below y[e] latter Place it sends out a navigable Creek from y[e] North side which communicates with y[e] Dacca River or Beurygonga.[2] Here, the Tides flowing up it increases in breadth to near half a mile in most places Between y[e] head of the Dacca Creek & its conflux with the Megna it receives the two Branches of the Issamutey[3] River on y[e] South side, & the Beurygonga & Luckya Rivers on y[e] North side, by which time it becomes a mile & quarter broad.

The Issamuty River is formed from two small Branches of the Ganges which run out from the North side near Hadgigunge. It is navigable all the Year for large * Boats. Its breadth is about 200 yards & Course very serpentine.

We begun the Survey of the Dolasery y[e] 4th. in y[e] Evening & continued it to the WNW till we passed the two Mouths of the Issamutty to y[e] Southward & Tagerpour[4] Creek to y[e] Nw[d]. The Tagerpour Creek leads from the Dolasery to the Dacca River & is 2½ Cubits deep at high Water during y[e] fair Season; but it is so narrow & the turnings in some Places so short that a large Boat cannot turn. Its Northern Outlet from the Dacca River is opposite to the Octagon Island,[5] & the Southern Outlet to y[e] Dollasery is at the Village of Tagerpour in sight of & within 5 miles of the city of Dacca, so near do the Dacca & Dollasery Rivers approach each other. The intermediate space is a very low Plain with some Villages in it. In y[e] wet Season it may be crossed in y[e] largest Boats. The Flood Tide in y[e] Tagerpour Creek comes from y[e] Dolaserry.

The Mouth of the Toolsey Creek or Westmost Branch of the Issamutty lies 3 miles West from Tagerpour. Thro' this Creek is y[e] common Route from Dacca to Hadgigunge. It is very narrow & crooked, but deep enough for the largest Boats * The Countrey on both sides of it is either Jungly or swampy. The length of this Creek is about 6 miles, & then you enter the largest Branch of the Issamuty which flows thro' a very fine pleasant Countrey. We finished the Survey of the Toolsey Creek & entered the great Issamuty the 8th. at Night.

* Beyond this the original is not paged The pagination is here denoted by asterisks.

[1] The Dhaleswari now runs out of the Jamuna or lower portion of the Brahmaputra, about 10 miles above Jafarganj.

[2] The Buriganga. [3] The Ichamati. [4] Thakurpur. Tagoorpour of Rennell's map.

[5] An island in the Buriganga opposite Dacca city, shown in Map No XII Bengal Atlas. It has now entirely disappeared.

From the 8th. to the 13th employed in tracing the Issamutty from Toolsey Creek to the great Ganges. The 10th. the Monsoon broke up,[1] having a strong Gale of Wind which veered from NE to S.

The Course of the Issamutty is extremely crooked, & the stream gentle. The Tides are scarce felt 3 Reaches above Toolsey. We noted 2 small Creeks that lead from it into ye Dolaserry at & a little below Sāāpour, but only small Dingeys can pass during the fair Season The Countrey on both sides lies moderately high, a few Jeels only excepted ; & it seems to be well cultivated. The Limits of the Provinces
* are described in the Maps. The Westmost head of the Issamuty (or that which comes out at Nabobgunge) is only 1 Cubit deep in ye dry Season ; but the other which comes out at Sabdychoar or Meggala is much deeper. These two Branches join together at Keerdupour near the Ganges.

The 13th. came back to the head of Toolsey Creek & the remainder of this day together with ye 14th. & part of the 15th. we surveyed the remaining part of this River (vt.) from Toolsey to the Dolaserry. There are few Circumstances worth remarking here, the Course of the River & nature of the Countrey being much the same as before The main Branch of the Isamutty joins ye Dollaserry at Pattergotta a small Village with 2 Mosques[2] which is situated a few miles below Tagerpour.

The 13th took an Obs. of ye Sun's Amplitude, by which the Variation is 1°-49′ Westerly.

The 16th. proceeded with the Survey of the Dolaserry & ye 17th. came to Sāāpour a large Village lying about 15 miles WBN from Dacca. The neighbouring Countrey is very low & full of Jeels, particularly Southward, in which direction there is scarce a Tree or House to be seen There are a few Brick Houses & an old Pagoda
* in Sāāpour. There is a small Creek which runs out of the Dolaserry at Sāāpour & communicates with the Isamutty. It is said to be navigable all the Year for Boats of a moderate size.

Four miles & half from Saapour a small River named Gadgically[3] runs out of the Dolaserry & communicates with the Dacca River. In the fair Season only small Boats can navigate it, & that at high Water, but in ye wet Season Boats of any size may go. The Place where this Creek seperates from ye Dollaserry is named Currua. A mile & half further Westward the Caagmar River[4] falls in : it is very small, & in ye fair Season only deep enough for Pulwars. The Countrey hereabouts is quite full of Jeels.

Pyelapour is ye next Village of note. It is situated on a high spot of Land & extends about a mile within the Southern Bank of the River. With respect to Saapour it lies NW¾W 10 miles (tho' by Water it is upwards of 13) & from Dacca

---

[1] See p 27.

[2] One of the mosques at Pathorghata was built in 1688 by one Unwar, a courtier of Aurungzib. (List of Ancient Mon. Beng., p. 218).

[3] Ghazikhali.

[4] Two creeks, the Heera and Conoi, are shown falling into the 'Dullaserry' a little to the west of the 'Gazycally' in the Bengal Atlas Map No. XII. The village of 'Caug-mary' is shown on Map No. IX at some distance to the NW., so the 'Conoi' is probably meant.

WNW$\frac{1}{4}$N 25 miles. The Countrey round Pyelapour is well cultivated and inhabited. Nearly opposite to the Village a small Creek from Caagmar[1] joins the Dolaserry, but it is shut up during y^e dry Season. From Pyellapour Westwards the Countrey is an * entire Swamp or Jeel, so that it was with difficulty we could ascertain the Bed of the River. These Jeels are a continuation of the great Jeels of Chatmol & Hurriol.[2]

The Village & Grove of Gwalpara lie WBN$\frac{1}{4}$N 7 miles from Pyelapour, but the Course of the River between the two Places is very crooked. This Village is the Boundary of the Provinces of Dacca & Radshy.[3] Here y^e River comes in two Branches named the Andyadaw and Curatty Gonga. The Andyadaw is the Northmost, & has the straitest Course, for which Reason we pursued our Route thro' it.

After going about 5 miles up the Andyadaw we came to Baljuree, where the Noigonga or Bailcoonsi River falls in. This River comes thro' the Jeels, & in its way communicates with the Sheebgunge & Rungpour Rivers.[4] The Village of Baljuree is known by two old red Pagodas lying a little to the Northward of it.[5]

Leaving Baljuree we enter the Comercally Creek which is narrow & communicates with several large Jeels. The Current is very rapid. At the end of this Creek which is about 2$\frac{1}{2}$ miles from Baljuree we come to the head of the Curatty Gongah * (a Southern River left at Gwalpara) & entered a fine high Countrey. From the Comercally we entered the Corki Creek which has a winding Course of about 2$\frac{1}{2}$ or 3 miles & then leads into a broad River named the Cantabotey. It is remarkable that almost the whole Body of Water which forms the Dolaserry is confined within y^e space of 70 yards breadth in its Course thro' the Corki Creek. The Cantabotey River after a Course of 5 miles leads into the great Ganges near Jaffiergunge after receiving the largest Branch of the Denospour River[6] & a small Creek from that of Sheebgunge.[7] We finished the Survey of this River the 23d.

The whole Course of the Dolaserry from its seperation from the Ganges to its Conflux with the Megna, the principal Windings included, is 75 miles. Of this we have now surveyed 63 miles, ye other 12 being surveyed before & about 41 of the Issamutey, besides the Toolsey Creek.

The 23rd. in the Afternoon entered the Rottingunge River or Arti[8] in order to *

[1] Caugmary of Rennell's Map No. IX, a district north of Atia. The name is not marked on modern maps.

[2] Rennell's Map shows a continuous line of Jhils extending north-westwards from the place where the Brahmaputra now joins the Ganges at Goalundo, along what was then the course of the eastern branch of the Atrai, or lower Teesta. The main stream of the Brahmaputra has broken across this low ground, and the face of the country is entirely changed.

[3] Rajshahi, now a Division under the Lt.-Govr. of E. Bengal and Assam. The portion now entered is called Bettooriah in the Bengal Atlas (Map No. IX). 'Raudeshy' is shown further west, the greater part of it lying south of the Ganges, about Murshidabad.

[4] The Atrai, Karatoya, and Tista.

[5] Probably destroyed since the incursion of the Brahmaputra. The face of the country hereabouts is entirely altered since that event. The 'Cantabotey' river is shown on the Atlas of India, sheet 120, as quite a small creek, the Kuntabuttee, not connected with the Ganges. The Dhaleswari now leaves the Brahmaputra or Jamuna 10 miles to the north of Jaffiergunge (Jafarganj). Fergusson gives a succinct account of the changes that took place in this region between Rennell's survey and his time in his paper on the Delta of the Ganges (Quart. Journ Geol. Soc., Vol. XIX, p 336).

[6] The Dinajpur R. or Atrai.

[7] The Karatoya.

[8] ? misspelling for Attri = Atrai R. This creek, which leaves the Ganges at Pubna, now goes by the name of the Ichhamati in some places and of the Attrai in others.

survey it & note the Northern Rivers that fall into it. We were employed on this Survey till the 28th. inclusive when we came into the great River by way of Pubna or Nasserpour. This River has a very serpentine Course, the distance through being upwards of 53 miles, whereas the Horizontal distance is not 28. Its breadth is from 150 to 300 yards, & depth sufficient for ye largest Boats during the dry Season. The Route from Jelenghee to Dacca is thro' this River, altho' the Passage by ye Ganges is 10 miles shorter. In going against the Stream this River is preferable to the Ganges, on account of their being good tracking Ground all the way, & few Sands; but in going down with the stream the other is preferable. The Countrey on both sides of this River lies high & is well cultivated; the Produce is Paddy, Cotton, &c.

A Branch of the Denospour River falls into this about 14 miles EBN from * Pubna at a Place named Boolbaria. In ye dry Season it is ye common Passage from Jelenghee to Nattour, Denospour, &c. Between Boolbaria & Rottingunge a small Creek runs out of the Arti into the Currumjar which is ye main Branch of the Denospour River & runs nearly paralel with the Arti.

The 29th. proceeded 2 Reaches up the Ganges to get information concerning the limits of the Radshy Province in order to make Lord Clive's Map as compleat as possible before his leaving Bengall. The 30th. returned to Boolbaria. On the Passage we were employed in preparing Maps & Journals for Lord Clive.

The 1st. December began surveying the Boolbaria Creek or Western Branch of the Denospour River, & at Night came into the Currumjar.[1] From hence proceeded with the Survey of the Denospour River to the place where Mr. Richards left off in July last.

Immediately above the head of the Currumjar River the great Jeels begin. These Jeels in ye wet Season are joined together, & form a prodigious Lake which * extends from the Western parts of Dacca to Nattour, a tract of about 80 English miles. In the dry Season they form several distinct Lakes. The Denospour River runs thro' the Western Part of these Jeels, frequently losing itself for several Miles, & dividing into a number of Branches. On the skirts of the Jeels are several considerable Villages particularly those of Sajatpour,[2] Hurriol, Chatmol, Cullum[3] & Nattour. In the shallow parts of the Jeels a prodigious number of tame Buffaloes are kept, by which means this part of the Radshy Countrey furnishes the neighbouring Provinces with Ghee.[4] The Countrey is incapable of any other Improvements for as it lies very low, the neighbouring Jeels make it a perfect Swamp.

The Village of Chatmol[5] lies in a high spot on ye SW side of the River & is situated from Pubna NBE 16½ miles, but by Water upward of 48 miles. This is

1 One of the numerous channels by which the Attrai emptied itself into the Ganges.

2 Shazadpour of Rennell's Map.

3 Chalan. The Chalan jhil or bīl is the largest in Rajshahi, measuring 21 miles in length from N.W. to S.E., and 10 miles in breadth It is a depressed basin, sunk below the level of the surrounding country. The average depth of water in the dry season, when the area is reduced to about 20 square miles, is 3 feet (Hunter, Stat. Acc. Beng., Vol. VIII, p. 25).

4 Clarified or boiled butter.

5 Chatmohur of Atlas of India, Sheet 120, and in Stat. Acc. Beng., Vol. IX, p. 297.

y[e] first principal Village in the Route from Pubna to Denospour. Hurriol[1] lies on y[e] East side of the Jeels & about 6½ miles NE from Chatmol. The nearest River to it is the Baganudi or Chatmol River† with which it communicates by means of the Jeel.

†Two miles Northward from Chatmol a Creek from Surda[2] joins this River, but it is not navigable during y[e] fair Season.

At Sittalya 9 miles NNW from Chatmol the River divides into two distinct * Branches, the Westmost flowing thro' a fine high Countrey, & the other thro' a Jeel. The Western River leads to Nattour the Capital of the Radshy Province, the other to Cullum & Denospour. As the River near this place divides into a great number of Branches it will be impossible to convey an Idea of their Courses without the Map, to which I shall refer.

Nattour[3] is situated on a very small River whose Course is in general about East & it is said to be a Branch of the Ganges which seperates somewhere above Bolio.[4] It is not navigable in y[e] dry Season, so that Boats at that time cannot come within 5 miles of the Town where a small Branch of the Denospour River comes. Nattour has a large Bazar but is a Place of no Trade. The Rhany Bowany or Rajah's House is y[e] only Brick Buiding in y[e] Town; this is surrounded by a high wall & a Ditch, but not after the manner of a Fortification. Two miles NE from Nattour is Diggypattia a Village belonging to Dyram.[5] This Village contains several * Brick Houses, & a large Pagoda. The Countrey round Nattour lies very low. Nattour lies in Latitude 24°-24′-30″ North & bears from Muxadabad ENE 47 miles.

Cullum[6] a large Village lies on y[e] Eastern Bank of the great Denospour River & at the head of the large Jeels. With respect to Nattour it lies EBN 11 miles. This is the first Place where we could with any certainty determine the breadth of the River,[7] for farther down it either mixes with y[e] Jeels or seperates into several Streams, so that no Idea can be formed of the quantity of the Body of Water. Above Cullum it is in general 200 or 220 Yards broad & deep enough for y[e] largest Boats, excepting at one certain Place which I shall take notice of hereafter. The Stream is not rapid, nor is y[e] Water of the muddy colour of the Ganges & Baramputrey. This River has a great many names given it, the People of every District giving it a particular Name. *

1 Hureeal in the same Atlas Sheet. The E. I. Co. had a factory at 'Hurriaul' in 1784, and the French traded here from 1766 to 1770 (Bengal, Past & Present, Vol. III, No. 2, p. 360).

2 A village on the Ganges below Rampur Boalia near Charghat. The creek is the Baral R. Its mouth is closed by a sand bank which obstructs the passage for several months in the year (Hunter, Stat. Acc. Beng., Vol. VIII, p. 24).

3 Nattor, the residence of the hereditary Rajas of Rajshahi. At this time it was the largest and wealthiest zemimdari in Bengal, and it was about five times the size of the present District, extending from Bhagalpur on the West to Dacca on the east, and including a large territory on the south bank of the Ganges. The estate was at this time in possession of a woman, the Rani Bhawani, whose failure to pay the revenue demanded by the English led to the gradual break up of the estate, and the Nattor family now ranks only third or fourth in Rajshahi in respect of wealth (Hunter. Imp. Gaz., Vol. XI, p. 429. Annals of Rural Bengal, p. 58). For a complete account of the character and career of the Rani Bhawani *see* Cal. Review, Vol. LVI, p. 9, *seq*.

4 Rampur Boalia, a large and important centre of commerce on the Ganges.

5 Dayaram, the Dewan and trusted adviser of the Rani Bhawani (*see* article in Cal. Review cited above).

6 Chalan, at the head of the Chalan jhil (*ante* p. 82).

7 The Atrai. At this time the volume of water must have been very much greater than it is now, for the main stream of the Teesta took this course on its way to join the Ganges. The clearness of the water is no doubt due to the deposition of the silt in the numerous jhils through which the river flows.

Between Boutan & Raage Gunge [1] it is named the Teesta, from thence to Bandegotta the Attri; between that & Cullum the Gole nuddy; & afterwards the several names of Baganuddy, Ballaser, & Currumjar.

Mr. Richards had surveyed the River from Raage Gunge to Cullum as beforementioned, but for want of an Instrument for taking the Latitudes the latter part of the Survey was not sufficiently exact; for this Reason we proceeded up the River & took the Latitudes as far as was necessary. We finished the Survey as far as Cullum the 9th. of December.

From the 9th. to yr 13th. proceeded up the River whose Course is from the NW to SE. taking yr Latitudes at several places. The last Observation was at Baumanpara near Conchon,[2] the Latitude of which was 24°-53′ North. The Course of the River from hence to Raage Gunge is nearly North & ye distance determined by the Latitude of Raage Gunge.

At Baumanpara the River is 300 yards broad & sufficiently deep. About 12 miles below this Place the River changes its general Course from South to SE & at the same Time seperates into 2 Channells, & the Northmost of these again into several others. By the Waters being divided into so many Streams it happens that none of them are navigable for Boats of 2 Cubits draught of Water. This shallow place is at Kalcour 4 miles above Bandegotta. At Bandegotta the two principal Channells join again. The Countrey round this Place is an entire Swamp.

Having finished our Observations the 13th. we proceeded down the River again in order to survey a Branch of it which turns off to the Eastward near Chatmol & receives the Gorregott & Rungpour Rivers.[3]

All our leisure Time since we left Dacca has been employed in compiling a general Map for Lord Clive. After all the Observations that we could make before his Lordship's setting out, the Map would remain very imperfect without we were supplied with Copies of several Maps from Calcutta, & it being too late to wait for these, I determined to go to Calcutta as soon as the Survey of the abovementioned River should be compleated.

The 16th. at Night arrived at the head of the Eastern River, & the next day Mr. Richards proceeded to survey it whilst I was employed on the Map. This River after a very serpentine Course thro' the Jeels leads to Sajatpour a large Village situated at the conflux of the Rungpour & Gorregott Rivers. It is necessary to observe that Seerpour & Sheebgunge are both situated on the Gorregott or Coretya River; & that Nulshi & Bailcoonsi are on that distinguished by ye name of the Rungpour River.

We had not Time to survery the Currumjar River as I intended, by reason of the sudden departure of Lord Clive. We left Sajatpour & proceeded for Calcutta the 20th. of December. We arrived at Jelenghee the 25th. at Noon. I observed that we could make no further Progress than from 18 to 22 miles a day in the great River altho' our Boats were light, & the Dandies kept at work the whole Day. We

[1] Dinajpur.

[2] About 45 miles S. of Dinajpur.

[3] The Karatoya and the Ghaghat. The latter becomes the Bengali R. in the lower part of its course and flows parallel with the Brahmaputra for a considerable distance.

lightened the Budgarows at Jelenghee, being informed that some Places in ye River * were very shallow. This however we found to be false as there was not less than 2 Cubits Water. The 28th. in ye Evening got clear of the Jelenghee River, having gone from 30 to 38 miles p. day. Took an Observation of Latitude in ye next Reach below Gwareea & found the Lat. 23°-26′ N.† The 30th. in the Evening arrived at Calcutta. We had been employed on the Map the whole Passage.

† Refraction allowed 23° 26′ 40″.

From the 30th. of December to the 6th. of Feby. inclusive staid at Calcutta. The greatest part of the Time, that is to say, till ye 24th. of Jan^y^., we were employed in compiling & copying Maps for Lord Clive. His Lordship carried home a Map of Bengall & part of Bahar on a Scale of 10′ to an Inch 5 foot by 3 ; & another Map containing ye Ganges &c. from Patna to Kanoge [1] on the same Scale.[2]

---

1 Kanauj. The ancient capital of the Gupta dynasty, situated near the Ganges in Farukhadad District, in the United Provinces.

2 Lord Clive left Calcutta on the 29th January, 1767.

JANUARY, FEBRUARY 1767.

The 1st. of Jan. 1767 I was appointed Surveyor Genl.[1] & the Govr. (Mr. Verelst) appointed the several Surveyors that were to be employed under me (Vt.)

Capt. Lewis DuGloss	Lieut. ——— Carter.
Capt. John Adams	Ensign Wm. Richards.

The three first had each a particular part of the Countrey alloted him to survey, & myself (with Mr. Richards as an Assistant) had another part. Mine was to be: first, the Roads from Calcutta to Hadgigunge; next, the Cosa or Cosee River from its Conflux with ye Ganges to the Northern Frontier of Bengall.

The 6th. Feby. sent ye Baggage off to Dumdum,[2] the same Evening I joined it, in order to begin the Survey next Day from Gowreepour Bridge;[3] Capt. Cameron having surveyed as far as that Place.

The 7th. began the Survey, and at Night came to Barrasett,[4] which is 7m 3.5fr from Dumdum. This Countrey is a part of the Kistnagur Province.

After leaving Barrasett we seldom found the Roads good, they being excessive
Plan No. 1. narrow, rough, & crooked, & very frequently running across Padda Fields, so that
* when the ground is ploughed up there are no Traces of a Road to be found.[5]

At the end of the Journal I have added a Table of the Roads with the distances

[1] *See* Introduction, p. 1. Concerning this appointment Malcolm says:—"Among other eminent men whom he (Lord Clive) patronised, he found Rennell, then a lieutenant of engineers, employed in various surveys, encouraged him to complete the general survey and map of Bengal, communicated to him all such previous surveys as were to be found in the public offices, furnished him with a proper establishment (though before this he seems to have had only two assistants, Ensign Richards and the Armenian who was killed by the Sunyasis at Deenhotta), gave him every assistance in his power, and finally, young as he was (he was just turned 24) bestowed on him the office of Surveyor-General, which seems to have been created for him. Clive's mode of trusting officers in whom he could repose confidence, and his means of securing the speedy and effectual execution of the orders he gave, are illustrated by one of his letters to Rennell (4th October, 1765, *see ante*, p. 51). He had ordered a general map of the provinces to be completed. 'If you have occasion for any assistants, name them, and I will order them to attend you'" (Life of Clive, Vol. III, p. 162). Sir C. Markham quotes a letter of Rennell, referring to Ensign Richards:—"I have now company at all times; and luckily for me, the gentleman proves a very agreeable and cheerful companion" (Life of James Rennell, p. 46). To the other three assistants the only reference I can find is an order of Mr. Verelst's dated April 14th 1766, directing Mr. Plaisted (*see ante*, p. 38) "the Surveyor of the Burdwan province to procure and transmit to him a particular account of the Bunds, and further to join Mr. DeGloss who is upon the same Service at the Bunds of Mandergatchee and Bulrampore" (Wilson, Old Fort William, Vol. II, p. 177); and Mr. Firminger informs me that in a letter to the Board of Revenue, dated April 1771, the Supervisor of Birbhum asks for a reinforcement for the escort of Capt. Carter, "who was engaged in the survey of the bordering lands of Beerbhum and Bhagulpur, inhabited by chooars, who prevented him from proceeding further." Mr. Plaisted had been transferred from Chittagong to Burdwan in August 1765 (*Ibid.*, p. 174). The Bunds were embankments on the Rupnarain R.

[2] Dum-Dum, a military cantonment 4½ miles N.E. from Calcutta, the headquarters of the Bengal Artillery from 1783 to 1853. Lord Clive had a country house here, built on the remains of an older house and a mound, from which the place takes its name *damdama*, a raised mound or battery. The original house was a shooting box of Siraj-ud-daula. The house is still in existence and occupied as a private residence (Hobson Jobson, p. 330; Bishop Heber, Journals, Vol. 1, p. 35; List of Ancient Mon. Beng., p. 58).

[3] Three miles N.E. of Dum-Dum.

[4] Barasat, a resort of the Calcutta 'bucks' at this period, and closely connected with the names of Sir Philip Francis, Machrabie, etc. (*see* Busteed, Echoes from Old Calcutta, p. 135; Bengal, Past and Present, Vol. II, p. 509).

[5] The present Bengal Central Railway follows this road very closely as far as Jessore.

between each Stage, as well as that of the principal Topes[1] & Tanks, by which a Detachm[t]. may regulate their Marches, so as to halt at proper Places for procuring Shelter & Water.[2]

The 8th. surveyed 7½ miles of the Road, which runs pretty strait to the NEBE. The Countrey in general is open & well cultivated, the Produce Padda, Gram, &c.[3] There are a great Number of Tanks near the Road, & a fine Tope of Coconut & Betel Trees at Chaldibarya 6 miles from Barrasett. There is another good Tope with a Tank, at Joypool, 7½ miles from Barrasett.

The 9th. surveyed 8½ miles thro' an open Countrey. We found good Tanks at the distance of every 1½ or 2 miles. The Villages very poor, & the Land ill cultivated. At Belgurree 2½ miles from Joypool we crossed a small Nulla ; it is nearly dry at this Season, but in y[e] wet Season it is deep & rapid. This part of y[e] Countrey lies high, & is not overflown during * the rainy Season. We passed 3 fine Topes this Day; one at Plan No. 2 Jawberria 5½ miles from Joypool, & y[e] other 2 at Hottybur 3½ miles from Jawberria.† Near y[e] last Tope is a good Tank & a small Village named Chunderhāāt.

† Between Jawberria & Hottybur is a fine Road raised above y[e] level of the Countrey.

The 10th. surveyed about 8¼ miles, the road very crooked. We have seen no considerable Villages since we left Calcutta. After going 2 miles & half thro' a well cultivated Countrey, we came to a large Plain of about 2½ miles extent from SW to NE, & about twice that length from SE to NW. The Jubbunaw[4] Creek runs along the NE side of this Plain. We crossed this Creek at Mullicpour. It is a Branch of the Hughly River & runs out of that River nearly opposite to the Town of that Name. It falls into the Issamot River a few Miles SE of Mullickpour, & in y[e] wet Season is deep enough for the largest Boats. At this Season it is only 3 foot deep.

After crossing this Creek we passed thro' a remarkable thick Wood which skirts y[e] Eastern Bank of it. This Wood is full half a mile thro', & the path very narrow & intricate.

Leaving this Wood we entered another large & well cultivated Plain. There * are many Villages & Tanks within it, & near the middle of it a large Swamp. In y[e] Evening came to Coyah where there is a good Tank, but no Grove.

The 11th. surveyed about 9¼ miles, the Countrey made up of extensive Plains with some large Villages & a few Swamps. The Arable Lands seem to be all Cultivated either at one Season or another, but at present there is very little of any kind of Grain growing. In our Route this Day we passed thro' the Villages of Dogassia & Mullicpour : they both of them afford good Water & convenient Shelter. The latter of the Villages is large & the Residence of the Jemitdar[5] of these Parts.

1 Tope, a grove, usually of Mango trees. Hobson Jobson says that the term is only used by Europeans and is unknown to the natives of Upper India. It is derived from Tamil 'topu' (p. 934).

For an interesting discussion of the use of the word Tank in India *see* Hobson Jobson, p. 898. The word seems to be both Indian and European in use and derivation.

2 *See* below p. 94.

3 Gram, from Portuguese grão, *i.e.*, grain. A kind of vetch used as food for horses all over India. (*Ibid.*, p. 392).

4 The Jabuna, a creek leaving the Hughli at Kanchrapara, and running eastwards into the Ichamati (Issamot), a branch of the Matabhanga, not to be confounded with the river of the same name in the Pabna district.

5 Jemitdar is probably used here for Zemindar, a landowner.

In the Evening came to Bongong[1] a middling Village situated on the Western Bank of the Issamot River. At this Place there is a remarkable fine Grove; & from the side of the Issamot there is a very pleasant Prospect, the River being transparent & serpentine, & flowing through a Countrey made up of pleasant Meadows interspersed with Groves & Villages.

* The Issamot River is a Branch of the Comer Creek[2] whose head is at Custee[3] on y South side of the Ganges. The Issamot has a very winding Course as appears by a Sketch of it taken by one of my Assistants in ye Year 1765. It runs by Buxypour, & Sibnybas,[4] & from hence runs to the Southward & into Sunderbound. It is not navigable for large Boats till some Time after ye Waters have begun to rise; however at the crossing Place at Bonegong it is 12 Cubits deep & near 160 yards broad. The Tide rises about one Cubit.

Capt. Cameron having surveyed a part of this River together with ye Company's Lands, I sent Mr. Richards to trace it from hence to the place where Cameron left off, & afterwards to proceed to Jaynagore by way of Culna, describing the Roads, Rivers & Country thro' which he passed, & to join me at Jaynagore.

This Morning copied & sent a Plan of Channell Creek[5] to the Governor agreeable to an Order received from him last Night.

* The 12th. 13th. & 14th. halted at Bonegong; the first day with an intent to refresh the People, & the two following on acct. of the Weather, which was very squally & rainy. The 13th. Mr. Richards set off on his Survey.

Plan No. 3. The 15th. surveyed about 4½ miles of the Road. This space was extremely crooked & rough; we also crossed 2 Creeks besides the Issamot. About ¾ of a mile from ye East Bank of the Issamot is the Village & Tope of Jaöwpour. The Tope is a remarkable fine one, & chiefly of Mango Trees. The Nowbory a Creek is crossed about a mile & quarter from the Issamot; it is only 2 foot deep. The Hokker is a mile & half farther, & must be crossed in Boats; from the crossing Place the Road lay along the Southern Bank of it to the place of our Evening's Halt, which was at the Village of Nomosgah. About half a mile Northw^d^. from this Village is a large Jeel. We have every Day variable Winds & frequent Squalls & Showers, the Weather which commonly preceeds the setting in of the Southwardly Winds.

* The 16th. surveyed 11 miles, the Course in general EBN. The face of the Countrey here has various Appearances, some parts Jungly, others Woody, & a large part Open cultivated Plains. Seven miles from our last Night's Halt we came to the Batena[6] Creek which is crossed at the Village & Chokey[7] of Jadopour. The Batena is about 4 foot deep & 160 yards broad. This as well as the two last Creeks is a Branch of the

[1] Bangaon, now the headquarters of a subdivision of Nadiya district.

[2] Now known as the Matabhanga, one of the three 'Nadiya rivers.' It leaves the Ganges at Maheshkunda, about 10 miles below the mouth of the Jalangi. The Kumar diverges from it at about 40 miles from the point where it leaves the Ganges and flows to the S.E.

[3] Kushtia.

[4] The Sibnibashi of Bishop Heber (Vol. I, p. 91). At the time of his voyage, 1824, the river channels had altered and he could not identify them from Rennell's map.

[5] The southern route for boats proceeding from Calcutta to Khulna and Barisal.

[6] The Bhetna. [7] *Chauki*, a police station or posting house.

Issamot River. The Countrey People inform us that there is no good Water near y^e^ Road between Nomosgah & Jadopour. In the Evening we came to the Grove of Gutcally, which lies $3\frac{3}{4}$ miles from Jadopour. This Wood is full half a mile broad, but not very close. We halted at the East side of it, but could find no good Water. Thro' this Wood runs a deep Gully which forms y^e limits of the Kistnagur[1] & Jessore Provinces.

The 17th. in the Morning surveyed $5\frac{1}{4}$ miles; in y^r Afternoon I was obliged to stay in, being ill of a Fever. The Road now runs to the NEBE its proper Course towards Hadgigunge. A mile & half from last Night's Station came to the Tank & Grove of Bannyel. They are both remarkably good. About a mile & half farther on we crossed the Kobbatuck or Koba Duke River.[2] It is said to be a Branch either of the Comer or Issamot, & is navigable from hence to Sunderbound for y^r largest Boats. The Tide flows up above the Ferry, & the River is about 130 yards broad. On the East side of the Ferry is the Village of Jigergutcha or Jingergutcha where there is a Grove of Peepel Trees.[3] Plan No. 4 *

We stopt at a Tank situated in y^e midst of a thick Wood $2\frac{1}{4}$ miles from Jigergutcha. The Road hereabouts is intersected by several deep Gullies.

The 18th. in the Afternoon continued the Survey & went about 3 miles. The Countrey in general is open & well cultivated; in the Groves there are great numbers of Coconut Trees, & a kind of Trees named Cazir-Gatch[4] from whence they make a coarse kind of Sugar. In the Evening halted at a good Tank near Mallunchee.

The 19th. surveyed 8 miles of the Road, At Pullugot $1\frac{3}{4}$ miles from Mallunchee crossed the Mookterserai River; we crossed the River in Boats, but a little way below the Ferry it is fordable. The Current of this River is very slow. *

About a mile beyond the River is the Residence of the Jessoor Rajah.[5] His House is surrounded by a large Grove of Coconut Trees, & is only visible from the NE ward. Here are two good Tanks, & a small Village named Chansera. From hence the Road leads across Padda Fields to Neelgunge or Leelgunge, a Bazar lying on the Western side of the Boyrub River. At this Place is a remarkable fine Mango Grove.

The Boyrub River[6] is very deep at the crossing Place, but farther down it is shallow in many Places. Altho' it lies full as near the Sea as the Kobatuck, yet the distance by the River is so great by reason of its serpentine Course, that the Tides do not reach this Place. This is the River that runs by Daudpour and Culna. Its breadth at Neelgunge is 90 yards. Plan No. 5.

1 Krishnagar, now a subdivision of Nadiya district.

2 The Kabadak R., an offshoot of the Matabhanga. It forms the boundary between the districts of Nadiya, the 24-Parganas, and Jessore.

3 The Pipal, *Ficus religiosa*.

4 Khajur gachh, the bastard date palm, *Phœnix sylvestris*. The manufacture of sugar from this palm has since reached large proportions in Jessore district. A full account of it will be found in Sir. W. W. Hunter's Stat. Acc. of Bengal (Jessor), Vol. II, pp. 280-298. Jhingergachha (Rennell's Jigergutcha) is one of the principal centres of the trade.

5 The residence of the Jessor Rajas is at Chanchra (Chansera of text), about a mile south of the Civil Station. It formerly had a rampart and fosse surrounding it, but the remains only are traceable. The Raja at this time was Srikant Rai, but at the time of the Permanent Settlement he lost the greater part of his estate. He died in 1802 (Hunter, *loc. cit.*, pp. 202, 204).

6 The Bhairab, a tributary of the Madhumati.

At Night came to Dytulla a Dauk's stage[1] $3\frac{1}{4}$ miles from Neelgunge. The Boyrub * runs by the South side of this Village. The Countrey here lies very low & is covered during most part of the rainy Season. There is a large Jeel lying to the NNE of Dytulla & within sight of that Place.

The Boyrub River is the Limit of the Jessore and Radshi Provinces.

The 20th. surveyed near $9\frac{1}{2}$ miles, the Road excessive crooked & rough. The first two Miles lay along the Northern Bank of the Boyrub & thro' a very close Countrey. From hence the Boyrub turns off to the SE. & runs by Daudpour to Culna Bunder.[2] Passed thro' the Jemitdary of Pukarya which belongs to Jessore, & at Noon came to the River Sittarya.[3] This River is crossed at Doccalee, where it is about 200 yards broad, & very deep. The Countrey People can give me no Account of the Source of this River; they say it comes from a Jeel, by which I understand that it runs thro' a Jeel in its way to this Place. It falls into the Nobo Gonga. The Tide does not come up to this Place. The Countrey hereabouts is full of Jeels & Swamps.

From the Sittarcea we went 3 miles over a Jungly Plain which is said to lie under * Water during the wet Season. At this Time it has a very unpromising Appearance. At Night came to the Village of Serampour, where we had our Water from a small Jeel, there being no Tanks in the Neighbourhood. Here we enter another Jemitdary belonging to Jessore.

The 21st. surveyed $8\frac{1}{2}$ miles, the Countrey chiefly made up of waste Lands and Woods. About a Mile beyond Serampour we came to a fine Tank at y[e] end of the large Plain mentioned yesterday. About 9 miles from the first Sittarya we came to another River of the same Name. The Hircaras informed me that it is the same River, but that is impossible as both the Rivers ran to the Right as we crossed them.[4]
Plan No. 6 The Tide flows up this second River & I enquired the Time of Tide, which likewise served to confirm me in the Opinion of its being a different River from the former. This second Sittarya is crossed at Gunagotta a Dauk's Stage lying y[e] East side of the River. The Countrey People inform me that this River passes thro' the Mohamedshi * Countrey in its way to this Place, & that it falls into the Nobo Gonga about 7 Coss to the Eastward. The Western Bank of this River is covered with a very thick Wood; the Eastern Bank & y[e] Countrey adjoining is low & swampy.

A Mile & half from Gunagotty crossed the Judacally Creek, thro' which the Tide flows up from the Sittarya. It is 4 foot deep at High Water.

Eastward from this Creek the Countrey is both Swampy & Jungly. At Night we halted at Simylya, & had our Water from a small Jeel.

The 22nd. surveyed $7\frac{3}{4}$ miles thro' a dismal Jungly Countrey infested with Tygers. About $4\frac{1}{4}$ miles from the Judacally Creek we came to the Nobogonga[5] or Lobo Gonga, a deep & rapid River. The Ferry is at Pultya, at which Place a large

---

[1] A relay post for the mail runners; also known as a chauki (chowkey).

[2] Khulna, an important town lying at the head of the Sundarbans, formerly the headquarters of the Company's Salt department. Bunder=A port or quay.

[3] The Chitra. This appears to be an old offshoot of the Matabhanga, like the Nobogunga into which it flowed.

[4] This is correct, there were two rivers named Chitra. The eastern branch is now called the Katki (Kutkee of Atlas of India Sheet 120).

[5] The Nobogunga, an offshoot of the Matabhanga in Nadiya district. It is now completely dry at its head, and

Creek falls into the Nobogonga. The River is from 140 to 180 yards broad & very deep : The Tide rises near 3 Cubits at Pultya. This River is the same that I traced part of in my way down the Southern Creeks, & at the place where I left off surveying it is known by ye name of the Burrasaat River.[1] This is the first navigable Branch of * the Ganges that we meet with to the Eastward of the Jelenghee River.

The Pultya Creek is said to come from a large Jeel which lies about 6 miles WNW from Pultya. The Jeel is named Berille.

After crossing the Nobogonga our Road lay thro' a prodigious thick Wood or Jungle for ye space of a mile & three quarters, the Nobogunga running close on the left of it. There are many Tygers in this Jungle.

At the end of the Jungle lies ye Village & Stage of Nohatta, from whence the River turns off to the Northward. The Road from hence lies thro' an open cultivated Countrey. At Night we halted at ye side of a Jeel near the Grove of Luckypour ; about ½ a mile farther on was a small Tank in the Grove.

The 23rd. surveyed near 10 miles, being obliged to go farther than usual on Account of the scarcity of Water. Passed thro' the Village of Mohamedpour which is by far the most regular & neatest that we have seen since we left Calcutta.[2] Immediately to the Southw^d^ of this Village there is a very fine large Tank. It is up- * wards of 700 yards long, & about two thirds of that in breadth. The Countrey round Mohamedpour lies excessive low. At this Season it is swampy in many places. Mohamedpour is upwards of 7½ miles from Nohatta.

After leaving Mohamedpour Grove we came on a large Plain which lies so low that it is a Lake or Jeel during great part of the Year. It is named Beelseral or Seral-Jeel. There are a number of Pools & Swamps at this Time, & about a mile & half from Mohamedpour is a Creek called Manickdaw : it is very shallow.[3]

At the end of this low Plain which is near 5½ miles from Mh^d^pour we came to the Burashee River. This River though excessive deep is not more than 50 yards broad at the Ferry. It is a Branch of the Comer & is navigable all ye Year for very large Boats. Its outlet from ye Ganges is opposite Charbagat Island, & it falls into Sunderbound * a little above the Herengotta River.[4] The Ferry is between Mosudgotta & Doagotta.

is drying up year by year. On Rennell's map it is shown as a continuation of the Gorroy or Garai R. which leaves the Ganges at Kushtia.

[1] *Ante* p. 21.

[2] Mohamedpour remained a large town till 1836, when it was devastated by a fever introduced by prisoners employed on the Dacca-Jessor road, and it has since become an insignificant village. It was founded at the end of the 17th century by Sitaram Rai, a landholder of Bhushna, and under him became the capital of the district. There are the remains of a quadrangular fort surrounded by a ditch, the southern portion of which forms the tank mentioned by Rennell. An account of the antiquities of the place is given by Hunter in his Stat. Acc. of Bengal, vol. II, p. 212, and in the List of Ancient Mon. Bengal, p. 126. For an account of the career of Sitaram Rai, *see* Bengal, Past and Present, Vol. V, p. 236.

[3] Rennell does not mention the Madhumati, on the R. bank of which Mohamedpur now stands. At this time the name was given only to that portion of the river which lies below the mouth of the Nabaganga. It is the southern continuation of the Garai, which leaves the Ganges at Kushtia, and it enters the sea by the Haringhata estuary. When the Ganges broke south into the Garai channel, early in the nineteenth century, the Nabaganga and Barasia (Rennell's Burashee'), its natural outlets to the sea, were unable to carry the surplus water, and a new channel was opened through a small creek, the Alangkhali (Ellenkhali of Fergusson. Quart. Jour. Geol. Soc., XIX. p. 335). Afterwards the name Madhumati was extended to the new channel (Hunter, *op. cit.*, p. 174).

[4] The Haringhata estuary, or "Deer ford."

Plan No. 7. The 24th. surveyed upwards of 9 miles. In ye Morning came to Jaynagore[1] which lies on ye Western Bank of the Comer Creek, & about 2 miles by the Roads from Doagotta. The Comer & Burashee approach each other so near as to leave an Isthmus of only a mile & half broad. Jaynagore is a large Village, & has a Bazar, together with some good Bungaloes in it.

From Jaynagore the Road goes in general along the N.W. side of the Comer, & is consequently very crooked, however the Bengalas are fond of travelling by the sides of Rivers, partly I suppose for the convenience of Water, & partly because the River Banks are commonly higher than ye rest of the Countrey.[2] The Countrey hereabouts is open & very well cultivated, & the River winding thro' it adds to the beauty of the Prospects. At Night we crossed the Comer opposite to the Village of Gopalpour. Gopalpour is 7 miles from Jaynagur.

* The Comer Creek is a Branch of the same River from whence the Burrashee proceeds. It begins to be navigable for large Boats about the middle of July, & then a Passage is open from Jaynagur to Hobbygunge, the Comer falling into the Hobbygunge or Arika River.[3] Its bed is about 160 yards broad, but the Water at this Season is confined to a Channell of 40 or 50 yards & is scarce knee deep in many places. It has a remarkable winding Course, as I experienced in 1764, when I passed through it in my way to Dacca.[4]

This Day we had a fresh Breeze of Wind at South, & the first that I have taken notice of for the Season.

The 25th. surveyed 9¼ miles: the first 2½m. was along the S. E. Bank of the Comer, when having passed Commipour the River turns off to the Westward, & the Road to the Northward, for near a mile & half, & then runs along the Southern Bank of the * Harri Gonga.[5] The Isthmus formed by the two Rivers is little more than a quarter of a mile broad. The Harri Gonga runs out of the Ganges nearly opposite to Rottingunge Creek, & from hence runs by Hadgigunge, & falls into the Ganges again a few miles below that Place. Its bed is from 200 to 250 yards wide but it is in many Places too shallow for Boats of a moderate size. The Dacca Road goes along the side of this River for about 2 miles, & then the River winding round to the N. E. we lost it for about 3 miles till we came to Furridpour a Dauk's Stage.[6] From hence the River widens, occasioned by some Sand Banks & Islands lying in ye midst of it. The Countrey hereabouts is very well cultivated, but it lies very low, & must be overflown during a great part of the Year. We halted about a mile below Furridpour. The Southwardly Wind seems to be settled.

[1] This place is shown as quite an insignificant village, Golla Jynugur, in the Atlas of India, Sheet 120. The branches of the Barasia and Kumar which flowed on either side of it are now silted up.

[2] For the causes of this *see* Fergusson, Quart. Journ. Geol. Soc., Vol. XIX, p. 324. The still water of the jhils checks the velocity of the water, flowing outwards across the banks of the rivers, when the latter are in flood, and compels them to deposit the bulk of the silt along the banks.

[3] The Arial Khan. A branch of the Bhubaneswar, now one of the main channels of the Ganges.

[4] *Ante* p. 22.

[5] Also known as the Mara Padma. According to tradition the Ganges formerly took this course instead of the present more easterly channel.

[6] Now the head-quarters of the District of Faridpur.

The 26th. surveyed $5\frac{1}{4}$ miles & came to Hadgi Gunge.[1] The first two miles lay along the side of the River mentioned yesterday; from thence the Road turns to the E. S. E. & goes very strait to Hadgi Gunge. The latter part of the Road lay along the S. W. side of a long Jeel, a small Branch of which we crossed about a mile & quarter from Hadgigunge. *

The whole distance by the Roads from Dumdum to Hadgigunge is 133 miles 3 furlongs; & if Dumdum be as is reported 6 miles from Calcutta the whole distance will be $139\frac{1}{2}$ nearly.

I staid at Hadgigunge till the 2d. March waiting for Mr. Richards. During this time I was employed in constructing & copying a large Map of Bengall for the Governor. The 2d. of March finding that Mr. Richards had but just left Culna, I set off for Dacca to get a supply of Men & Boats for the next Survey.

The Passage by Water from Hadgigunge to Dacca is about 69 miles at this Season. The Route is thro' Meggala Creek & into the Issamuty at Kardupour; then by way of Nabobgunge & Churan; thro' Toolsey Creek & into the Dollaserry; by Tagerpour & Fattylur, & up the Beurygonga to Dacca. The 4th. arrived at Dacca & continued there till yᵉ 11th. The two last days I was detained by reason of my Dandies[2] running away. Plan of yᵉ Ganges. *

During this time I finished & sent away the Governor's Map, & procured a new sett of Boats & Coolies. Mr. Richards arrived the 7th.

The Northwest Squalls began the first of the month, & we have had several days of Northwardly Wind since that Time.

The 11th. in the Morning left Dacca in order to drop down to the Mouth of the Ganges & proceed to Jelenghee by way of the Southern Creeks. My Intention was to send Mr. Richards by way of the Burashee & to go myself by way of the Nobogonga or Burrasaat River, & to meet Mr. Richards at the head of the Comer Creek.

On my leaving Dacca I began to reduce another Map of the Ganges for the present Governor, Mr. VanSittart & some other Gentlemen having carried off all the Plans that I had made of the Ganges in 1764.[3] The Map I now began was intended to be on a Scale of 3 British miles to an Inch, & to contain all the several Branches of the Ganges from Jelenghee to the Sea: also the River Megna from its Conflux with the Ganges to Dacca, together with the Environs of that City. The whole was to be on 3 Sheets of Imperial Paper. Mr. Richards was employed in correcting & reducing his Route from Bongong to Mohamedpour. The 11th. at Night we came near Rajabarry.[4] *

The 12th. the bad Weather obliged to stay at Rajabarry great part of the Day.

The 14th. in yᵉ Morning arrived at the head of Badarashon Creek which leads out of the great River oppsite Rajanagore, & runs by Hobbygunge into the Goanuddy

[1] *See* note p. 22.

[2] Boatmen.

[3] These are perhaps the maps referred to by Sir C. Markham in a note on p. 55 of his 'Memoir of the Indian Surveys':—"The originals are now in the Geographical Department of the India Office. They were taken home by some official and treated by him as private property, till they were accidentally discovered in the collection of a lady of rank, and purchased for £100 by their lawful owners, the Court of Directors (Bombay Quarterly Review, Vol. III, p. 140)."

[4] At the junction of the Dhaleswari with the Meghna.

River. I directed Mr. Richards to take a Plan of it, whilst I was employed on yᵉ Map

The 16th. in yᵉ Forenoon we came into the Goanuddy River by the abovementioned Creek. The distance thro' is about 20 miles. During its Course it receives 2 other * Branches of the Ganges, the Creek from Sajatpour, and the Comer which runs by Jaynagur. At its first separation from the Ganges it is scarce 150 yards broad, but below HobbyGunge it is near a quarter of a Mile broad. It is deep enough for the largest Boats during the whole Year & thro' it lies the common Route from Sunderbound to the great River.[1] In one place this River approaches within a mile & quarter of the Ganges, & at the same Place a narrow but deep Creek joins the two Rivers. This Creek is named Jaffierabad, & is used by the Boats that go from Dacca to Sunderbound. This whole Countrey is fertile & well cultivated. It belongs to the Province of Dacca.

In our way to Sutalury[2] we surveyed the Western Branch of the Goanuddy River called the Lolcherra Creek. This Creek runs out of the Goanuddy River about 2½ miles below the Village of Goanuddy, & is at first scarce broad enough for 2 Boats to pass abreast of each other, but after a few miles it increases to a considerable breadth & * leads into yᵉ Main River again. This survey of the Route from Goanuddy to Sutalury renders the Map of the Ganges pretty compleat, save only that the Course of the Burrashee & Nobogonga are wanting.

The 17th. in yᵉ Evening arrived at the head of the Sutalury River. The Burrashee River is said to fall in below SujaGunge, which is the Reason that we go so far about.[3] I directed Mr. Richards to survey the Sutalury River from the Place where I left off in 1764,[4] & to continue it to the Burrashee, I being ill of a Feaver.

The 20th. finding myself very considerably weakened, & having no Prospect of getting rid of my Disorder without proper Assistance I left Mr. Richards to pursue the Survey according to the proposed Plan, & set out for Dacca in yᵉ Evening. We were then near SujaGunge. This part of the Countrey lies so low, that at High Water Mark the level of it is not 2 foot above the level of the Water. The Countrey seems * but poorly cultivated & as badly inhabited. The Flood Tide runs to the Westward thro' the Sutalury & SujaGunge Rivers. The 23d. in the Afternoon arrived at Dacca: on the Passage I was able to do some work on yᵉ Map of the Ganges, & towards making an Abstract of my Journals for the Governor.

[1] The route now taken by steamers during the dry season runs further E., through the Nayabhangi R., which connects the Arial Khan above Barisal with the Meghna.

[2] Jhalakati, headquarters of a police circle 10 miles W.S.W. from Barisal. On Rennell's maps this is shown as much the more important place.

[3] The Barasia or Madhumati river, as it is called in its lower course, falls into the Haringhata estuary at Firozpur, where the river from Barisal (the Sutylury R. of Rennell) joins in. This is now on the steamer route from Calcutta to Dacca and Assam.

[4] *Ante* p. 36.

Names of Places.	Distances. M.	F.	Dec. Pts.	Shelter.	Water	
*From Dumdum to Gowreepour Bridge ..	2	7	·9	...	Nulla .	Good Road.
Barrasett	4	3	·6	Groves ..	Tanks ..	High Road.
Kolpukareea Nulla almost dry	2	..	·3	...	....	Road across Pad[a]. Fields.
Dollapukrey	3	5	·2	....	Tank ..	Smooth Road.
Chaldybarrya	..	4	·4	A fine Tope ..	...	Good Road.
Joypool	1	2	·7	Good Topes .	Tanks ..	Good Road.
A small Nulla almost dry ..	1	..	..	....	....	Rough Road.
Belguree Nulla very shallow ..	1	5	..	....	Tanks all y[e] way.	
Jawberria or Chawbarrya ..	3	..	.	Fine Tope ..	Water near ..	Good Road.
Commature	2	..	..		A Jeel near ..	Very good Road.
Chunderhaat .. .	1	5	..	Good Topes ..	Tank ..	Very good Road.
Janapool	1	3	..	....	Sev[l]. Tanks ..	Good Road.
Enter on Mullicpour Plain ..	1	1	.	....	...	Tol[e]. Road.
End of the Plain. Mullicpour. Cross the Jubbunaw Creek in Boats	2	3	..	Fine Topes ..	River ..	Tolerable Road.
Coyah a fine Village ..	3	2	..	....	Tank ..	Across a large Plain.
Chanpara	3	3	..	Tope ..	Bad Water ..	Good Road.
Dogassia	1	7	..	Tope & Village	Tanks ..	Rough Road.
Callipour	1	2	..	Large Village ..	Tank ..	Across Pad. fields.
Bongong on the River Issamot crossed in Boats.. ..	2	7	..	Very fine Topes	River ..	Road across a Plain.
Jaöwpour Tope Chawgarrya ..	1	..	..	Rem[e]. fine Tope	Creek near.	
Nowbonga Creek fordable ..	..	3	·5	....	....	Bad Road & close Countrey.
Hakkor Creek crossed in Boats	1	4	..	Woody ..	....	Rough Road.
Nomosgah Vill. ..	1	4	..	Large Vill. ..	Creek ..	Tolerable Road.
Porabarry	1	2	·5	Small Topes ..	..	Bad Road.
Jadopour	5	6	..	Groves ..	Batenau Creek crossed in Boats.	Mostly a close Jungly Countrey.
Gutcally Grove	3	3	·5	Thick Woods ..	Bad W[r]. ..	Tol. Road.
A Gully to be crossed ..	..	3	..	do. ..	....	Bad Road.
Bannyel Tank & Grove ..	1	4	..	Thick Wood ..	Fine Tank ..	Across a Plain.
Kobaduck River crossed in Boats. Jigergutcha the East side	1	5	..	Peepel Grove ..	River ..	Jeels in y[e] Road.
A Good Tank	2	1	..	Wood ..	Tank ..	Good Road.
Pullugott on the Mookterserai fordable but crossed in Boats	4	6	..	....	River ..	Close Countrey.
Chausera the Jessore Rajah's House	1	..	..	Groves ..	Tanks ..	Rough Road.
Neelgunge	2	..	..	Fine Tope ..	R. Boyrub crossed in Boats.	Bad Road.
Dytulla	3	2	..	Thick Wood ..	Boyrub R. ..	Jungly Countrey.
Side of the Boyrub ..	1	4	..	Thick Woods ..	River ..	Bad Road.
Doualee .. .	5	..	..	Thick Woods ..	River Sittarya crossed in Boats.	Mostly a crooked bad Road.
Miles ..	79	6	·6			

* This is the Table, or abstract of the route from Dumdum to Hajiganj, referred to on p. 87.

Name of Place.	Distances. M.	F.	I	Shelter.	Water.	
Miles ..	79	6	·6			
A large Tank at ye end of a Plain	3	7	..	Vill. near ..	Tank ..	Across a dismal Plain.
Gunagotta	4	7	·5	Thick Woods ..	R. Sittarya crossed in Boats.	
Judacally Creek Fordable ..	1	5	..	....	....	Low swampy Plain.
Nobogonga River. Pultya Village	4	1	·5	Thick Woods ..	The River crossed in Boats.	Mostly a Jungly or swampy Countrey.
Nohatta	1	7	..	Woody ..	The same R. ..	Thro' a thick Jungle.
A fine Tank in a Grove ..	4	..	..	Grove ..	Tank ..	Pass several Jeels.
Mohamedpour	3	4	..	Large Village ..	Tank ..	Swampy Countrey.
Manicdaw Creek Fordable ..	1	4	·5	No Shelter ..	Creek ..	Low Plain.
Mosudgotty. River Burrashee ..	3	7	..	Groves ..	River crossed in Boats.	Low swampy Plain.
Jaynagur	2	..	..	Large Village ..	R. Comer ..	Rough Road.
Jāāmpour	4	2	..	Large Vill. ..	R. Comer ..	Good Road.
Gopalpour. Cross ye Comer in Boats	2	6	..	Groves ..	River ..	Rough Road.
Connipour	2	4	..	Small Vill. ..	R. Comer ..	Crooked Road.
To the Harrigonga ..	1	2	..	...	....	Good Road.
Leave ye River	2	..	..	....	....	Along ye Bank R.
Furridpour	3	..	..	Groves ..	Harrigonga close on ye L.	Good Road.
Pāātpassar Hāāt	2	2	..	Groves ..	do. River ..	Good Road.
Cross a small Jeel. Fordable ..	2	6	..	....	....	Low Countrey.
Hadgi Gunge	1	2	..	Large Vill. ..	River.	
Miles ..	133	2	·1			

Editor's Note:—Many of the observations recorded in the succeeding pages of the Journal have been incorporated in Rennell's 'Memoir of a Map of Hindoostan' and in his 'Description of the Roads in Bengal and Behar', a small volume printed in 1778 "by order of the Honourable the Court of Directors." The routes inserted in the latter volume are indicated by the numbers in brackets. I have also added in brackets the modern spelling of some of the names, where it seemed necessary.

Burdwan to Banchburria[1]—

To Bussool	7·6
Chaulkund or Maymary	12·4
Borinchy	5·7
Purrua[2]	5·1
Bansbarria	10·2
	41·4

DIMENSIONS OF THE PROVINCES &c.[3]—

Bengall NW to SE 465 Eng. Miles—

	EM.		Propn.
Bengall dim. ..	315 by 315 or square miles	99,225	99¼
Bahar ..	210 by 210	44,100	44
Awd[4] ..	270 by 120	32,400	32½
Ellahabad[5] ..	144 by 93	13,392	13½
The King's[6] ..	180 by 36	6,480	6½
France ..			174

British Territories	143¼
Sujah Dowlah's	46
King's	6½
France	174

New Calculation—

British Provinces	142,000 sq. miles.
England	60,000 ,,

1 Bansbaria, a town on the Hugli, 27 miles N. of Calcutta, celebrated for its temples. The road follows the Grand Trunk Road pretty closely.

2 ? Pundua, the capital of the ancient Hindu kingdom of Paundravardhana.

3 This list is revised and amplified in the 'Memoir,' p. cxiii.

4 Oudh.

5 Allahabad, at this time in the possession of Suja Daula, the Nawab of Oudh.

6 The Emperor of Delhi, Shah Alam.

FROM COSSIMBAZAR.[1]

Patna (55)—

	M.	F.
Bomineah	10	6
Duanserai	8	0
Comrah	10	4
Sooty (Suti)	8	2
Downapour	11	1
Furrucabad (Furrukhabad) ..	7	6
Falkypour	8	2
Oudinulla (Udhua Nullah) ..	3	4
Rajamohl (Rajmahal) ..	8	0
Siclygully	18	6
Terriagully	12	4
Pialapour	9	0
Colgong	10	2
Boglipour (Bhagalpur) ..	17	4
Sultangunge	17	4
Goorgut Nulla	4	6
Monghir	18	4
Suradgegurrah	17	4
Ruinulla	10	4
Doomrah	7	2
Bar	26	0
Boycauntp[r] (Baikanthpur) ..	20	0
Jaff. Kan's Gard.[2]	10	0
Patna Factory	5	0
Miles ..	281	1

Burdwan (92 & 103)—

	M.	F.
Chunapour	2	7
Bobtah	8	0
Daudpour	6	4
Plassey	6	3
Cutwa	12	4
Ninghen Serai	13	6
Burdwan	21	3
Miles ..	71	3

Jellinghee & Dacca (84 & 99)—

	M.	F.
Bally	5	5
Dultabazar	2	5
Azimgunge	11	4
Jellinghee (Jalangi)	10	0
Horrisongkor (Harisankra) ..	11	2
Cometpour cross the Ganges ..	20	0
Pubna	6	3
Sujanagore	12	4
Rottingunge	15	0
Jaffiergunge (Jafarganj) cross the little Ganges	9	3
Niabondura cross the Issamuty ..	28	0
Churan	9	4
Pattergotta (Pathorghata) cross the Dollaserry	10	0
Dacca	6	0
Miles ..	157	6

Jellinghee—

	M.	F.
2[d]. Road To Gunee ..	2	6
Rypour ..	6	0
Bagretpour ..	7	0
Mohamedpour ..	5	4
Jellinghee ..	9	7
Miles ..	30	1

Bolia[3] (63)—

	M.	F.
To Mutejyl[4]	2	3
Cuttorah	2	0
Seetaram Pani	3	6
Titalya	3	2
Murcha	9	2
Codalcotty Gott[5]	1	6
Cross the Ganges to Nabobgunge	2	4
Bolia	2	6
Miles ..	27	5

2[d]. Road—

	M.	F.
To Bally	5	5
Titalya	6	6

[1] The British Factory at Murshidabad.

[2] Jafar Khan's Garden.

[3] Rampur Boalia, on the N. bank of the Ganges, above Jalangi.

[4] Motijhil. Lord Clive had his residence here. The Jhil is an old bed of the Kasimbazar river (Cal. Rev., Vol. XCIV, p. 335).

[5] *Ghat*, a landing place, or ferry.

	M.	F.
Murcha	9	2
Bolia	7	0
Miles ..	28	5

Bogwangola[1] (13)—

	M.	F.
To Mutejyl	2	3
Cuttorah	2	0
Palasbarry	5	1
Baderpour	4	3
Bogwangola	5	0
	18	7

Meenkoot & Denagep^r.[2] (26)—

	M.	F.
Bomineah	10	6
Banniagong	4	3
Sackral	3	4
Meenkoot	4	4
Cross the Ganges to Godagary ..	3	0
Chappygunge	15	0
Okilpour	14	4
Daudpour	8	0
Titalya	4	6
Nishanpour	8	4
Dourgunge	7	3
Nysintah	10	2
Pransagur	7	7
Ramsagur	7	2
Denagepour	5	6
Miles ..	115	3

Ballitunghee[3] (123)—

	M.	F.
To Chunapour	2	7
Lowdah	6	3
Manicknagore	4	6
Callytulla	2	5
Batebarya	3	2
Ballitunghee	6	0
Miles ..	25	7

Birbohen[4] (120)—

	M.	F.
To Callyongunge	13	0
Seerpour	6	2
Bowdgong	8	1
Telloah	7	2
Cotemolysure (Kot Mauresh-war)	2	5
Bajetpour	4	4
Angergurrya	6	0
Soory	6	2
Nagore	15	7
Miles ..	69	7

Mauldah (60)—

	M.	F.
To Meenkoot	23	1
Cross the Ganges to Godagary	3	0
Chappygunge	15	0
Bangabarry cross the Maha-nada	16	0
Mauldah	14	0
Miles ..	71	1

Rungpore (64)—

	M.	F.
To Bolia	27	5
Bowanyguuge	25	0
Belloar cross the Denagepour River	10	0
Currihey	14	0
Naddyol	22	0
Goragott	14	0
Burradirgah	20	0
Rungpour Factory ..	17	0
Miles ..	149	5

Rangamatty & Gwalpara (12 & 32)—

	M.	F.
To Rungpour	149	5
Curygong	25	0
Poonkur	17	0
Dubarye (Dhubri) ..	12	0

---

[1] Bhagwangola, a river mart on the Ganges N.E. of Murshidabad.

[2] That these notes were written some considerable time after the Journal itself is shown by the changes in the spelling—Dinajpur is always 'Denospour' in the earlier pages.

[3] A town on the Jalangi R., S.S.E. of Murshidabad, represented in the Atlas of India by two small villages, Ballee and Toongee.

[4] *See* note, p. 101.

		M.	F.
	Rangamatty	14	0
	Dudekoar	15	0
	Gwalparah	26	0
	Miles ..	258	5

Calcutta (92)—

		M.	F.
	To Chunapour	2	7
	Bobtah	8	0
	Daudpour	6	4
	Plassey	6	3
	Augurdeep	14	0
	Beltully	10	4
	Jahanagur	6	6
	Summenger	7	0
69	Mirzapour	7	0
	Amboa	6	4
	Insurah	7	0
72·6	Niaserai	9	4
	Banchbarya	4	4
	Chandernagore	8	0
	Bankibazar	6	6
	Calcutta	19	0
	Miles ..	130	2

2d. Road by Kistnagur (92)—

	M.	F.
To Plassey	23	6
Bickrampour	10	4
Niahaat or Bellya ..	11	3
Kistnagur cross the Jellinghee	9	0
Texal Ferry	10	7
Runnagott (Ranighat) ..	10	0
Burrua or Hell	13	1
Amedungah	13	5
Barrasett	7	2
Dumdum	7	4
Calcutta	6	0
Miles ..	123	0

Birkuty at the foot of the western Hills[1] (116 & 87)—

	M.	F.
To Teretcoondah	6	4
Sonkoe	15	4
Baderpour	14	0
Birkuty	3	6
Miles ..	39	6

	M.	F.
To Ametpour[2] (91)	6	2
Augurdeep	8	0
Pattolee Tank	3	0
Beltully	3	7
Jahanagur	7	1·82
Summutgur	4	0·18
Merzapour	4	2·27
Culna	4	0·59
Amboa	2	5·60
Inchurah	6	5·75
Niaserai	8	7·37
Bansbaria	4	4
Miles ..	63	4·58

[1] The Rajmahal Hills. Berkati is now an insignificant village (Atlas of India Sheet 113) S. of Muheshpur.

[2] A road leading along the western bank of the Baghirathi to Calcutta. The river is crossed at Agurdip, S. of Plassey.

GREAT ROADS of BIRBOHEN.[1]

	M.	F.
From Nagore to Deogurh[2] (57)—		
NW. To Dudapauny Gott ..	4	5
Cohorut	6	2
Coryaum	4	4
Jallyne	8	4
Coonjuree	7	2
Operbanda	5	2
Sarhaut	7	4
Suramma	11	4
Deogurh	11	4
	66	7

	M.	F.
Burdwan to Kiewgong—		
Mayalkote	20	5
Mirryalah	8	6
Kiewgong	7	1
	36	4

	M.	F.
To Comerabad[3] (252)—		
N. Lettabanny Gott ..	5	2
Baharow	3	4
Mobog Gaut	5	4
Futtapour	4	0
Comerabad	2	4
	20	6

	M.	F.
NE. to Molatty—		
To Bolio Gott[4]	6	6
Carracoondy	8	2
Dijoucha	4	2
Damrah	7	6
Molatty	3	7
	30	7

	M.	F.
ENE. to Margong—		
To Bolio Gott & Carracoondy ..	15	0
Perauagong	6	4
Pursundpour	7	0
Billaspour	5	4
Margong	5	6
	39	6

***To Soory,[5] 3 Roads—**

	M.	F.
EBS. North Road—		
To Bolio Gott	6	6
Battua	4	5
Soory	4	4
	15	7

	M.	F.
Middle Road (the best) (49)—		
To Dulebpour Gott	7	5
Caddya	6	7
Soory	1	5
	16	1

	M.	F.
South Road—		
To Bucclesore hot Wells[6] ..	7	2
Serampour Gott	1	4
Soory	9	0
	17	6

	M.	F.
SE. to Kistnagur & Elambazar[7] &c. (147)—		
To Bursaul Gaut	4	1
Niagott	2	4
Dubraagepour	6	7
Kissenagur	3	1
Gowrahya	4	3
Goorshya	6	0
Paher	2	5
Elambazar	1	1
Curuagore	7	4
	38	2

---

1 Birbhum. Orme spells it Berbohin (History, Vol. II, p. 168).

2 Nagar or Rajnagar was the capital of the Hindu princes of Birbhum prior to the conquest of Bengal by the Muhammadans. It lies W. of Suri, the present head-quarters of the district. Deogarh lies to the N.W. in the Santal Parganas. For the legend of its foundation *see* Hunter, 'Annals of Rural Bengal,' p. 191.

3 *i.e.*, from Nagore. Koomrabad is on the Mor R. to the north. Rennell notes:—"By this Pass the Mahrattas entered Bengal in 1742" (Roads, p. 252).

4 A ferry on the Mor R., not to be confounded with Rampur Boalia, on the Ganges.

5 Suri. Now the head-quarters of the district.

6 These are the Bakeswar hot springs, situated about a mile south of Tantipara, between Suri and Nagar. There are numerous hot jets in the bed of the stream, and the air is impregnated with sulphuretted hydrogen. The locality is a noted place of pilgrimage (Hunter, Stat. Acc. Beng., Vol. IV, p. 322; Oldham, Mem. Geol. Surv. Ind., Vol. XIX, Pt. 2, p. 42).

7 On the Ajai R.

SE. to Supour[1]—

	M.	F.
To Kissenagur	16	5
Jaunabaz	7	5
Rupour	6	5
Supour	6	3
	37	2

SBW.

To Lacaracoonda[2] & Okera—

	M.	F.
To Bandy Gott	3	5
Immumgur Gott (Imamghar Ghat)	1	4
Bahdee	2	3
Lacaracoondah	3	2
Ajy R.	4	6
Okerah	7	2
	22	6

SW. to Pachet[3] (90)—

	M.	F.
Lacaracoondah	10	7
Luckaupour	6	7
Jamgong	9	4
Aiturah	6	0
Damoodah R.	6	4
Pachet	7	6
	47	4

NNE From Soory to Molatty—

	M.	F.
To Mohamedbazar	7	6
Dyoucha	3	1
Damrah	7	6
Molatty	3	7
	22	4

NE. to Margong—

	M.	F.
To Peranagong	9	0
Purchandpour	7	0
Billaspour	5	4
Margong	5	6
N.B.—This is y[e] great Road to Rajmol[4]		
	27	2

NE. to Boudgong (169)—

	M.	F.
To Amgergurrya	6	2
Bajetpour	6	0
Cotemolysure	4	4
Telloah	2	5
Boudgong	7	2
N.B.—This is the Road to Mux: (adabad).		
	26	5

E. to Deckabary, Jummucandy, &c.[5] (251)—

	M.	F.
To Bidelyparah	6	5
Hautinagore	6	4
Deckabarry	6	7
Cottree or Bellya ..	5	0
Moneegong	6	1
Jummu Bazar	4	0
	35	1

ESE. to Gomhi[6]—

	M.	F.
To Purrunderpour	5	1
Issarpour	6	4
Chowtah	3	4
Laatpour	4	2
Gomhi	5	0
	24	3

SE. to Bahary[7]—

	M.	F.
To Purrunderp[r].	5	1
Jaunipour	3	3
Parpour	2	5
Omdarrah	7	5
Bahary	6	0
	24	6

[1] Sheopur, near Surul, once the centre of the E. I. Co.'s trade in the district.

[2] Called Sakarakunda by Hunter. There is a warm spring here, temp. 85°, with the ruins of a curious old Hindu temple (*Ibid.*, p. 322).

[3] Or Panchet, a well-known hill in the Raniganj coal-field.

[4] Rajmahal, on the Ganges.

[5] Towards Berhampur.

[6] Towards Katwa on the Bhagirathi.

[7] Near Surul.

SSE. to Surrool & Supour—

	M.	F.
To Purrunderp[r].	5	1
Gurgurrya	3	5
Saturya	6	3
Surrool Factory	4	3
Supour	3	2
	22	6

SBE. to Curnagore (Burdwan Road) (49)—

	M.	F.
To Comah	4	7
Coostigerya	5	4
Hanserra	3	5
Roopour	4	6
Ramnagur	2	1
Curnagore	4	4
	25	3

Another Road—

	M.	F.
To Parbutypour . ..	6	0
Munguldy	4	1
Billetty	4	0
Roopour	3	4
	17	5

To Ramnagur &c.—

SW. to Kistnagur & Cotah—

	M.	F.
To Poleserrah	3	5
Kisnagur	8	0
Cotah	5	4
	17	1

CROSS ROADS of BIRBOHEN.

From Luckanpour to Jallyne[1]—

	M.	F.
To Serascooondah	7	2
Nallah	6	0
Chowjurah	7	3
Jallyne	2	0
	22	5

Futtyp[r].[2] to Dyoucha—

	M.	F.
To Muncalgur Pass	9	4
Purtabpour	2	6
Jinderpour	5	7
Dyoucha	4	4
	22	5

Purchundp[r]. to Jummu C.[3]—

	M.	F.
To Cotemolysure	3	0
Saneckpour	7	3
Cunderrah	6	5
Jummu Candy	6	7
	23	7

[1] Running N. W. from Lakhanpur, a small village near the Ajai R.

[2] A village on the Mor R., N. of Nagar. Dyoucha lies to the north of Suri.

[3] A cross road leading towards the Bhagirathi from the Rajmahal road. Cotemolysure stands for Kot Maureshwar, a pargana of Birbhum.

WESTERN GREAT ROADS.

From Cossimbʳ. to Jummucand. Surrool Aurung &c.[1] (90 & 130)-

SW.	M.	F.
To Moketerpour Chokey ..	6	0
Gokorrun	6	7
Cusbaspour	1	4
Jummu Candy ..	5	6
Assoah .. .	6	1
Curroondah	8	2
Noaddah	3	4
Omdarrah	8	0
Surrool Aurung ..	6	5
	52	5

From Cossimbaz. to Burdwan by way of Jummucandy (90)—

	M.	F.
To Jummucandy	20	1
Assoah	6	1
Tarrapour	3	7
Culluah	3	3
Rye .. .	5	7
Saznaure	4	6
Monglacote (Moghalkot) ..	8	3
Arrawah	4	6
Saggra	4	1
Massundy	3	6
Burdwan	8	0

Great Northern Road from Burdwan to Furrucabad[2] (90 & 238)—

From Burdwan to

	M.	F.
Massundy	8	0
Saggra .. .	3	6
Arrawah	4	1
Mungulkote	4	6
Saznaure	5	0
Rye	4	6
Cullua	5	7
Tarrapour	3	3
Assoah	3	7
Moneegong	3	4
Muyser	2	7
Cargong	3	3
Nagore Atty	4	3
Seerpour	2	7
Bogaryaparah	3	4
Pazgong	2	3
Sonkoe . ..	7	4
Bircoonda	2	6
Sheikdiggy	2	3
Mirzapour	2	4
Jungipour	4	4
Sooty	8	6
&c. &c.		

NE. Birbohen to Jungipour[3]—

From Magore to—

	M.	F.
Bolio Gott	6	6
Carracoondy	8	2
Peranagong	6	4
Purchundpour ..	7	0
Billaspour	5	4
Margong	5	6
Ningha	4	7
Bahdur	4	6
Sonkoe	6	0
Mirzapour	7	5
Jungipour	4	4
	67	4

Nᵒ. Margong to Noangong[4]—

	M.	F.
To Nulhatty	10	4
Kanpour	7	0
Noangong	9	2
	26	6

Nagore to Rajmol (251)—

	M.	F.
To Peranagong, Purchandpour & Margong as before ..	39	6
Nulhatty	10	4
Kanpour	7	0
Noangong	9	2
Omrapour	6	7
Purtabgunge	5	7
Downapour	5	2
Furruckabad	7	6
Fulkypur	8	2
Oudinulla	3	4
Rajamohl	8	0
	112	0

[1] In Birbhum. Formerly the centre of the Company's trade in that district, and the site of an Aurung, or Factory.

[2] On the Ganges below Rajmahal.

[3] On the Bhagirathi above Murshidabad. This road is not marked in the Bengal Atlas.

[4] Part of the road from Jamu Khandi to Rajmahal.

Cossimb[r]. to Sooty (73)— Western Road.			M.	F.
To Muradbaug	..	..	6	3
Ghysabad	..	..	6	6
Bellyah	..	..	5	1
Mohamedp[r].	..	..	4	1
Belgottah	..	..	7	0
Sooty	..	..	8	5
			38	0

Burdwan to Surrool (72)—			M.	F.
Oregong	..	..	15	0
Gobindpour	..	..	6	6
Supour	..	..	9	4
Surrool	..	..	3	1

ITINERARIES.

GREAT ROAD FROM MOORSHEDABAD TO DELHY, MEASURED BY ORDER OF THE KING.[1]

	Coss.
From Moors. to Duanserai	7
Aurangabad	10
Furrucabad	8
Rajamohl (Rajamahal)	8
Sicly gully	8
Shawbad	8
Kahalgong	10
Bogolpour (Bhagalpur)	12
Janghira	9
Monghyr	9
SuroodgeGurrah (Surajgurh)	9
Derreahpour	12
Barrah	9
Bykuntpour	10
Patna	5
Beckaramabad	12
Mungulpour	8
Punnarah	9
Doudnagur	8
Gotelee	9
Shahuserabad[2]	7
Zelautabad	10
Monea	9
Curruah	9
Mogulla Serai (Mughalsarai)[3]	10
Baranushy (Benares)	5
Tornaushabad	9
Mando Sing	9
Hundea	11
In(nal) Serai	8
Elliabad (Allahabad)	3
Ameninchem Serai	10
Shazadabad	6
Chuveer Serai	12
Belunda Canarp^r.	12
Korah	12
Shahunabad	12
Moolump^r.	9
Moosapagur (Muzafargarh)	9
Boogulee Mydan[4]	10
Sicanderah	9
Attypour	12
Etagooah	14
Meelypour	12
Surrungabad	12
Raja ke Tallow[5]	12
Ahmedpour	12
Agra	12
Gogattah	8
Muttorah (Muttra)	4
Suller Serai	12
Horisha	12
Shungoon	12
Ferisdabad (Faridabad)	12
Delhy	12
Coss	519

N.B.—Bindarabund[6] is 3 coss W. from Muttura—

[1] Shah Alam was Emperor of Delhi during the period of Rennell's career in India. The road ran along the south bank of the Ganges to Patna, then up the Son to Daudnagar, where this river was crossed. Thence across country to Mughalsarai and over the Ganges at Benares. Along the north bank to Allahabad, where the Ganges was again crossed, and up the Doab to Agra, crossing the Jumna at that place. It is shown on Maps IX and X of the Bengal Atlas.

[2] Sasaram. Rennell's form of the name is derived from the Afghan Sher Shah Suri, the conqueror of Humayun and afterwards Emperor of Delhi, whose tomb is situated here.

[3] Sarai, a house for the accommodation of travellers.

[4] Maidan, an open space or plain covered with grass.

[5] Talao, a tank or reservoir The name signifies 'The King's tank.'

[6] Brindaban. The traditional habitation of Krishna in his youth, and a famous place of pilgrimage.

Midnap^{r}. to Jellasore (30 & 103)—	Coss.
Carickpour	2
Narangur	6
Culnagur	4
Ranyserai	2
Dantoon	2
Jellasore	4
	20

Midnap^{r}. to Gongacally [1] (248)—	
Patra	3
Shawpour	5
Cassejurah or Purtap^{r}.	4
Gongacally	6
	18

Jellasore to Ballasore (30)—	
Multanny	3
Bustah	3
Gurpuddah	2
Ramchandap^{r}.	2
Ballasore	3
	13

Ballasore to Cuttack (30)—	
To Surow	10
Caunsbansi Br.	2
Baderuck on ye Sollundree R.	7
Chundee Bridge	2
Chura Kooty	2
Domnagur	2
Georgepour	3
Mogadanny	1
Churrua R.	1
Barwah	1
Bahmounee R.	2
Comreea R.	1
Gulgulgottee Br.	1
Gingootty R.	1
Gobria R.	1
Hurryp^{r}.	2
Pudamp^{r}.	2
Cuttack	2
	43

Cuttack to ye Sea (31)—	Coss.
Cautjuree a large R.	1
Balcantha Tanna	5
Noar Pipley	5
Daudmocundp^{r}.	2
Jancandyp^{r}.	4
Attara Nuddy	3
Jaggernaut [2]	1
	21

Midnap^{r}. to Balramp^{r}. (168)—	Miles.
To Mudipour	3
Dermah	2
Derwah	2
Pirtapour	4
Bulramp^{r}.	2½

Burdwan to Soopour (72)—	
3 Tanks bet. ye Road & ye Vill. of Tallit	3
Kipalpour to Balessy Baug [5]	4
Curry R. to Khizop^{r}.	3
Oragong	4
Nulla & Slough to Govenp^{r}.	6
Bilea	2
Cunoor R. to Buxy Baz.	4
Ajy to Supour	2
	28

Midnap^{r}. to Calcutta—		Coss
Muncagur	Mid. Dist.^{r}	3
Daira	Mid. Dist.^{r}	4
Buckleshaw	Mid. Dist.^{r}	5
Doannee	Mid. Dist.^{r}	5
Cuncadee	Mid. Dist.^{r}	3
Mancohar (45)		5
Bognaun		4
Pullareah		3½
Seesburreah		2
Buzbuzeah (Budge-Budge)		2
Douahpurrah		2
		38½

1 On the Tamluk road.

2 The famous temple at Puri.

5 Bagh, a garden.

	Coss.
Midnap^{r}. to Burdwan (103)—	
To Shawpour	8
Chitwa	5
Bally Duan G^{r}. (Gunge) ..	9
Woochalen	8
Burdwan	8
	38

	Coss.
Ano. Route—	
Amely	4
Asseramp^{r}. or Asshrifpour ..	3
Jaukerah	3
Beubanp^{r}.	$2\frac{1}{2}$
Cottah	$2\frac{1}{2}$
Pucka Serai	3
Balchan	3
Uchalan	2
Burdwan	6
	29

	Coss.
Another Route—	
Amily	4
Bulchunserai	5
Mobaruck Munzil	5
Beubanp^{r}.	5
Assarapur	5
Amily	3
Midnap^{r}.	4
	31

PURGANNAHS OF BIRBOHEN.[1]

Sarhaut.[2] Cutch.[3] at Sarhaut 50 miles NWbW from Soory. Dim. 22 by 17 miles. All Hilly & Woody. The Ajy forms the Western Boundary.

Carryah.[4] Cutch. Luckanpour 20′ WSW from Soory. 20′ by 10. Hilly & Woody, only a few cultivated spots in the Valleys.

Chonit. Cutch. Oudgerya 19′ WbN from Soory. 22 by 11. The Northern part Hill & the rest Woody.

Belputtah.[5] Cutch. Comerabad in the Hills 25′ NW from Soory. 24′ by 15. All Mountainous. It is bounded on the North by the Districts f the Herboe (?) Rajah[6] & on ye East by Sultanabads.

Baharon[7] or Mohamedabad. Cutch. Barrow on the River More 15′ NW from Soory., 14′ by 8, the Northern part Mountainous & ye rem^r. a thick Wood.

Noney.[8] Cutch. Dyoucha on the River Derkah 9½′ NBE from Soory. Dim. 12 by 9. Jungley & barren, all except a spot between Dyoucha & Jinderpour. Forges for Iron are wrought at Dyoucha & Mh. bazar.[9] The ore is brought from the Malarp^r. Purgannah.

Herpour.[10] Cutch. at Gwallerra 9½′ West from Soory. 11 miles by 10. The City of Nagore lies in the West part, & is skirted on each side by a prodigious Wood. The hot Wells are 6 miles SE from Nagore. There are fine cultivated spots at Rannypour & Gwallerrah, the rest of the Purgannah is a thick Wood.

Malarpour.[11] Cutch. at Damra 16 miles NEbN from Soory. 11′ by 7′. The middle part Cultivated, the rest barren or Jungley. Iron Mines are wrought near Damra & Forges at Damra & Mysara.

Kirny.[12] Cutch. at Boggarshola[13] in Sallump^r. Purgannah. This is a small P. & chiefly a Jungle. Dim. 7 miles by 5. It joins Herpour on the Southwest.

---

1 A list of the fiscal divisions or Parganas of Birbhum is given in Hunter's Statistical Account of Bengal, Vol. IV, p. 421 *seq.*, from which, and the new edition of the Imperial Gazetteer, the details given in these notes are taken.

2 Sarath Deogarh. Now transferred to the Santal Parganas district, 952 sq. miles.

3 Cutch. = Cutcherry (Hind. Kachahri), an office of administration or court house.

4 Apparently this pargana, with the next, form the pargana of Kundahit Karea, now included in the Santal Parganas (Hunter, op. cit., Vol. XIV, p. 377), area 406·35 sq. miles.

5 Marked as a subdivision of the Santal Parganas on the Atlas of India Sheet No. 113, now included in the Dumka subdistrict.

6 I can find no mention of this Raja in any of the old records. On Rennell's map of Birbhum, No. II of the Bengal Atlas, this part of it is bounded on the N. by a district called 'Hendooa.'

7 Baharan, mentioned by Hunter but no particulars given.

8 Nani, Nonee of Atlas of India. Area 51·23 sq. miles. In 1852 there were still 30 iron smelting furnaces at work at Deocha, and as many more for refining it. The ore is a brown haematite obtained from lateritic deposits.

9 Muhammad Bazar, a village situated between Suri and Deocha.

10 Haripur Tappa. Area 103·14 sq. miles. The hot springs mentioned are those of Bakeswar (*ante* p. 101).

11 Mallarpur. Area 36·49 sq. miles. There were 4 iron furnaces at Dhamra in 1852.

12 Khirni. Area 32·53 sq. miles.

13 Bajasula in Shah Alampur pargana.

Cuttungah.[1] Cutch. Soory or Hyderabad. The Western half barren or Jungly, the rest a fine open fertile Countrey. Soory lies on the Skirts of the Jungle & about 3 miles from the southern Bank of the River More. Dim. 11′ by 8′.

Burra.[2] Cutch. Boggarshola in Sallump^r. Dim. 5½′ by 3.′ It borders on the Ajy & is clear & fertile.

Sallumpour.[3] Cutch. Boggarshola 18 miles SW from Soory. Dim. 12½ by 7. Open Countrey & fertile. On the N. it is bounded by the great Wood, & on the South by the Ajy.

Jinnijol.[4] Cutch. Saapour 9 miles SbW from Soory. Dim. 10 by 6½. The NW corner a Jungle, but the rem^r. a fine Countrey. Iron Mines are wrought at Kistnagur.

Selmboom.[5] Cutch. Paher near the W side Ajy & 19 miles SbW from Soory. 12 miles by 7. All arable Land save a Wood of 4′ extent near Elambazar.

Supour.[6] Cutch. Soopour a large Town on the Ajy 22′ SSE from Soory. The Talook belonging to the Town is reckoned a Purganna of itself, tho' but 3½′ by 2½.

Barbucksing.[7] Cutch. Baharee 23′ SE from Soory. Dim. 12′ by 5½ chiefly arable Land, & remarkably open. The NW part consists of high Downs interspersed with Jungle. The Factory of Surrool lies in this part & is only 3′ NW from Supour. This P. produces much Cotton.

Burkoondah.[8] Cutch. at Cosbah 13′ SEbS from Soory. 8½ by 4½. It is chiefly high barren Downs.

Allinagore.[9] Cutch. Jaunipour 9′ SE from Soory, & on ye Baccasore River. Dim. 13 by 4½. The Land mostly barren.

Cootubpour.[10] Cutch. Gomhi 23′ ESE from Soory, & on the South side Baccasore or Queyah River. 11 by 4 miles. The Land in the western parts high & barren the eastern parts cultivated. This is a District of ye same name bordering on it belonging to Radshi.

Acburshi.[11] Cutch. Peranagong 9′ NE from Soory. 4½ by 4. It consists chiefly of high barren Downs.

Savack Mowlisher.[12] Cutch. Mettyarah 9′ ESE from Soory. 10′ by 6. The SW part high Downs, the rest clear, fertile Land.

1 Khatanga. 81·54 sq. miles.

2 Bara Taluk. 36·79 sq. miles.

3 Shah Alampur. 76·62 sq. miles.

4 Zain-ujial. 68·21 sq. miles.

5 Senbhum. 93·90 sq. miles. The patch of jungle or wood near Ilambazar was still in existence in 1852.

6 Supur Taluk. A 'Talook' in Bengal is a tract of proprietary land, sometimes not easily distinguished from 'Zemindaries' (Hobson Jobson, p. 894). Area ·22 of a square mile. In Rennell's time it probably included the small pargana of Sheopur.

7 Barbaksingh. 65·40 sq. miles.

8 Bharkanda. 32·63 sq. miles.

9 Alinagar. 59·40 sq. miles. The Bakeswar R. runs through the northern portion.

10 Kutabpur. 45·75 sq. miles.

11 Akbarshahi. 27·55 sq. miles.

12 Maureshwar Sabak. 61·94 sq. miles.

Dowrah Mowlisher.[1] Cutch. Same name 15′ ENE from Soory. 13 by 6½. Open Countrey & arable Land.

Surroofsing.[2] Cutch. Deckabary 19′ East from Soory. Its figure is extremely irregular & many Talooks of it lie in the midst of Radshi. Its Dimensions may be reckoned 12 by 10. The Lands are chiefly arable & produce Paddy & Cotton.

The Talooks of Purrunderpour & Omdarrah[3] are called Purgannahs likewise. The first borders on Cuttungah and the latter on Cootubpour. NB.—The Purgannah of Futtypour* & Jem^y.[4] of Burkoondah lie in the midst of Birbohen.

* Belonging to Radshi.

The general Dimension of Birbohen is 64 miles by 36 & contains 2304 square miles or Beagers[5] 4,605,440. The Arable Land may be reckoned 646 sq. miles or Beagers 1,250,656.

From Agra to Delhy.[6]

	Miles.
To Jundipour	10
Mootra (Muttra)	8
Chautra	10
Hoorhul	12
Pulwall	12
Furreezabad	12
Delhi	12

1 Maureshwar Dari, divided into two portions by pargana Mallarpur. 146·60 sq. miles.

2 Swarupsinh. 85·35 sq. miles

3 Purandarpur. 13·79 sq. miles. Omdarrah is not mentioned by Hunter or shown on the Atlas of India.

4 Jemitdary, a corruption of Zemindary, an estate.

5 Hind. *Bigha.* A measure of land area, varying greatly in different parts of the country. In Birbhum it was about one-third of an acre. The present area of the district is 1752 sq. miles, of which 1056 sq. miles are cultivated.

6 These places are shown on map No. X. of the Bengal Atlas. The road runs along the right bank of the Jumna.

Note.—The weather table that follows covers the period of Rennell's third expedition and is referred to on p. 44.

referred to on p. 44.

MAY 1765. Dacca & ye Baramputrey.

D.	Winds. AM.	Winds. PM.	Weather.
R.1	Var. ..	....	Fine W^r. all day. Ev. close. Some Rain in ye Night.
2 3 4	Wind in ye Morning from ye NE, ye rem. of ye day W & SW.		Remarkable fine Weather.
5	W ..	....	Weather very hot all day.
R.6	Squall ..	W ..	Morning very hot. At Noon squally & rainy.
R.7	Variable	....	Much Rain.
R.8	S. SSE	Var^e. SE	Much Rain. At Night a hard Gale at SE.
R.9	SSW. S.	W. S.	Morning cool. Afternoon hard Squall & Rain.
10	SE ..	NBE Var^e.	Morning dry. At Noon hard Gales SE. Aft. & Night squally. No Rain.
11	S. SE ..	NNW ..	Fresh Gales. At 10 PM a Squall.
12	SW ..	SSW ..	Fresh G. & Cloudy. Dry W^r.
13	SSW. SW	WSW ..	Mostly fresh Gales.
14	SSW ..	SBE. S ..	Weather as yesterday.
R.15	SE. S ..	Calm ..	Morning cool. Aft. very hot.
16	S. Calm ..	Calm ..	Excessive hot all day.
17	Var^e. &	Calm ..	Mostly excessive hot.
18	Calm SSW.	Var^e. & Squally.	Morning drizling Rain Aft. close & sultry. R.
19	NE	ENE ..	Heavy Rain. R.
20	Var^e. from NE to East.		Flying Showers, Wind fresh. R.
21	SE. S.	SSW. SW.	This day a hard Gale var. as p. margin. R.
22	SW SSW	NNW Squall.	Fresh Breezes all Day. At Night a slight Squall. R.
23	SBE ..	SE ..	Much Rain. R.
24	SEBS ..	SE ..	Very fresh Gales. Dry W^r.
25	SSW	SE	Fresh Gales & cool Weather.
26	SE. E^t...	SSE ..	Cool Weather. Very Cloudy.
27	SE S NE	S SSE	Morning fair. At Noon Squall from ye NE & Rain. R.
28	NE SE	Calm Var.	Forenoon cool & Cloudy. Aft. & Ev. very hot.
29	S SE	Calm ..	Forenoon cool. Aft. & Night very hot.
30	Calm ..	SW Calm	Morning Foggy. Sultry Weather.
31	SE Calm	Calm SSW	Morning Foggy. All day very hot.

Rain 13 Days in May.
8 Days very hot Weather.

JUNE 1765, Baramputrey.

D.	Winds. AM.	Winds. PM.	Weather.
1	Calm ..	NE Calm NNE.	Morning Foggy till 7. Most of the day very hot. Night cool.
R.2	ESE ..	Calm NE	Mostly cool W^r^. At Noon Rain.
R.3	Calm S	NW NW. SW.	Mostly cool. Ev. much Thunder & Lightning, Rain Night.
4	SE ..	SEbE ..	Fresh Breezes & Cloudy.
5	SE ..	ESE ..	Mostly fresh Breezes & cool.
6	SE. SSE	S ..	Forenoon cool. Aft. very hot. A fine Night.
R.7	Calm SSE	Squall SE	Morning Foggy. Much Rain in y middle of y day.
8	SE ..	SE ..	Fresh Breezes. Cool Weather.
9	SE SSE	SBE ..	Fresh Breezes & frequently squally.
10	SBE ..	to S. ..	Very fresh Gales. Cool Wea^r^.
R.11	Calm NE ENE.	East ESE	Rain during the greatest part of the Day.
R.12	East ..	ESE .. Calm	Much Rain.
R.13	East ESE	SW NNE.	Forenoon rainy, the Aft. variable Weather.
R.14	ESE ..	ESE S	The Day fair. At 10 Night began Rain, & a stiff Gale.
15	ESE ..	SE ..	Rain all ye Forenoon. R.
16	East ESE	SE Calm	Cloudy & cool Weather all Day. In ye Evening some Rain. R.
17	SE ..	SEBS ..	Squally & Rainy all Day. R.
18	SE to ..	EBS ..	Fresh Breezes with frequent Showers. R
19	ESE EBS	SEBE ..	Rainy Morning, a fresh Gale of Wind. R.
20	ESE	SE ..	Fine Weather.
21	N NNW Calm	Calm ..	Some Rain in ye Morning, the rem^r^. of the Day calm, the Weather fine R.
22	SE SBE	NBE ..	Fine Weather all Day.
23	S SBE Calm.	ENE Calm.	Forenoon fine Weather. Afternoon very hot. Some Rain in ye Night. R.
24	SE East	EBN ..	Morning & Night rainy. Mid. of the Day cool. R.
25	ESE ..	SE. SSE	Rain the most part of the Day. R.
26	S. ..	SSE ..	Rain half of the Day Wind moderate. R.
27	S. ..	SEBS ..	Pleasant Weather.
28	ESE East	SSE ..	Much Rain during the Forenoon. R.
29	S. ..	SSE SE	Thick Cloudy Weather all Day.
30	WBS S SE	SE ..	The Morning Hot. The rem^r^. of the Day rainy. R.

19 rainy Days in June.

JULY 1765, Baramputrey.

D.	Winds. AM.	Winds. PM.	Weather.
R. 1	SSE	SE	Most part of the Day rainy, the Night also.
R. 2	ENE / Calm	NEBE / SSE.	Thick Cloudy Weather with some Showers.
3	S / SE	SSE / Calm	Cloudy. Mid. of ye Day hot, y remr. pleasant Wr.
R. 4	SSE to	ESE	Much Rain.
R. 5	SE / SSE	NBE to S	Several heavy Showers.
R. 6	SE / Calm	SE	Most part of the Day heavy Rain.
R. 7	SE	SSE	Rain great part of ye Day.
R. 8	SSE	SE	Hard Rain in ye Morning & several Showers aft.
R. 9	SE	S / SSE	Much Rain, Wind modt.
R. 10	S to	SE	Morn. & Ev. rainy. Mid. of ye Day pleast. Wr.
R. 11	SE / Calm	SSE	Morn. rainy. Most part of ye Day Fair. Rain all Night. Squall fr. ye SSE.
R. 12	SSE / SE	Calm	Forenoon rainy. Clear Aft. & Night.
R. 13	SE / Calm	SSE	Forenoon rainy. Aft. & Ev. fair. Rain in y Night.
R. 14	SE / Et.	ESE	Pleasant Wr. all Day. At Night Rain. & a Squall from ye ESE.
R. 15	SE	SE	Mostly fresh Breezes. Only one Shower this Day. Some Rain in ye Night.
R. 16	Et. / SE	SSE	Morning & Ev. rainy. ye remr. of the Day fair. Wind fresh.
17	SE / ESE	Et. / SEBE	Forenoon Wind squally, ye Weather dry till 8 PM, then some heavy Rain. R
18	ESE / Et.	EBN / Et.	Fresh Breezes, some Rain in ye Forenoon. Aft. fair. R.
19	Et. / EBS	SE	Morning ye air cool. During ye Forenoon some Rain. Rain in ye Night. R.
20	EBS / SE	ESE	Morning fair. Wind very cool. Much Rain in ye Forenoon. R.
21	SEBE.	ESE / Calm	All Day fresh Gales, & some flying Showers. Night calm. R.
22	SE	BE	Very fresh Breezes. Fine Weather.
23	ESE / SE	Calm	Forenoon fresh Breezes. Aft. calm & hot. Clear Wr.
24	SE	Calm	Mod. Wind with Showers. Aft. quite calm. Fair Night. R.
25	Calm / NBW.	N / Calm SE.	Forenoon Calm, hot Wr. at Noon a Breeze NBE. All Night fresh Gales.
26	ESE / East	EBS	A hard Gale all Day at EBS. & ESE. Much Rain. R.
27	SEBE / SE	ESE	Squally & Rainy all Day. R.
28	SSE / SE / SEBE	SE	Morning clear, the remr. Squally & Rainy. R.
29	SE / SBW	S / SSE	Fresh Gales & Squally. Much Rain. R
30	SSE	SBW	Very Squally & Rainy all Day. R.
31	S / SBE	SBW	Weather nearly as yesterday. R.

27 rainy Days in July.

BEARINGS AND DISTANCES.

From Culpee[1] to Ninedally near Badutolah Point	...	... N 4-15 E. 30·75
Do	& Gowreepour Bridge[2]	.. E 30-30 N. 13·1
Do.	& Hadgigunge	.. E 33-25 N. 113
Do.	& Luckipour	.. E 39-15 S. 67·9
Do.	& Jurilgunge[3]	.. E 7-10 S. 48·4
Do.	& Islamabad R. Mouth[4]	.. S 24 E. 48·2

Nudya to Pattolee[5]	..	..	23
Augurdeep	..	..	32½
Cutwa	..	..	42½
Plassy	..	..	62
Satti	..	..	82½
Meeneasa	..	..	95
Cossimbazar	..	..	105
Saddekbaag	..	..	118½
Bellya	..	..	130
Jungip^r^.	..	..	148
Sooty	..	..	157½
Ganges	..	..	163

Jel(enghee) to Sooty—

Bagwangola		..	38
Meenkoot		..	45
Sooty	..	..	61½

---

[1] A village on the Hugli 8 miles below Diamond Harbour. A road is shown on Rennell's map of the Hugli. No. XIX Bengal Atlas), running north to Calcutta. Ninedally and Badutolah Point are not marked on Rennell's map of the Hughli (Bengal Atlas No. XIX) and I have not been able to identify them.

[2] Near Dum-Dum.

[3] On the road from Lakshmipur to Chittagong.

[4] Mouth of the Karnuphuli R.

[5] This list is entered in pencil.

ASIATICK RIVERS.[1]

	°Lat.	Length of Course.
Kian Kew (China)	73	38
Hoanho do.	67	34
Amur do.	28	19
Cambodia	26	
Ava	24	
Ganges	24	
Burrampooter	24	
Indus	14	
Lena	29	
Wolga	24	
Oby	26	
Jennisea	25	
Euphrate	21	
Africa.		
Nile	32	
Europe.		
Danube	17	
Rhine	6½	
America.		
Amazons	69	
Missisipi	40	

[1] This list was evidently the basis of the calculation of the proportionate lengths of course of some of the most noted rivers of the world given in Rennell's 'Memoir of Hindoostan.' p. 337.

The list as given there runs—

European rivers—

Thames	1
Rhine	5¼
Danube	7
Wolga	9½

Asiatic rivers—

Indus (probably)	6¾
Euphrates	8½
Ganges	9½
Burrampooter	9½
Nou Kiau or Ava river	9½
Jennisea	10
Oby	10½
Amoor	11
Lena	11½
Hoanho (of China)	13½
Kian Keu (of ditto)	15½

African river—

Nile	12½

American rivers—

Missisipi	8
Amazons	15¾

MEMORANDUMS FROM THE FIELD BOOKS.

Purgunnahs in ye Rangamatty Phousdary[1]—

Currybarry.	Beesnee.	Julkur.
Burrahazary.	Batyamarry.	Turya.
Measpara.	Solaā	Guredalaa.
Hobberagott.	Biddagong.	Saappour or Chawppour.
Bickally (Garrows)	Purbutjoär.	Patyladaw.
(Chief Place Ombue).[2]	Jammyra.	Saupour (Descouya).

Other Places (or Gotts)[3] belonging to Rangamatty,
Allumgunge, Tombacubary, Jeekeer.

Dewangunge is in the purgunna of Jaffiersee.[4]
Chilmary in Baharbund.

Pora Doar,[5] a Place in Boutan lying to ye NE of Catchubary.

Sackatee in Assam 1 day E 15 S from Commerputa.[6]
Guahatty in ye Assam Countrey on ye Baramputrey, 3 Days by Pulwar from Gwalpara.

6 Rajas under the K. of Assam. Revenues of ye Bisnee Raja 6,000 Rup. P. Ann. He pays an Annual Tribute of 60 Elephants to ye Bengall Nabob.[7]

Cobytukan a Chokey 1½ par above Mallansa, & near ye Village of Sunederdee. Nagarabara Purg.[8]

Ombue Hills from Commerputa E 30-30 S. 36 miles.

1 Faujdari, a district under a military governor. Rangamati was the frontier district bordering on Assam, now the Goalpara district. Most of the 'parganas' of Rennell are now permanently settled estates under various Rajas or Zemindars. The following are those mentioned in the District Gazetteer of Goalpara published in 1905:—

Karaibari.	Parbatjoar.
Mechpara.	Jamira.
Habraghat.	Taria.
Bijni.	Chapar.

2 Ombue probably stands for Um Bu (Um, Khasi=water), a small stream in the Khasia hills.

3 A landing place or 'Ghat.' Often applied to a river-side village.

4 On the Bengal Atlas map No. V the Pargana in which Dewanganj (on the Brahmaputra below Chilmari) is situated is called Patladah. now the Patiladaha estate.

5 Perhaps Paro, the head-quarters of the Paro Penlop, in Western Bhutan (Lat. 27°-23'; Long. 89°-27').

6 Kamarpota and Shakhati were both villages on the frontier line of Assam, the former lying on the Brahmaputra. Gauhati is now an important place. A day's march in Assam is considered to be from 10 to 12 miles.

7 The Imp. Gaz. states that under Moghul rule the Raja of Bijni paid a *tribute* of Rs. 5,998, afterwards commuted to an annual delivery of 68 elephants. The estimated rent-roll of the estates at present is 2 lakhs of rupees.

8 These villages were across the frontier of Assam on the south bank of the river. For the definition of 'par' see p. 127.

The Bisnee Rajah's Residence at Bisnee on the R. Bonaash 2½ days by Boat from Jugygupa. 1 Day by Land. Catchubary in Boutan from Jugygupa 2½ days Land. Sering 1 day farther. Aāndypour the Thibet Rajah's Residence 2 days from Sering. In all 5½ days from Jugygupa. Rajah's Name Mocun-Naran. Roco-Cotta a Place on the Bonaash 4 days up from Jugygupa.[1]

Rangamatty & Cutchubary 2 days by Land.

Howeragott on the Keestry River 2 Par from Gwalpara.

Deelma a Garrow's Town 1½ Day from Howeragott.[2]

Commerputa & Howeragott 1 Day.

RIVER PASSAGE FROM CALCUTTA UPWDS.

	Calcutta[3]—	M.	
	To Ghyretty	17	¼
	Chinsurah	8	
	Hoogly	2	
	Niaserai	7	½
	Chogdah	7	
	Puleeah Haut	14	½
	Culna	12	
82¼	Nuddeah	14	
	Kistnagur	10	¼
	Rookpour Creek	15	
	Taegaree	12	½
	Putimary	10	½
	Notyputah	13	
	Ballitunghee	12	¼
	Buxypour	5	
	Peeapour	15	¼
	Boyrub Creek	15	
117	Head Jellinghee	8	¼
	Head Surda Reach.. ..	12	½
	Cutlamary opposite Bowlia	9	
	Bogwangolah	17	
	Meenkoot	7	¼
62½	Head Coss^r. River.. ..	16	¾
261¾			

	M.	
To Nuddea as before— ..	82	¼
Augurdeep[4]	33	
Cutwa	10	¼
Plassey	20	
Satty	21	½
Jumjumcolly	16	¼
Cossimbazar	6	½
Saddekbary	13	
Bellyah	16	¼
Jungipour	17	
Sooty	10	
Head R.[5]	4	¾
	250	¾
	261	¾
Difference	11	
Furrookabad[6]	24	
Oudinulla	11	¼
Raujimol[7]	7	
Sielygully	18	½
Terriagully	11	¾
Pointee	8	
Colgong	18	
Boglipour (Bhagalpur) ..	17	¼
Sultanp^r.	18	

[1] None of these places are marked on the Atlas of India Maps, but Wandipur (Aandypour) is mentioned as one of the chief towns in Bhutan in the Imp. Gazetteer. The relations of the British with Bhutan did not arise till 1772, six years after the date of Rennell's visit to Goalpara (*see* Memoir of Hindoostan, pp. 301, 302).

[2] Howeragot (Habraghat) village is shown on Rennell's Bengal Atlas No. V, 10 miles S. of Goalpara Neither village nor stream are marked in the Atlas of India, but Dilma (Deelma) is shown in the Garo Hills 22 miles S. of Goalpara.

[3] *Via* the Jalangi R. [4] *Via* the Baghrathi.

[5] Junction of the Bhagirathi and Ganges.

[6] Up the Ganges from the head of the Bhagirathi. [7] Another spelling of Rajmahal.

	M.	
Monghir	26	
Sur(agegurra)	19	
Ruinulla	8	½
Der(riapour)	14	
Bahr	21	
Bykuntpour	24	
Patna	14	
	260	¼

	260¼
	261¾
Miles ..	522

Moneah[1] .. ..
Buxar .. ..
Gazypour .. ..
Benares .. ..
Chunar .. ..
Merzapour .. ..
Mouth Townse R. .. ..
Ellahabad .. ..

Calcutta to Dacca—

To Head Jellinghee[2]	199	¼
Horrisongkor (Harisankra)[3] ..	9	
Chocula	10	
Shaapour	14	½
Comitpour	11	¾
Custee (Kushtia)	6	
Pubna	8	½
Boolbaryah Creek	23	
Soondry	19	
Rottingunge	8	¾
To the Ganges	5	¼
Jaffiergunge	6	¾
Comercally	7	
Gwalparah	7	¾
Pialapour	12	
Saapour	14	
Callyteer Creek	7	¼
Dacca	11	½
Miles ..	382	¼

Dacca to Gwalparah[3]—	M.	
Demrah	14	
Molaparah	5	
Jamalpour	20	
Akedallah (Ekdala) ..	8	½
Saghordee	17	
Dugdugga	12	
Callygunge	22	
Cassergunge	11	
Bygonbarry (or Maimansingh)..	7	
Pykerhaut	17	
Sanashygunge	13	
Dewangunge	22	
Chilmary	20	
Baggoa	20	
Arrya-curyah	11	¼
Dubarye	19	
Rangamatty Gaut.. ..	11	
Jughigupah	34	
Gwalparah	5	¼
Miles ..	289	

To Meercaserai[4]—	11-4
Seetacoon	12-4
Cuddumrusil	13-4
Islamabad (Chittagong) ..	12
	49-4

Dacca to Luckipour[5]—		
Fattylur	6	¼
Fringybazar	7	½
Rajabarry	14	
Chandpour	11	
Luckipour	28	½
	67	¼

1 These distances are not entered in the original text.

2 Down the Ganges to Pabna, through the Ichamati R. to Jafarganj, and then along the Dhaleswari to Dacca.

3 Up the Lakhmia R. and along the old Brahmaputra to Dewanganj.

4 From the crossing of the Fenny R. east of Lakshmipur.

5 Down the Meghna.

Dacca to Silhet[1]—	M.
Fringybazar	13 ¾
Allynya	14 ½
Gagatyah	18 ½
Corallya	17
Gusipour	11 ½
Sunerampour	8 ½
Cottilbar	18
Lacki	11
Allipour	19 ½
Azmerigunge	8
Moradpour	11 ½
Momadnuggur	11
Currimgunge (Karimganj)	3 ¾
Gussyah	16
Jummulabad	16
Solagur	21
Pannyle	16 ¾
Chattuck	8 ½
Digley	12
Silhet	18 ½
	275

Distances from Luckipour to the Fenny.[2]

	M.	F.	P.
To the Nulla	4	0	29
To Hazarypara	8	1	5
Chandergunge	2	5	12
Currimpour	7	1	19
Colinda (Kaliyandi)	7	5	5
Little Fenny	8	2	14
Cassidya Haat	0	5	8
Meerjapour Bazar	4	7	5
To ye Fenny	2	7	39
	46	4	16

Here follow some arithmetical calculations in pencil, now almost indecipherable.

LATITUDES.

	°	′
From Ironside.—Calcutta	22	33 N
Chinsera	22	53
Burdwan	23	11
Cossimbazar	24	4
Muxadabad	24	11
Nabobgunge	24	29
Goah	24	35
English Bazar[3]	24	53
Maulda	24	55
Purneah	25	40
Modduban[4] (the end of my Survey, *sup. Capt. Adams's*)	25	41
N.B.—Campbell's[5] Map—		
Ellah(*abad*)	25°	25′
Ben(*ares*)	25	17
Pat(*na*)	25	37

[1] By the Burigunga, Little Meghna, Meghna and Surma rivers.

[2] See pages 75 to 78 of journal.

[3] Near Malda.

[4] I cannot identify this place.

[5] ? Donald Campbell, Captain of a cavalry regiment in the service of the Nawab of the Carnatic, and author of 'A journey overland to India, comprehending his shipwreck and imprisonment with Hyder Alli, and his subsequent negociations and transactions in the East" (London, Cullen & Co., 1795).

LONGITUDE OF PLACES FROM D'ANVILLE'S MAP.[1]

	Place		°	′
	Cape Comorin	From Paris Et.	94	45
	Pt. Din		87	18
	Bombay		89	25
	Delhi		94	55
	Corragenabad		97	40
	Pt. de Galle, Ceylon		97	48
	Pondicherri		97	25
	Agra		95	45
	Madras		98	3
	Allahabad (Iliabad, Helobas)		99	..
	Pt. Gordeware		100	10
	Benaras		100	18
	Pt. Palmiras		104	45
	Patna		102	18
	Muxadabat		105	53
	Calcutta		106	5
Corrected .. 108 5	Dacca		107	20
109 41	Islamabad		108	34
	Great Andaman middle		109	30
	S. Nicobar I.		110	55
	Negrais		111	..
	P. Ronda near Achien		112	18
	Ava		114	18
	P. Pinang (Str. Malacca)		116	18
	Siam City (or India)		118	30

OBSERVATIONS OF LATITUDE & VARIATION OF THE NEEDLE 1764, 1765.

Time Observed.		Places' Names.	E. Variatn. °	′	W. Variatn. °	′	Latitude N. °	′
1764.								
May	13	Negareen Jelenghee R.	3	3				
	21	Jelenghee R. Head..	..	..				
	27	Silah, Ganges	..	36				
June	3	Jawnpour near Custee	1	8				
	28	Serampour in ye Chunnunah	..	54				
October	1	Rottingunge	..	..	1	..		
	3	Gondaëly	.	..	1	10		
	16	Coberpour	..	..	1	2		
	20	Jattapour	..	..	..	38	23	27
	23	Seneckondy	..	..	..	16		
Novemr.	10	Pokera	..	..	1	6		
	16	Rypour	..	..	..	55		
	25	Nagulpara	..	..	1	10		
	27	Monerpour	..	..	1	..		
Decemr.	28	Kesserpour	..	..	1	14		
1765.								
Jany.	21	Daadpour I. Megna	..	..	1	7		
Feb.	8	Luckypour	..	..	.	..	22	55
May	13	Allynya in ye Megna	..	..	..	37		

[1] D'Anville's map of India was produced in 1752. All the figures given are much too far East.

Time Observed.		Places' Names.	E. Variat^{n}.		W. Variat^{n}.		Latitude N.		
			°	′	°	′	°	′	
Feb.	9	Solacally Creek Megna *Omitted in Place*	..	..	1	30			
June	22	Ossunpour	..	..	..	38			
July	21	Chilmary	..	..	..	..	25	25	Medium of ye last 2 observ^{s}. 25-27.
	23	do.	..	..	..	..	25	28	
	25	do.	..	..	..	..	25	26	
Octo^{r}.	25	Sunacalley	..	..	..	32	..	..	
	18	Bolasa	..	..	..	..	23	52	
	23	Osuupour	..	..	..	..	24	26	
	25	Bagunbary	..	..	..	..	24	45	
	28	Cuttermary	..	..	..	58	..	..	
	29	Dewangunge	..	..	..	55	..	..	
	30	1½ mile N. of the Parallel of do.	..	..	..	..	25	11	
Nov^{r}.	7	⊙[1] Above Baggua	..	..	..	..	25	43	30
		Near do.	..	..	..	46	..	..	
	21	Same Place	..	..	..	51	..	..	
	..	Chilmary 4th. Observation ..	..	..	..	..	25	29	
	28	Soatterpour near Gwalpara ..	..	..	..	52	..	..	
	25	⊙ 100 near Rangamatty ..	..	..	..	..	26	4	

			Lat.	N.	
			°	′	″
Dec.	18	Beejurah .	26	24	..
	23	Japarachor near Rangamatty.	26	2	30
	24	⊙ 2 near Bagolamarry	26	6	..
	25	Dheer Hill ..	26	8	45
	27	⊙ 14 opp. Chanduchoar	25	51	15
	28	⊙ 22 opposite to Cossabatcha.	25	41	15
1766.					
Jan^{y}.	4	At Gurygong Factory	25	46	45
	22	Nabobgunge ..	25	43	..
	23	Gungepour ..	25	46	30
	24	Jaffiergunge ..	25	48	30
	25	Bambund ..	25	55	45
	26	Banchdaw ..	25	58	45
	27	Dam: Choc: ..	26	5	..
	28	Dewangunge ..	26	5	30
	29	Curume ..	26	8	30
	30	Taledar ..	26	16	30

1766.			Lat.	N.	
			°	′	″
Feb^{y}...	4	Sanashygotta ..	26	32	30
	5	⊙ 32 near ye Ballasun	26	29	30
	6	⊙ 49 Dulelly ..	26	22	..
	10	⊙ 23 Balagury ..	26	4	30
	11	⊙ 38 ...	26	4	..

N.B.—All ye above Latitudes want 50″ allow^{ce}. for Refraction so that they should be 50″ more N.

1767.					
Nov...	25	Lat. Baggoa Hadleys Qud^{t}. wth. refraction ..	25	41	22
		Land Qud^{t}. ..	25	39	15
		Var. new Theod^{e}. ..	..	12	Wt.
		Foot Isl^{d}. below Gwareea ..	23	26	..
		Calcutta ..	22	32	30

[1] ⊙ Is the usual field note-book sign for a surveying 'station.'

MEMORANDUMS.

A Coss of Indistan[1]

1760) 4000 (2·480 yds. or
3520
——
480

2¼ miles nearly.

200 yards—1 Zarieb.
20 Zariebs—1 Coss.
————
4,000 yd. in a Coss (Capt. Polier).

Ganges rises 30 feet Perpendicular in ye Rains, measured at Jelenghee.

Boats 20 days from Patna to Jelenghee.

No Coconut Trees (or very few) on ye Banks on ye Ganges.[2]

Price of Calcutta Boats

of 90 Maund. Hire pr. Month.

4 Dandies	.. 12
1 Mangy[3]	.. 4

Variation of ye Needle near Negarin in ye Jelenghee 3°-3′ East by Knight's Compass.

Rising of ye Rivers* in ye Rains.

1764				
May 19th.	..	1¾	Cubits	Jelenghee.
,, 29th.	..	3	Cubits	Sappour.
June 4th.	..	4	do.	Custee.

*Jelenghee & Ganges.

From Mr.————'s Journal. Entered Channell Creek 7th. March. Came to Sewtylewry 25th. do. May 19th, left Hobbygunge, the 20th. entered the Puddaw,[4] Came thro' Rottingunge & Pubna Creeks.

From Maudapour to Boostna or Goostney 3 days by the Chunnunah & Comer Creeks. In ye dry Season only Boats of 100 Maund can go from Maudapour to Boostna.[5]

---

1 Originally Sansc. '*krosa*', a call, the distance to which a man's call could be heard. It varies much in different parts of the country, but is generally taken to be about two miles (Hobson Jobson. p. 261). For a discussion of the length of the Coss, *see* Rennell 'Memoir of Hindustan,' p. 4, and note, p. 151.

2 There are cocoanut plantations in many parts of East Bengal, and the tree ascends both the Ganges and Brahmaputra to a considerable distance.

3 Manjhi, the headman or steersman of a boat.

4 The Padma or Padda is the name given to the main channel of the Ganges from the head of the delta to its conflux with the Meghna. The route taken was the southern route through the Sunderbuns. The name of the traveller is not given.

5 Maudapur was at the head of the Chandua (Chunnunah) river, and Bhushna on the Barasia, a little to the east of Muhammadpur. In the Bengal Atlas, No. 1, it is shown due north of the latter town.

Boats of 3500 Maund loaded, draw	..	4½	Cubits.
300	.. ..	2½ & 2	,,

From Moanpour in ye Chunmunah Creek to Hobbygunge by Land 4 days, Culna 7 do.

*Silet River is called ye little Megna.

*This means ye Creek leading from Corallya to Allynya; ye Silet R. being called the Surma.

Dimensions of ye great Gun at Dacca [1]—

			Feet	I.	
Diameter at Muzzle		.. ..	3	1	
Do.	Breech	.. ..	3	2½	61,673 lb.
Do.	of ye Trunnions	..		11½	or Tons 27 9.
Do.	of ye Bore	.. ..	1	3½	
Length		.. ..	22	6	Wt. of Shot 474 lb.

H. Water at Dacca full & change nearly VII½ Hours.

---

1 Further particulars of this gun are given in Rennell's 'Memoir of Hindustan,' p. 61. "It was made of hammered iron; it being an immense tube formed of 14 bars, with rings of 2 or 3 inches wide driven over them, and hammered down into a smooth surface; so that its appearance was equal to that of the best executed piece of brass ordnance. although its proportions were faulty.

Whole length	.. ..	22 ft. 10½	inches.
Diameter at the Breech ..	..	3 ,, 3	,,
,, 4 feet from the Muzzle ..		2 ,, 10	,,
,, the Muzzle	..	2 ,, 2½	,,
,, of the Bore	..	1 ,, 3½	,,

The gun contained 234,413 cubic inches of wrought iron; and consequently weighed 64,814 pounds avoirdupois or about the weight of eleven 32 pounders. Weight of an iron shot for the gun 465 pounds."

The dimensions and weight vary somewhat from those given in the text, but the entry in the Journal was probably merely a rough note.

Rennell further remarks that the gun "has since fallen into the river, together with the bank on which it rested."

I have been supplied by my friend Mr. H. E. Stapleton of the Educational Dept. with particulars of the great gun now preserved at the Chauk (an open place in the middle of the city) at Dacca, whence it is appears that this is not the one described by Rennell. The dimensions of the existing gun are quite different, being:—

Length	.. ..	11 ft. 0 ins.
Diameter at Muzzle	..	1 ,, 7½ ,,
,, ,, Breech	..	2 ,, 3 ,,
,, of Bore	..	0 ,, 6 ,,

Mr. Stapleton has also kindly sent me a translation of a passage in the Tarikh-i-Nusratjaugi, published in 1908 by Babu Harinath Dé (Memoirs, As. Soc. Beng., Vol. II, No. 6) confirming the statement of Major Rennell that one of the guns had been lost in the river, and giving some account of their history. The translation runs:—"The big cannon which was placed at Sowari Ghat and the other cannon which, together with two big cannon balls, went down into the water at Mughlani Char, were built for the purpose of training the soldiers of the Khankhanan Mouzzim Khan (*circa* 1660) in their handling, and also for serving as a protection against danger. * * * * * In 1246 A.H. (1830-31 A.D.) Mr. Walters the Magistrate had the cannon at the Sowari Ghat taken away from there and placed in the Chauk."

There is another big gun at Murshidabad, the dimensions of which are nearly the same as those of the one now at Dacca. An inscription in this states that it was made in the reign of Shah Jahan and governorship of Islam Khan (*circa* 1637) at Jahangirnagar (Dacca) by Janarjan blacksmith (Cal. Rev., Vol. XCIV, p. 339).

Different Quality of y^e^ Strata, of Soil in y^e^ neighbourhood of Jelenghee River.[1]

1st.	..	$1\frac{1}{2}$ feet	Fine Mould.
2d.	..	2 ,,	Brown Heavy Sand.
3d.	..	$1\frac{1}{2}$,,	Light Sandy Earth.
4th.	..	$1\frac{1}{2}$,,	Clayish Earth.
5th.	..	$1\frac{1}{2}$,,	Stiff Clay.

A Boat of 4,000 Maund seen in y^e^ Chunnunah Creek drew $4\frac{3}{4}$ Cubits Water. Burthen in Tons 141, Dra^t^. in Feet 6^F^ 10^I^.

May 10th. 1764. A small Nulla at Chogdah (in Hugghly R.) not inserted in y^e^ Map.

June 4th. Chain measured at Jamalpour & found 6 inches too long.

Septr. 1st. Chain measured at Dacca found 8.5 In. too long or 56^F^. 8^I^. in an Eng. Mile[2].

Mem^d^. The Waters at Dacca at their greatest Height the 15th. of Septr. 1765. They did not rise above a Cubit from ye beginning of August to that Time.

In ye year 1764, the Waters were fallen more than 3 Cubits ye 19th. September.

Berrisgunge from Jelenghee	..	..	5 Coss.
Chocculo do.	..	..	13 ,,
Custee from Calcutta	..	..	6 days by Land.
Culna from Custee	..	..	10 days, Boat.
Comercalli from Custee	..	..	8 Coss.
Jaynagore from Custee, by way of y^e^ Creek		..	8 days Boat.
Mola[3] from Hadgygunge	..	..	1 day by Boat.
Dacca	..	..	3 do.
Jelenghee	..	..	3 do.
Pubna	..	..	1 do.
Paunchiferra	..	..	2 do.
Jelenghee	..	..	3 do.
Do. by Land	..	..	$1\frac{1}{2}$
Jochillampour & Maudapour	..	..	6 Coss.

Noatchygonga Name of y^e^ R. from Rungpour to Jaffiergunge.[4]

Bummisore Nuddy do. y^e^ Creek from y^e^ great River to do.

Corattygonga do. from Bummisore tow^d^. Dacca.

[1] This is the only geological section in the Journal. It is of interest only as showing what such an acute observer as Rennell might have done in this way, if his opportunities had been greater.

[2] *See* Introduction, p. 4.

[3] Mola, a small village on the Ganges above the mouth of the Chandna R. All these places are on or near the Ganges Padma. Most of them are mentioned in the Journal of the first Expedition.

[4] The lower channel of the Karatoya R.

Allachypour,[1] & Mullopara pour.[2]
Coratcally. Name of ye Creek from Saleenagore to Hadgygunge.

Hadgygunge from	Connipour ..	..	1½ par. by Land.
	Hobbygunge ..	..	1 day Boat.
	To do. & then to Jaynagore		1½ do.
	Jaynagore ..	..	½ day Cossid.[3]
	Connipour ..	..	1½ pour do.
	Hobbygunge, Land	..	1½ or 2 days.

Creek from Mousudabad[4] to Dacca dry in ye Month of November—

Mongulcundy & Rajanagore ..	..	1 day.
Amidabads[5] E. from Luckypour ..	..	1¾ Land.
Hadgygunge	..	3 pour.

Jattypour Octo. 20th. 1764. ⊙ Mer. Alt. 55°-48′[6]
Height above ye level of ye W. 5½ feet.

Bromgumge to Seibgunge	..	..	5 or 6 hours Land.
Comerpour }	from Hobbygunge	..	2 pour. } Land.
Bickerampr. Purg.[7] }	Luckypour	..	1½ day. } Land.
Gonganagore I.[8] }	from Luricool	..	1½ pour.
Amidabad }	Rajanagore	..	4 hours.
Rypour from Goanuddy	..	..	1½ pour Land.

Gozarya in ye Ganges[9] High Water full & change IX hours—
Soynary near do. ⊙ 55 saw a white Pagoda N 37°-45′ E.
Tyger I. south P^t^ a white Pagoda N 30°-15′ E. 3½′ or 4′.
Baramputry Point Decr. 5th. at Noon ⊙ Mer. Alt. 44°-33′.
Height of ye Eye 5 foot.

Little B. Gunge[10] H. Water full & change 4^h^ 45′.
Conederopour } Jungle Island } do. 5 hours.

Litt. B. Gunge opposite ye Creek, Tide ran to ye Southward at 10′ past 11 h. Moon ½ day old.

[1] Elaichipur, opposite Goalundo. [2] For definition of pour or par *see* p. 127.
[3] Arab. *kasid*, a courier or running messenger (Hobson Jobson, p. 262). Connipour is on the Kumar R. west of Hajiganj.
[4] On the Ganges opposite Hajiganj.
[5] Ahmirabads of map No. 1 in the Bengal Atlas; a pargana of Noakhali District.
[6] *See* p. 29. Jattrapour of map XVI, Beng. Atlas.
[7] A pargana in the Dacca district.
[8] West of Rajanagar.
[9] A small island due S. of Rajanagar.
[10] Little Bakarganj, near the old conflux of the Ganges and Meghna.

Tarrachoar (in ye Creek bet. ye E. & W. Branches of ye Ganges) H. W^r . 9h.
Goanuddy, just above do. a small Creek to Basundra
Hautcola 4 hours.

Kalkenny Creek[1] from Hobbygunge 6 hours (false)
In 4 h. come into ye great R. by do. Creek.

Backergunge from Culna	..	3	days.
Sewtylewry	..	½	day.
Gubindapour	..	1	day.
Buckinagore	..	1½	days.

Luckypour (Dec^r . 20th. 1764) ⊙ Mer. Alt. 43°-20′.
Height of ye Eye 6 foot.

Experiments for finding ye distances of ye Bengall Par or Pour.[2]

Medium Pour 5½ Eng. Miles Days Journey 22 E. Miles on a strait line, tho' nearly 25 by the Roads.	1½ Pour	7 British Miles.
	3 do.	15 ,, ,,
	6 do.	35 ,, ,,
	2 do.	9½ ,, ,,
	4 hours	3½ ,, ,,
	1½ pour	10¼ ,, ,,

Luckypour Feby. 4th. ⊙ Mer. Alt. 50°-47′.
Height of ye Eye 6 foot.
Lat. of Lukypour by a good 6bs. 22°-55′ N.

Chundergunge more than half-way from Luckypour to Colinda.

Serampour & Soylerhaut[3]	..	1	pour.
Cotalpour & Rajabarry	..	2	pour.
Golychel & do.	..	1½	do.
Noadda ⊙ 55 near it, Rajanagore		1½	do.
Chiddypour Mulputgunge[4]	..	½	a pour.
Rajanagore	..	2	pour.

Daadpour I. (Jan. 21st.) ⊙ Mag. Amp. at setting W. 20 30 S. Var^n . 1°-7′ W.

Moral Feringybazar	..	2 pour.
Comarya Chandpour	..	½ a day.
Nursingpour Luckypour	..	1 day Land.

Solacalley Creek Variation West^ly. 1°-30′.

1 A branch of the Kumar R. south of 'Hobbygunge.'

2 The Par (Hind. pahar) or Pour (Pahar, Pore, Pyte) is strictly a measure of time, equal to a fourth part of the day and of the night (Hobson Jobson, p. 736).

3 Across the neck dividing the old Ganges from the Meghna, S. of Rajabari.

4 On the old Kirtinasa R.

Mulputgunge	Rajanagore	. 1	pour.
	Rajabarry	..	do.
Sonergam[1]	from Kallagatchy	.. 1	pour.
Meercadim[2]	Nundakitchel	.. 3	Hours, land.
	Meergunge	.. 2	do.
	Mulputgunge	.. 3	pour.
	Dacca	.. 2	do.

Doarsanny[3]

near do. ⊙ 30 Saw	Rajabarry Pagoda W.	38-30 S.
	a sharp Pagoda	17-10—
	like another do.	10-54—

Allynya,[4] May 13th, Mag. Var^{n}. 0°-37′ West^{ly}.

Nishenpour to Dacca 1 day by Land.

Pobaregong to Sonergung	..	1 par SW.
Dacca	..	3 par.
Sheangacandy ⊙ 97	} To Ossunpour	2 par.
Lautangore to Dacca	..	1 day.
Osseetpour to Nursing	..	½ a par.[5]

Nursingdee Creek to ye Baramputrey .. 2 pour.

First Reach Baramputrey called ye Poggolah—

Chor-subadee & Nursing	..	1 pour.
Ouësalabo[6] & Dacca	..	2 days by Land.

Corallya. River[7] near it comes from Silet. Sujetpour lies 3 or 4 days up it. The Water of ye same Colour as that of ye Jeels. Called the Megna.

Toank[8] or Toak Banaar R. { Creek runs out of ye Baramputrey near it. The Creek soon after receives another from ye Baramputrey & afterwards falls into the Luckya River, Baugunbary 4 or 5 days up ye Creek, by Pulwar.

[1] Sonargaon was the ancient Mahomedan capital of Eastern Bengal, from 1351 to 1608, when the seat of Government was transferred to Dacca. (Hunter Stat. Acc. Beng., Vol. V, p. 71; List of Ancient Mon. Beng., p. 208) 'Kallagatchy' lies at the mouth of the creek connecting it with the Meghna, marked Burrampooter Cr. on Map No. XVII of the Beng. Atlas.

[2] Close to Firinghi bazar. [3] South of Rajanagar.

[4] Close to Daudkhandi at the mouth of the Little Meghna.

[5] These places are all on or near the Meghna above Dacca.

[6] A village on the Narsingdi creek N.E. of Dacca.

[7] The Titas R., draining the jhils of the Tippera District.

[8] Tok, a small village on the old Brahmaputra opposite Agarosindur. The Banar R. leaves the Brahmaputra above Maimansingh, at Baiganbari

Osunpour. From do. to Chilmary & Gwalpara—

		To Moddepour ..	..	1	day Et. side River.
		from do. to Cassergunge	..	1½	do. Et. side.
		to Bozerapour	..	1½	Wt. side.
	Dewangunge	to Dobagunge	..	1	Wt. side.
Baggua 1		to Chilmary	..	1½	do.
Chandchor 1	Dubarye	to Dowhly	..	2	do.
Rangt. 1		to Jagagupa	..	2	
Dudekoar 1		to Gwalpara	..	½	
Jugygupa 1					

Creek to Rangamatti runs out above Dowhly.

Sosongo Mountain opposite Chilmary.

Chandpour. ⊙ 31 near it. Sosongo Hill bore N. 5°-45′ Et. distant by Estimation 9 or 10 nautic Leagues.

Chornuddy Island. ⊙ 53 on ye N. side of it. Sosongo Peak N. 9°-30′ Et.

Seltya, Dacca from do.	..	3	days by Land.[2]
Borya & Buzerapour	..	2	days Land.

Assistant's Intelligence recd. down Dugduga Creek June 26th. & 28th.[3]

Habbetnagore a large Village.	To Banagong	..	5	Par or Pour.
	Lilliedapour	..	1	do.
	Asmarygunge	..	4	days.
	Akarasonda	..	3	do.
	Silet	..	5	do.
	Delolpour	..	3	do.

Junglebary[4] a large Village.	To Kanna Dugdugga	..	3	Par.
	Adampour	..	2	days (Water).
	do.	Land	1	day.
	Osunpour	..	1½	day.
	Asmarygunge	..	1½	do.
	Silet	..	7	do.

---

1 Kailas (3375 ft.), in the Garo Hills. The distance in a direct line from Chandpur is 145 miles.

2 On the bank of the old Brahmaputra, below Maimansingh.

3 The 'Dugduga' creek run into the old Brahmaputra near 'Ossunpour,' and connected that river with the Meghna (Map No. VI, Bengal Atlas). Habbetnagore is probably the Hybutnuggur, close to Kishorgunj, of Atlas of India Sheet 125 S.W.

4 Junglebary was on a branch of the same creek to the E. of 'Ossunpour.' Asmarygunge (Ajmirigunj) is a large trade centre in the Habigunj district, South Sylhet, on a branch of the Surma R.

Place	Route		Distance
Hazaradee.[1]	To Deroa	..	2 Hours.
	Kalpassa	..	4 do.
	Licklee	..	2 Par.
	Asmarygunge	..	2 Par.
	Akarasonda	..	1½ do.
	Adampour	..	2½ (Water).
Dellyapara.	To Assmere(gunge)	..	3 Par.
	Delolpour	..	3 do.
	Akarasonda	..	1 Day.
	Adampour	..	1 do. (Dingey).
	Abdulapour	..	Land 2 Par. Water 1 Day.
	Silet ..	..	6 Days.
Licklee. A Pagoda at that Place.	To the Megna	..	2 Par South.
	Baramputrey	..	2 do. S. 20° W.
	Adampour	..	Water 2 Days. Land 1½ Par W. 38° S.
	Abdulapour	..	2 Par S. 20° W.
	Firridpour This Creek falls into ye Baramputrey, then		1½ Par.
	Akarasonda	..	Land 3 Par.
	Asmarygunge	..	1 Day.

⊙ 34 R. Base of Mount^{n}.[2] E. 35 N.

Baganbarry. ⊙ 35 opposite to it. The Peak of Sosongo bore N. 40°-45′ E.

⊙ 39 Do. Mountain N. 35°-40′ E.

N.B.—At this ⊙ ye top of ye Peak was seen very distinctly.

The long Range of Mountains.[3]

L. Base	N. 9° W.
1st. L. Peak	4-40.
2d. do. the highest of all	2.
Round Hill	13-15 E.
⊙ 42 Sosongo	N. 32°-30′ E.
R. of all ye dist. Mountains seen[4] ..	E. 26° N.

Saampour. ⊙ at ye Hāāt Tree[5] of Saampour

Sosongo .. E. 21 N.

[1] Neither Hazaradee, Dellyapara, nor Licklee are marked on Rennell's maps.

[2] Probably Sosongo Hill or Kailas.

[3] The Tura Range of the Garo Hills. Highest peak Nokrek, 4652 ft.

[4] The Khasi Hills.

[5] A tree in the Market place (Hât).

Jamalpour in ye Luckya River.[1]	Dacca from do. ..	Land 3 Par.
	Nursindy ..	do. 2 Par. / Boat 1 Day.
	Sultansuddy ..	Land 1½ Par.
	Sagordee ..	do. 3 Par.
	Akarasonda ..	do. 1 Day.
	Noranda Creek ..	do. 2 Hours.
	Mullopara ..	do. 2 Par Et. side R.

1765 Mr. Galloway's Intelligence 21st. Octor.[2]

Curygong or Gurrygong[3] is situated on ye little River Dherla, which has its Source in ye Bootan (Badtan) Countrey & falls into ye Baramputrey on ye west side about one day or 20 miles above Chilmary. The Place's Name where ye River joins ye Barampy. is Bagway or Boggua. The Dherla is navigable for large Boats all ye Year. Course fr. ye Wt. & WNW. Curygong is situated with respect to Chilmary WNW or NW dist. 30 miles, or one day Journey for a Cossid. It is said to be nearly ye same distance from Dewangunge as from Chilmary.

Rungpour lies SW or South Westerly from Curygong, ye distance one day's Journey for a Cossid or 25 or 30 miles. (14 Coss said to be). There is a good Road all ye way. Rungpour is 4 days Cossid from Muxadabad.

Curesa is 6½ Coss to ye N. wd. of Curygong, & lies on ye frontier of Baär.[4]

Tangrapara[5] ⊙ 78 near it. Mount Sosong E 6°-10′ N or True E 7°-5′ N.

Rungpour lies from the Mouth of the Teesta Creek near Manusmerra W 23°-30′ N distce. 32·2 E. miles.

Manusmerra & Olyapour W 29-45 N 10·05 E M.
Olyapour & Tytari W 11 N 5·73.
Tytari & Rungpour W 13 N 16·5.

From Olyapour W 12°-20′ N. 22·2.

From Tytari W 13° N 16·5.

The Estimated Distance from Rungpour to Olyapour is 12½ Coss. The true distance by the Road is 24 Miles, & the distance on a Line 22·2, so that a Coss must be reckoned about 1·8 Miles on a streight Line. By ye Roads it nearly agrees with 2 Miles, the common Calculation.[6]

[1] A village below the junction of the Lakhmia and Banar rivers

[2] On the 21st Octr. 1765 Rennell was surveying the 'Bernya' creek (*ante* p. 52) between the Lakhmia and old Brahmaputra rivers, at the beginning of his expedition to Goalpara. I can find no mention of Mr. Galloway elsewhere.

[3] Kurigram, on the right bank of the Dharla R. in the Rangpur district.

[4] Cooch Behar.

[5] A village on a large island in the Brahmaputra below Chilmari.

[6] *See* ante p. 123.

A Journey of Mr. Walker's.[1]

Notes	Route		Bearing	Distance	Remarks
	From Rungpour to Gora Gatt	..	S½W	17 Coss.	These 3 Places lie on yᵉ same River.[2]
	To Gooangunge	..	SSE	6	
4 Coss to the NNE of Rungpour is yᵉ Monaash Creek,[3] & a Coss farther Eᵗ· is yᵉ Teesta.	To Seebgunge	..	SBE	6	
	To Jamalgunge	..	W½S	10	On a small Creek.
	To Shawpour	..	SW	5	Do.
	To Saamgunge	..	N.	6	Do.
	To Budall	..	N½E	2	
Guzgotta is 4 Coss from Rungpour, & lies on the Monaash.	To Buxygunge	..	NE	6	
	To Nabobgunge	..	NBE	7	On a small Creek.
	To Rungpour	..	NNE	13	

Mr. Walker's Route from Rampour Bolio to Gorygott[4]—

From Bolio to Bobbanygunge[5] NE 13 Coss.

To Bullowah .. .. 5 do. Here he Crossed the Purnabubah River which comes from Raasgunge & Denospour.[6]

From Bullowah to Carrihey .. 7 Coss a large Village.

to Naddiol .. 11 do. do.

to Gorygott 7 do. do.

Mr. Walker's Intelligence—

In yᵉ District Of Denospʳ.	From Rungpour to Raasgunge	WSW	..	21 Coss.
	From do. to Fazydunga[7]	NWBW	..	22 do.
	To yᵉ Boutan Countrey	N.	..	30 or 35 Coss.

Computed Distances—

	From Olyapour[8] to Gurygong	..	6	Coss.
A Par is here reckoned 3 Coss or 5.4 miles on a streight Line.	to Rungpour	..	12½	do.
	to Raasgunge	..	3	days Travellᵍ.
	to Baggoa	..	6	Coss.
	to Chilmary	..	12	do.

Stages—From Olyapour to Curygong—

To Maldywary	2 Gurry[9]	2 Par.
Cotipour	2 do.	
Durgapour	2 do.	
Lowwa	2 do.	
Potyapar	2 do.	
Malwanga	6 do.	

[1] To the south of Rangpur. [2] The Karatoya. [3] The Manas, now a branch of the main channel of the Teesta.

[4] Rampur Boalia, on the Ganges, to Goraghat, an old military outpost of the Muhammadans, south of Rangpur.

[5] Bhawaniganj. [6] Rajganj and Dinajpur.

[7] A village on the Teesta to the south of Jalpaiguri.

[8] Ulipur, in the peninsula between the Dharla and Teesta rivers.

[9] Ghari, a clepsydra or water clock, measuring 24 minutes, the eighth part of a 'Par' or 'Pour.'

Collyana—Consuma on ye R. Mallyjole.[1]
Continagore[2] on the Doppaw R.
Corenaw on the P. Bubaw.[3]
Raunpour on the Mohananda-Chera.[4]

(Mr. Walker.)

1 The Malijol is an artificial canal connecting the Atrai with the Dhapa (or Doppaw of Rennell), a tributary of the Purnabhaba (Hunter, Stat. Acc. Beng., Vol. VII. p. 361). Buchanan Hamilton says that it was dug by a Mahomedan Chief named Sadut Ali, and until the Teesta deserted its old channel in 1787, carried a large quantity of water (Martin, Eastern India, Vol, II, p. 597).

2 Kantanagar, a celebrated temple dedicated to Kantaji, 11 miles north of Dinajpur, on the Dhapa R. The temple is built on the ruins of a fort belonging to Virat Raja, one of the heroes of the Mahabharata.

3 The Purnabhaba R., on which Dinajpur is situated.

4 Probably the Chiramoti, a tributary of the Mahananda.

APPENDIX A.

RAJNAGAR AND LURICULE. (*See* Journal, pp. 31, 39.)

I am indebted to Mr. F. D. Ascoli, of the Indian Civil Service, for the following information collected while he has been engaged on the settlement of the District of Faridpur :—

Rajnagur :—This place was swept away by the Kirtinasa river in 1871-2, and Luricule by the same river nine years later, together with Jaopsa pagoda. The ground on which they stood has since re-formed, and that course of the Kirtinasa is now practically dry.

Rajnagur was built by Raja Raj Ballabh, who flourished in the second quarter of the eighteenth century. Originally a poor man, he acquired a large fortune as peshkar (agent) of the Nowarrah mahals at Dacca (lands, the profits from which were used for the maintenance of the fleet), and built a house at Rajnagnar, which was at that time a 'bhil' or lake, called Bhil Deema. This he drained, and covered the site with extensive tanks and buildings, which were added to by his sons and grandsons. The most notable buildings were the temples Naba Ratna (nine spired); Pancha Ratna (five spired); Saptadas or Shata Ratna (seventy or one hundred spired); and the Ekeesh or Ekabinsha Ratna (twenty-one spired). A description of these with a photograph and several drawings has been published in a Bengali work, the History of Bikrampur, by Jogendra Nath Gupta. Old men of the locality remember to this day the beauty of the architecture of the place.

Luricule or Noreekole :—These names are identical, ল and ন being readily interchangeable in Bengali. The old name of the place was Sripur Shahabunder and it is mentioned by Ralph Fitch, who visited it in 1586, as an important town, where "great store of cotton cloth is made."[1] Since the place was swept away by the Kirtinasa the land has been re-formed, and old men of the locality still remember the buildings, which were yet standing some 30 years ago. The principal buildings were a mosque, a ghat or landing place, and a masonry bridge over the Callygonga, not mentioned by Rennell; besides these there

---

[1] J. Horton Ryley, 'Ralph Fitch, England's Pioneer to India and Burma', London, T. Fisher Unwin, 1899, p. 118. It may be noted that Ryley identifies the 'Serrepore' of Fitch with Serampur, the former Danish settlement on the Hughli above Calcutta. But this cannot be the case, for Fitch says that Serrepore is six leagues from 'Sinnergan' (Sonargaon), the ancient Muhammadan capital of East Bengal, near Dacca, and it was on his way up the Meghna and Ganges, from 'Chatigan' (Chittagong) that Fitch visited Serrepore. It is correctly identified by Blochmann (Journ. As. Soc. Beng., Vol. XLII, Pt. 1, p. 230) as "Sherpur Firinghi, marked by Van den Broucke a little south of Idrakpur, on the Dalasari" (T. H. D. L.)

were the ruins of many brick houses, one of which may have been the Portuguese Church. It appears that the name of the place was changed to Luricule about 150 years ago, which would agree very well with its derivation from the title of the Marquis of Louriçal, as suggested in the note on p. 39.

Traces of the Portuguese are still to be met with in the neighbourhood. They were great traders in the days of Akbar, as Fitch relates, and were employed by Raja Raj Ballabh in managing his estates. Two distinctly Portuguese names still exist near Luricule, *viz.*, Howla Gonzales, an old land tenure in the neighbouring 'mauza' of Kamarpur, and a tank at Naria (a mile west of Mulfatganj), called Dorta Dighi (or Da Orta's Tank), after a 'Firinghi' still remembered in the locality for his kindness and liberality.

Finally, it may be noted that the 'Chiddypour Creek', which passes by Luricule, is the real Callygonga River; the river marked as the Callygonga in Rennell's Atlas is the Naya Nadi Rathkhola, *i.e.*, the 'New Chariot Path River,' so called because in the early part of the eighteenth century this was the path, so it is averred, along which the chariot was drawn at the Sripur Rath-jatra festival. The deepening of the path led to the formation of the creek, and it has finally become the bed of the mighty river Kirtinasa.

APPENDIX B.

(*See* Journal, p. 62.)

The Revd. W. K. Firminger has very kindly placed at my disposal the following letter of Rennell's, which he has recently discovered among the Records preserved at Murshidabad. Godagary, near which place the incident occurred, is on the left bank of the Ganges, due north of Murshidabad:—

To Richard Becher Esq.
Chief of the Controuling Council of Revenue
at Murshidabad

Bowanygunge

Decr. 9 1770.

Sir,

I beg leave to lay before you a Complaint against Caddar Beg, a Mogul & Zemindar of a small District named Pulsah, lying about 5 Coss inland from Gadagary. I am employed on a Survey of the Roads, etc., on the North side of the Ganges, & halted near Pulsah, the 5th instant, at Noon. A few minutes after our Arrival the Villagers came arm'd, & threatened to fall upon us. I asked them if they had any Complaint to make. They abused me, told me no, & insisted that I should go away. We soon dispersed them without making use of any Weapons, as I never suffer a Sepoy to fire till matters come to an Extremity. Whilst they were in the action of running away, we caught one of them, a Burkundass, who had entangled himself in the Jungle. I enquired of him who the Village belonged to, & (after disarming him) sent him with a message to Caddar Beg, informing him of my Business in these Parts.

From this Time none of my People enter'd the Village, altho' everything seemed quiet: yet, about two hours afterwards, a Mogul (Caddar Beg) appear'd on Horseback, & with him a very great Rabble, some of them armed with Matchlocks, and the rest with Pykes and Swords, etc Without sending me any Message, he came within Call and told me that he was come to fight me. I was obliged to have Recourse to my Sepoys, but hoping to end the matter with little Bloodshed, I aimed a single shot at the Mogul which, however, missed him, but killed a man close by him. This had the desired effect of making them retire to a greater Distance; but they kept us in continual Alarm by sending parties into the Jungles on every side of us: During this time the Mogul remained in Sight, and sent me several insolent Messages—one of them in particular so full of Abuse and Menaces that I thought myself fully authorized to chastise the Messenger, which I did. The rest contained hints of his Independence, together with Orders for me to depart. To one of these I replied by showing the Messenger the Sepoys, Arms, and camp Equipage, by which he might be assured that we belonged to the Company, for the Mogul affected to believe that we were Robbers. Even after this, he persisted in sending his Messenger, & using threatening Gestures, till, finding it had no Effect, he fell into the opposite extreme, and began to apologise for his Behaviour, which he imputed to his ignorance of my Station & Employment. You may imagine, Sir, that his Plea was extremely ill-grounded, after I had taken such Pains & exhausted my Patience to convince him. As he now acknowledged his Conviction, I desired his personal Attendance, which he declined.

I flatter myself, Sir, that the above Relation needs no comment to convince you of the great Affront I have rec'd, &, through me (as I humbly conceive) my Employers likewise. I have not yet laid an Acct. of it before the Governor, hoping that you will do me the justice the Case requires.

In these Expectations,
I remain with Respect, Sir,
Your most Obedient Servant,
J. Rennell.

LIST OF WORKS CONSULTED.

Allen B. C., Assam District Gazetteers. Calcutta and Allahabad, 1905.

Bengal, Past and Present. Journal of the Calcutta Historical Society. Calcutta, General Printing Co., 1897.

Beveridge, H., Old Places in Murshidabad. Calcutta Review, Vol. XCIV, p. 322; XCV, p. 195, 1892.

Blechynden, Miss K., Calcutta, Past and Present. London. Thacker & Co., 1905.

Blochmann, H., Contributions to the Geography and History of Bengal. Journ. As. Soc. Bengal, Vol. XLII, Pt. 1, 1873.

Blochmann, H., Remarks on the Sundarban. Proc. As. Soc. Bengal, 1868.

Buckland, C. E., Dictionary of Indian Biography. London, Swan, Sonnenschein & Co., 1906.

Busteed, Dr. H. E, Echoes from Old Calcutta. 3rd Edition, Calcutta, Thacker Spink & Co., 1897.

Fergusson, J., Recent Changes in the Delta of the Ganges. Quart. Journ. Geol. Soc., London, 1863.

Gait E. A., History of Assam. Calcutta, Thacker Spink & Co., 1906.

Gangetic Delta. Calcutta Review, Vol. XXXII. Art. 1, 1859.

Heber, Bishop, Narrative of a Journey through the Upper Provinces of India from Calcutta to Bombay, 1824-1825. 2 Vols., London, John Murray, 1828.

Hill, S. C., Bengal in 1756-1757. Indian Records Series, 3 Vols., London, John Murray, 1905.

Hill, S. C., Three Frenchmen in Bengal: or, the Commercial Ruin of the French Settlements in 1757. London, Longmans Green & Co., 1903.

Hooker, Sir J. Dalton, Himalayan Journals. 2 Vols., London, John Murray, 1854.

Hunter, Sir W. W., Annals of Rural Bengal. 5th Edition, London, Smith Elder & Co., 1872.

Hunter, Sir W. W., Imperial Gazetteer of India. 2nd Edition, 14 Vols., London, Trübner & Co., 1887.

Hunter, Sir W. W., Statistical Account of Assam. 2 Vols., London, Trübner & Co., 1879.

Hunter, Sir W. W., Statistical Account of Bengal. 20 Vols., London, Trübner & Co., 1875.

Hunter, Sir W. W., The Thackerays in India. London, Henry Frowde, 1897.

Imperial Gazetteer of India. New Edition, Oxford, Clarendon Press, 1907-1909.

Lettres Édifiantes et Curieuses, écrites des Missions Étrangères. New Edition, 26 vols., Paris, J. G. Merigot le jeune, 1781.

List of Ancient Monuments in Bengal. Calcutta, Bengal Secretariat Press, 1896.

Long, Revd. J., Selections from unpublished Records of Government for the years 1748 to 1757 inclusive. Calcutta, Superintendent of Government Printing, 1869.

Malcolm, Sir J., Life of Robert, Lord Clive. London, John Murray, 1836.

Markham, Sir Clements R., Memoir of the Indian Surveys. 2nd Edition, London, W. H. Allen & Co., 1878.

Markham, Sir Clements R., Major James Rennell and the Rise of Modern English Geography. Century Science Series, London, Cassell & Co., 1895.

Martin, Montgomery, The History, Antiquities, Topography and Statistics of Eastern India (compiled from the Surveys of Dr. Francis Buchanan-Hamilton). 3 Vols., London, W. H. Allen & Co. 1838.

Orme, R., History of the Military Transactions of the British Nation in Indostan from the year 1745. 2 Vols., London, John Nourse, 1778, 1780.

Plaisted, B. A., Journal from Calcutta in Bengal, by Sea, to Busserah. . . . . To which is added, An Account of the Countries, Cities, and Towns adjacent to Bengal, with a Map by Mr. Plaisted. London, T. Kinnersly, 1758.

Playfair, Major A., The Garos. London, David Nutt, 1909.

Rainey, H. J., The Sundarban. Proceedings, Asiatic Soc. Bengal, 1868.

Rennell, Major J., A Bengal Atlas, containing Maps of the Theatre of War and Commerce on that side of Hindoostan. Published by order of the Honourable the Court of Directors for the Affairs of the East India Company, 1781.

Rennell, Major J., Description of the Roads in Bengal and Behar. Printed by order of the Honourable the Court of Directors of the East India Company, 1778.

Rennell, Major J., Memoir of a Map of Hindoostan or the Mogul Empire. 2nd Edition, London, G. Nicol and W. Richardson, 1792

Ryley, J. Horton, Ralph Fitch, England's Pioneer to India and Burma. London, T. Fisher Unwin, 1899.

Stewart, C., History of Bengal. London, Black, Parry & Co., 1873.

Territorial Aristocracy of Bengal. Calcutta Review, Vol. LVI, Art. 1, 1873.

Vansittart, H., A Narrative of the Transactions in Bengal from the year 1760, to the year 1761. London, 1766.

Westland, J., Report on the District of Jessore. Calcutta, Bengal Secretariat Office, 1871.

Wheeler, J. Talboys, Early Records of British India. Calcutta, W. Newman & Co., 1878.

Wilson, Dr. C. R., Old Fort William in Bengal. Indian Records Series, 2 Vols., London, John Murray, 1906.

Yule, Col. H., and **Burnell, A. C.,** Hobson Jobson, a Glossary of Colloquial Anglo-Indian words and phrases. New Edition, London, John Murray, 1903.

INDEX

H

I

S

T

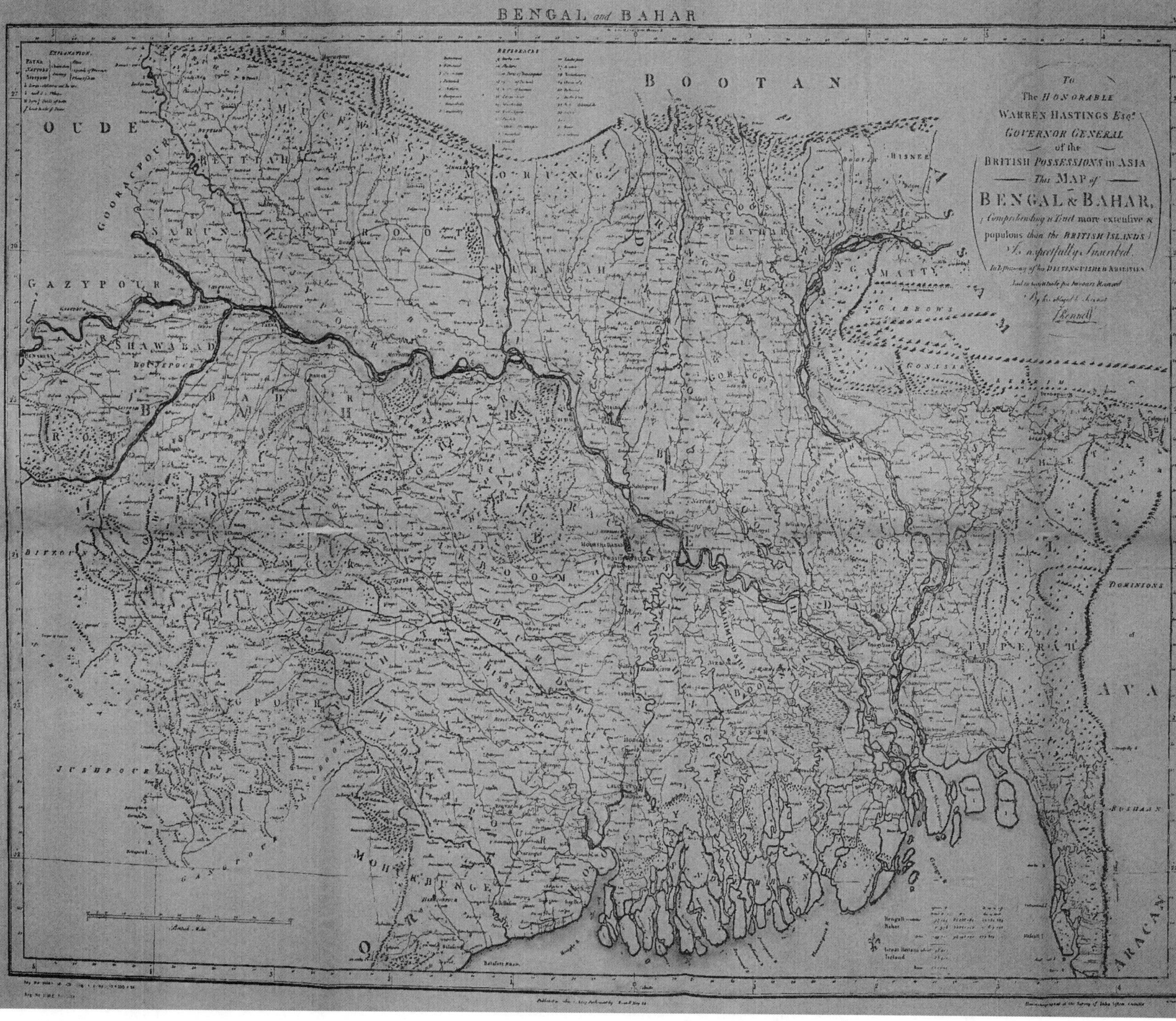
BENGAL and BAHAR
To
The HONORABLE
WARREN HASTINGS Esqr.
GOVERNOR GENERAL
of the
BRITISH POSSESSIONS in ASIA
This MAP of
BENGAL & BAHAR,
Comprehending a Tract more extensive & populous than the BRITISH ISLANDS
Is respectfully Inscribed,
In Testimony of his DISTINGUISHED ABILITIES
By his obliged & Servant
J. Rennell
BOOTAN
OUDE
GOORACPOUR
GAZYPOUR
SHAWABAD
BETTIAH
SARUN
PURNEAH
RANGAMATTY
ASAM
GARROWS
DOMINIONS of AVA
ARACAN
JUSHPOUR
MOHURBUNGE

Memoirs of the Asiatic Society of Bengal.

1905—1906.

I. *On certain Tibetan Scrolls and Images lately brought from Gyantse.—By* PROF. SATIS CHANDRA VIDYABHUSANA, M.A., M.R.A.S. (Price Re. 1-8; or 2s. 3d.)

II. *Sal-Ammoniac: a Study in Primitive Chemistry.—By* H. E. STAPLETON, B.A., B.Sc. (Price Re. 1; or 1s. 6d.)

III. *The Similarity of the Tibetan to the Kashgar-Brahmi Alphabet.—By* The REV. A. H. FRANCKE. (Price Rs. 2; or 2s. 10d.)

IV. *Alchemical Equipment in the Eleventh Century, A.D.—By* H. E. STAPLETON and R. F. AZO. (Price Re. 1-8; or 2s. 3d.)

V. *Malaysian Barnacles in the Indian Museum, with a list of the Indian Pedunculata.—By* N. ANNANDALE, B.A., D.Sc. (Price Re. 1-8; or 2s. 3d.)

VI. *Ashrafpur Copper-plate Grants of Devakhadga.—By* GANGA MOHAN LASKAR, M.A. (Price Annas 8; or 10d.)

VII. *Festivals and Folklore of Gilgit.—By* GHULAM MUHAMMAD. (Price Rs. 2; or 2s. 10d.)

VIII. *Notes on the Bhotias of Almora and British Garhwal.—By* C. A. SHERRING, M.A., F.R.G.S., I.C.S. (Price Re. 1-5; or 2s.)

IX. *Religion and Customs of the Uraons.—By* the late REV. FATHER DEHON, S.J. (Price Rs. 2; or 2s. 10d.)

X. *Notes on the Fauna of a Desert Tract in Southern India* (Herpetology and Entomology).—*By* N. ANNANDALE, D.Sc., C.M.Z.S., with a list of Mammals by R. C. WROUGHTON, F.E.S. (Price Rs. 2; or 2s. 10d.)

XI. *Amulets as Agents in the Prevention of Disease in Bengal.*—Compiled in the Office of the Superintendent of Ethnography, Bengal. (Price Annas 12; or 1s. 2d.)

XII. *Earth-Eating and the Earth-Eating Habit in India.—By* D. HOOPER and H. H. MANN. (Price Re. 1; or 1s. 6d.)

XIII. *On a Cup-Mark Inscription in the Chumbi Valley.—By* E. H. C. WALSH, I.C.S. (Price Re. 1; or 1s. 6d.)

XIV. *A Descriptive List of the Sea-Snakes* (Hydrophiidæ) *in the Indian Museum, Calcutta.—By* CAPTAIN F. WALL, I.M.S., C.M.Z.S. (Price Re. 1; or 1s. 6d.)

XV. *Common Saws and Proverbs collected, chiefly from Dervishes, in Southern Persia.—By* LIEUT.-COL. D. C. PHILLOTT. (Price Re. 1; or 1s. 6d.)

XVI. *The Common Hydra of Bengal: its Systematic Position and Life History.—By* N. ANNANDALE, B.A., D.Sc., C.M.Z.S. (Price Re. 1; or 1s. 6d.)

XVII. *Animals in the Inscriptions of Piyadasi.—By* MONMOHAN CHAKRAVARTI, M.A. (Price Annas 12; or 1s. 2d.)

XVIII. *Some current Persian Tales told by Professional Story-Tellers.—By* LIEUT.-COL. D. C. PHILLOTT. (Price Re. 1; or 1s. 6d.)

XIX. *The Dards at Khalatse in Western Tibet.—By* REV. A. H. FRANCKE. (Price Re. 1-6; or 2s.)

Supplement, Miscellanea Ethnographica. Part I. 1. *The Blow-Gun in Southern India* 2. *Miscellaneous objects from the Rámanád subdivision of the Madura district* 3. *Indian Weighing-beams.—By* N. ANNANDALE, D.Sc. (Price Re 1.)

Supplement, Miscellanea Ethnographica. Part II. 1. *Some Malayan Weapons—By* N. ANNANDALE. 2. *Plan of a Persian Gentleman's House.—By* LIEUT.-COL. D. C. PHILLOTT. (Price Annas 8; or 10d.)

Memoirs of the Asiatic Society of Bengal.

Vol. II.

I. *Cirrhipèdes operculés de l'Indian Museum de Calcutta.—Par* M. A. Gruvel. (Price Rs. 2; or 2s. 10d.)

II. *The Coinage of Tibet.—By* E. H. C. Walsh. (Price Re. 1; or 1s. 6d.).

III. *The Exact Determination of the Fastness of the more Common Indigenous Dyes of Bengal, and comparison with typical synthetic Dye-stuffs. Part I. Dyeing on Cotton.—By* E. R. Watson. (Price Re. 1; or 1s. 6d.)

IV. *The Saorias of the Rajmahal Hills.—By* R. B. Bainbridge. (Price Rs. 2; or 2s. 10d.)

V. *Mundari Poetry, Music and Dances.—By* Rev. Fr. J. Hoffmann, S.J. (Price Re. 1; or 1s. 6d.)

VI. *Tarikh-i-Nuṣratjangi.—By* Harinath De. (Price Re. 1; or 1s. 6d.)

VII. *The Exact Determination of the Fastness of the more Common Indigenous Dyes of Bengal, and comparison with typical Synthetic Dye-stuffs. Part II. Dyeing on Silk.—By* E. R. Watson. (Price Annas 12; or 1s. 2d.)

VIII. *Monograph on Sea Snakes.—By* Major F. Wall, I.M.S. (Price Rs. 5; or 7s.)

IX. *A Polyglot List of Birds in Turki, Manchu and Chinese.—By* E. Denison Ross, Ph.D. (Price Rs. 4; or 6s.)

X. *Notes on some Monuments in Afghanistan.—By* H. H. Hayden. (Price Re. 1; or 1s. 6d.)

XI. *On the Correlations of Areas of Matured Crops and the Rainfall, and certain allied problems in Agriculture and Meteorology.—By* S. M. Jacob, I.C.S. (Price Rs. 2-8; or 3s. 10d.)

Vol. III.

I. *Ramacarita by Sandhyakara Nandi.—Edited by* Mahamahopadhyaya Haraprasad Shastri, M.A. (Price Rs. 2; or 2s. 10d.)

II. *An Alchemical Compilation of the 13th Century A.D.—By* H. E. Stapleton, B.A., B.Sc. (In the press.)

III. *The Journals of Major James Rennell, F.R.S., First Surveyor-General of India.—Edited by* T. H. D. LaTouche. (Price Rs. 4; or 6s.)

Lisu Tribes of Burma-China Frontier.—By A. Rose and J. Coggin Brown. (In the press.)

Published by

Facsimile Publisher
Ashok Vihar, Delhi-110052 (India)
Website: www.facsimilepublishers.com

Distributed by

Gyan Books Pvt. Ltd.
5, Ansari Road, Daryaganj, New Delhi-110002 (India)
E-mail: books@gyanbooks.com, Website: www.gyanbooks.com

8 888000 878094